MYRIAD-MINDED SHAKESPEARE

Also by E. A. J. Honigmann

THE STABILITY OF SHAKESPEARE'S TEXT

SHAKESPEARE: Seven Tragedies – The Dramatist's Manipulation of Response

SHAKESPEARE'S IMPACT ON HIS CONTEMPORARIES

SHAKESPEARE: The 'Lost Years'

JOHN WEEVER: A Biography of a Literary Associate of Shakespeare and Jonson

THE TEXTS OF *OTHELLO* AND SHAKESPEARIAN REVISION

KING JOHN (*editor*)

RICHARD III (*editor*)

TWELFTH NIGHT (*editor*)

MILTON'S SONNETS (*editor*)

PARADISE LOST, BOOK 10 (*co-editor with C. A. Patrides*)

SHAKESPEARE AND HIS CONTEMPORARIES: Essays in Comparison (*editor*)

PLAYHOUSE WILLS 1558–1642 (*co-editor with Susan Brock*)

OTHELLO (*editor*)

BRITISH ACADEMY SHAKESPEARE LECTURES 1980–89 (*introduction*)

Myriad-minded Shakespeare

**Essays on the tragedies, problem
comedies and Shakespeare the man**

E. A. J. Honigmann

Second Edition

Published in Great Britain by
MACMILLAN PRESS LTD
Houndmills, Basingstoke, Hampshire RG21 6XS and London
Companies and representatives throughout the world

A catalogue record for this book is available from the British Library.

ISBN 0–333–72064–4

Published in the United States of America by
ST. MARTIN'S PRESS, INC.,
Scholarly and Reference Division,
175 Fifth Avenue, New York, N.Y. 10010

ISBN 0–312–17753–4

Library of Congress Cataloging-in-Publication Data
Honigmann, E. A. J.
Myriad-minded Shakespeare : essays on the tragedies, problem
comedies, and Shakespeare the man / E.A.J. Honigmann. — 2nd ed.
p. cm.
Includes bibliographical references and index.
ISBN 0–312–17753–4
1. Shakespeare, William, 1564–1616—Tragedies.   2. Shakespeare,
William, 1564–1616—Tragicomedies.   3. Tragicomedy.   4. Tragedy.
I. Title.
PR2983.H627 1997
822.3'3—dc21   97–26827
                                                                                            CIP

© E. A. J. Honigmann 1989, 1998

First edition 1989
Second edition 1998

This book is printed on paper suitable for recycling and made from fully managed and
sustained forest sources.

10   9   8   7   6   5   4   3   2   1
07   06   05   04   03   02   01   00   99   98

Printed in Great Britain by
The Ipswich Book Company Ltd
Ipswich, Suffolk

Contents

Acknowledgements

The 'Bibliographical Note' acknowledges my debt to the editors and publishers of some of the chapters, or parts of chapters, reprinted in this volume. In addition it is a pleasure to thank all colleagues and students, in many universities, who listened patiently to the lectures that are now printed for the first time. I cannot complain that I lacked criticism; I hope that I benefited from it.

It is also a pleasure to thank Kathleen O'Rawe and Margaret Jones for help with typing, and the staff of Newcastle University Library for expert advice and assistance. Harold Jenkins read through the typescript and made many valuable suggestions. My wife, as usual, helped as proof-reader and as the critic's critic, and generously gave this book more of her time than it deserved.

Note on texts and references

Quotations from Shakespeare, and line-references, are taken from Peter Alexander's *William Shakespeare: The Complete Works* (Collins, 1951). A single line-reference after a quotation is to the first line quoted. Other Elizabethan plays are usually quoted from *The Revels Plays* (Manchester University Press). Old-spelling quotations from Elizabethan texts are modernised, except that I retain old spelling when there is a special reason for doing so: I hope that this will not cause confusion.

Bibliographical note

Some of the essays in this volume are revised versions of earlier publications or lectures, or reprint parts of earlier publications, as indicated below. I am grateful to the editors and publishers for permission to reprint. I have not sought to disguise the fact that the lectures were written as lectures: my occasional exhortations to attentive listeners will not confuse the attentive reader.

1. 'In search of William Shakespeare: the public and the private man.' Partly based on a review in *The New York Review of Books*, vol. 31 (17 Jan 1985) pp. 23–6, and on 'Shakespeare and London's immigrant community *circa* 1600', in *Elizabethan and Modern Studies Presented to Willem Schrickx*, ed. J. P. Vander Motten (R.U.G., 1985). See also my *Shakespeare's Impact on his Contemporaries* (Macmillan, 1982) ch. 1.

3. 'The politics in *Hamlet* and the "world of the play".' From *Stratford-upon-Avon Studies 5*, ed. John Russell Brown and Bernard Harris (Edward Arnold, 1963).

4. 'Trends in the discussion of Shakespeare's characters: *Othello*.' From *Handelingen van het XXIX Vlaams Filologencongres* (Antwerp, privately printed, 1973). Some of the ideas in this chapter were later developed in my *Shakespeare: seven tragedies, the dramatist's manipulation of response* (Macmillan, 1976).

5. 'The uniqueness of *King Lear*: genre and production problems.' A lecture delivered on 23 April 1983 to the Deutsche Shakespeare-Gesellschaft West. Published in *Jahrbuch*, 1984.

6. 'Past, present and future in *Macbeth* and *Antony and Cleopatra*.' Partly based on a lecture delivered in Los Angeles, 1987, at a one-day conference on *Macbeth* sponsored by the University of California at Los Angeles.

7. 'Shakespeare suppressed: the unfortunate history of *Troilus and Cressida*.' Partly based on a lecture delivered to the Caltech-Weingart Conference at the Henry E. Huntington Library, 1982: see *Textual Criticism and Literary Interpretation*, ed. Jerome J. McGann (University of Chicago Press, 1985).

9. 'Shakespeare's mingled yarn and *Measure for Measure*.' A lecture delivered on 23 April 1981 at the British Academy. From *Proceedings of the British Academy*, LXVII (1983).

10. 'On not trusting Shakespeare's stage-directions.' Partly reprinted from *Shakespeare Survey 29* (1976), and partly based on a lecture delivered to the Renaissance Conference of Southern California, 1987.

11. 'Shakespeare at work: preparing, writing, rewriting.' Partly based on *The Stability of Shakespeare's Text* (1965), *passim*, and on 'Shakespeare as a reviser', in *Textual Criticism and Literary Interpretation*, ed. Jerome J. McGann (University of Chicago Press, 1985).

12. 'Shakespeare on his deathbed: the last will and testament.' A lecture delivered at the International Shakespeare Association World Congress, Tokyo, 1991, printed in the *New York Review of Books* (7 Nov 1991, pp. 27–30) and reprinted with additions in the Congress *Proceedings* (*Shakespeare and Cultural Traditions*, ed. Tetsuo Kishi *et al*, Newark, 1994), pp. 127–37.

Preface to the Second Edition

For some years now Shakespeare criticism has looked away from the plays and concerned itself with other though related matters – with ideology, the state of society, the Renaissance and similar abstractions. I find the best of this criticism exciting and sympathise with many of its aims, even if I do not see myself as a member of any one of the new critical movements. Readers of this book will, however, discover that while I am uneasy about identifying social institutions in the plays with their Elizabethan counterparts (chapter 3), I try to do justice to Shakespeare's own unease when he deals with 'power' and ideology (chapter 2) or with gender politics or the like (chapter 8). My life-long determination to question received thinking is perhaps most obvious in the chapters on Shakespeare the man (1, 11, 12) and in that on stage directions (10); I believe, though, that the same basic attitudes inform the less transparently radical chapters that try to explain how individual plays work, particularly the chapters on *King Lear*, *Macbeth* and *Measure for Measure* (5, 6, 9).

While this is a collection of essays that all grapple with timeless problems rather than with time-bound movements (New Historicism, Cultural Materialism, etc.), I recognise that problems and movements are linked. The problems force me to look at the plays, not away from them, and to investigate what I consider the building-blocks of Shakespearian drama – character, plot, language, genre, response – that is, questions that were asked by Shakespeare's first audiences and that will continue to intrigue the world in centuries to come. And, as we know that his contemporaries saw connections between the plays and Shakespeare the man, and that Heminge and Condell, the editors of the First Folio, already worried about the authenticity of his texts, I have boldly included chapters on these problems, which may displease those who say they believe in 'the death of the author' or that any text of *Hamlet* is as valid as any other 'as long as it works in the theatre'. In fact, I have added a twelfth chapter to this edition which brings together the author's personality and our interpretation of his text in a special way, and which also picks up threads from earlier chapters: the gentleness of 'gentle Shakespeare' (chapter 1); the integrity of a text and its revisions (chapters 7, 11);

the interconnectedness of the critical questions we have to ask (introduction and chapter 7).

To repeat: the essays not only by-pass fashionable movements, they also – I hope – avoid the jargon and tunnel vision that these movements too often encourage. I want a general reader, if such a creature really exists, to be able to follow the argument, and I want him or her to understand the problems rather than to accept my solutions.

Inevitably, I have changed or partly changed my mind on some issues. It may interest readers to know how and why. After 14 years of hard labour on a new Arden edition of *Othello* (Arden 3, 1997) I felt obliged to renounce my earlier endorsement of Nevill Coghill's argument for the revision of this play, and have also thought again about the revision of *King Lear*.[1] Nevertheless, the revision theory seems to me to have stood the test of time, in these two tragedies and as applied to Shakespeare more generally, even if some believers in Shakespearian revision appear to forget that other explanations of variant passages are also possible, and are sometimes much more likely.[2]

I have returned more than once to Shakespeare's social awareness and ideology, in reviews and scattered articles, and likewise in unpublished lectures on the *Sonnets* and on 'The Subversiveness of *Henry V*'. Even now, I would urge, after all the books and articles of the last dozen or so years, we still need to look more carefully at the Elizabethan social background and at its bearing on our interpretation of the plays.[3]

So far as I know, 'Trends in the discussion of Shakespeare's characters' has not received much attention. It may be worth pointing out that the 'attack on character' with which chapter 4 begins has continued, as has the defence of character.[4] This is another debate that is likely to go on in the foreseeable future.

The original version of my new chapter 12, first published in 1991 and now reissued in expanded form, has already drawn an interesting comment from Richard Wilson. According to Wilson's *Will Power Essays on Shakespearean Authority*, Shakespeare's will was not as eccentric as I suggested (I prefer the word unusual), because

the will to paternal power of Shakespeare's generation was grounded in a legal right to acquire property and determine its transmission which had not existed before and would never be so absolute again until the Wills Act of 1837. It was an authority that the dramatist exploited to the full when he revised his own will . . . (p. 209)

It is useful to be reminded that the structure of Shakespeare's will was influenced by historical developments. Nevertheless, Wilson concedes that 'it was Susanna, not, as custom dictated, her mother, who was made executrix of the will' (p. 210), and Shakespeare's other deviations from custom can now be more clearly understood with the help of a collection of wills, many of them previously unpublished, issued in the same year as Wilson's *Will Power*, namely *Playhouse Wills 1558–1642* (eds. E. A. J. Honigmann and Susan Brock, Manchester, 1993).

NOTES

1. See pp. 213–4, below; my *The Texts of 'Othello'* (1996), pp. 7–21; and my reviews in *New York Review of Books*, xxxi (1984), 16–18, and xxxvii (1990), 58–60.
2. Cf. my review of Grace Ioppolo, *Revising Shakespeare* in *Modern Language Review*, 88 (1993), 941–2.
3. Cf. my papers on 'Shakespeare and London's Immigrant Community circa 1600' (in *Elizabethan and Modern Studies*, ed. J. P. Vander Motten, Ghent, 1985) and on 'Social questioning in Elizabethan and Jacobean plays' (in *Jacobean Drama as Social Criticism*, Salzburg University Studies, ed. James Hogg, 1995).
4. Cf. John Drakakis, *Alternative Shakespeares* (1985), pp. 4 ff.; Peter Holland, 'The resources of characterization in *Othello*' (in *Shakespeare Survey*, 41 (1989), 119–32).

Introduction: Myriad-minded Shakespeare and the modern reader

> [Shakespeare] first studied patiently, meditated
> deeply, understood minutely, till knowledge,
> become habitual and intuitive, wedded itself to
> his habitual feelings, and at length gave birth to
> that stupendous power, by which he stands
> alone, with no equal or second in his own class.
>
> (Coleridge)[1]

My title, *Myriad-minded Shakespeare*, has a sting in its tail. We all
agree, I suppose, that Shakespeare's exceptional knowledge
contributed to 'that stupendous power, by which he stands
alone', but what of his reader's knowledge? How myriad-minded
must his reader be? In the theatre the plays are enjoyable
without any special knowledge whatsoever. I have seen twelve-
year-olds, unhampered by study of the play at school, entranced
by a performance of *Henry V*, and of some of the comedies. The
groundlings at the Globe, who are given a finger-wagging in
Hamlet ('groundlings who, for the most part, are capable of
nothing but inexplicable dumb shows and noise'), enjoyed even
Shakespeare's most sophisticated play, for we hear from a
contemporary witness of 'the vulgar's' delight in Shakespeare's
tragedies, one in particular: 'faith, it should please all, like Prince
Hamlet!'[2] Shakespeare himself, however, distinguished between
'the unskilful' in his audience and 'the judicious', adding that
one judicious spectator 'o'erweighs a whole theatre of others.' So
I rephrase my question: how myriad-minded will the judicious
spectator or reader have to be?

Shakespeare certainly expected the judicious of his own day to
'understand minutely', as Coleridge put it, the finer shades of
language, of social difference, and of contemporary intellectual
debate (e.g. concerning ghosts or melancholy in *Hamlet*). Four
hundred years later we have to labour to acquire this knowledge,

1

and it will sit less comfortably in our minds. In addition we have to evaluate the teachers who inflict this knowledge upon us, for they all offer different explanations and they cannot all be right. ('Are Hamlet's critics mad? or are they only pretending to be?') Today's judicious reader or theatre-goer, it seems, will have to be even more myriad-minded than his ancestors.

If that is an excessively daunting challenge, he can at least aim to be open-minded. Too many of the books published almost daily on Shakespeare, unfortunately, are the very opposite – narrowly restricted to a single approach. Either a specialist wishes to sell his thesis, or a generalist writes essentially the same essay about several plays, because he wants to sell a book. In this collection I attempt something different. It introduces the reader to the great variety of approaches to Shakespeare, dealing with genre, character, plot, the political and sexist implications of the plays, their sources, staging-problems, response problems, textual problems, the dramatist's character and biography, and so on, usually relating several of these narrower concerns to each other, to bring out the interconnectedness of all the critical and scholarly questions that we ask today. The method changes from chapter to chapter, but presupposes a reader who, if not myriad-minded, still wishes to be aware of the multiplicity of critical procedures. In short, this book may serve as an introduction to several (but not all) important 'specialist' approaches. As far as possible, however, I avoid surveys of recent research: instead, I plunge straight into problems, and show in passing that it is rarely safe to restrict oneself to a single specialist view. The open-minded reader learns that Shakespeare criticism is a *jeu sans frontières*.

This collection consists of several unpublished essays, and of others that are already in print (some in out-of-the way books and journals). I have excluded essays from my own books, and also work that would be too boringly technical for the general reader. For the reader's convenience I have concentrated on plays that are usually grouped together: five essays on tragedies, three on problem plays. To broaden the book's horizons I have added one essay on stage directions, illustrating the important consequences of textual study for producers and actors; another on Shakespeare as a writer and as a reviser, the latter a topic that has provoked heated debate in the recent past, and is likely to continue to do so; and a third one on Shakespeare's personality. This last may not seem strictly necessary, yet will be found to connect with others in the volume. My picture of a sometimes fastidious and private Shakespeare, as opposed to the popular one of a free and easy dramatist who was everyone's friend, and almost all things to all men, supports the argument that he took the trouble to revise some of his plays, worried about social and political issues, and did not resort lightly to 'bed-tricks' or irresponsible happy endings. If he was careless about trivialities, as they would seem, from his point of view – for example, omitting or misplacing stage directions, which he could easily put right in rehearsal – the signs abound of his artistic fastidiousness wherever it mattered. I hope that, among other things, this volume will sharpen our understanding of a self-critical dramatist.

And, perhaps, of self-critical criticism. For, though I began to back away from the notion of a myriad-minded reader as soon as it formed itself, I cling to it as an ideal. Shakespeare's plays teach many truths – one being that it is wise to look in all directions, not just in one direction. It is better to be Hamlet than Malvolio. Or – backing away again – Hamlet would be a better reader and critic. Unlike Malvolio, he is not guilty of 'the trick of singularity'; he takes an interest in everyone and everything, however insignificant in the world's esteem, even in plays – even in revised plays; he looks behind curtains, or guesses what is there without looking; above all, he distrusts easy answers and, like Polonius, willingly stoops to 'windlasses and assays of bias' to 'find directions out'. We, too, must learn to look, with Hamlet, in all directions. Myriad-minded Shakespeare deserves teachers – and actors, producers, readers – who willingly follow wherever the plays may lead.

1

In search of William Shakespeare: the public and the private man

Two images of Shakespeare have come down to us from the seventeenth century. One presents him as convivial, everyone's friend, familiar with the insides of taverns, quick in repartee, witty, a fluent writer, an extrovert; the other, as fastidious, sometimes unapproachable, sometimes tongue-tied, 'with what I most enjoy contented least' (Sonnet 29),[1] an introvert. Modern biographers take what suits them from both, offering us, for example, an easy-going poet indifferent to the fate of his own plays or, alternatively, one who revised some of his best work in minutest detail. The two images are not necessarily incompatible, but we should still ask whether we can safely trust both, or even one of them.

The early records that throw light on Shakespeare's personality can be divided into five groups: (1) contemporary allusions; (2) the Sonnets; (3) Shakespeare's many legal transactions; (4); the indirect evidence of the plays; (5) the Stratford bust and Droeshout engraving. Each of the five creates its own difficulties – for instance, unless an early allusion dates from the poet's life-time and can be traced to a source close to him it may have to be dismissed as idle gossip, even if something similar is reported by a seemingly independent witness. We hear of Shakespeare's drinking-exploits in the mid-seventeenth century, in a manuscript in the hand of Nicholas Burgh of Windsor ('Mr Ben Jonson and Mr Wm. Shakespeare being merry at a tavern . . .') and in the notebooks of John Ward, vicar of Stratford (1662–81) – 'Shakespeare, Drayton and Ben Jonson had a merry meeting, and it seems drank too hard, for Shakespeare died of a fever there contracted.' This was several decades after the poet's death, when his admirers were already making special trips to Stratford to see the tomb and talk to survivors who remembered him: stories about his deer-stealing, running away to London, later wealth, and so on, were now circulating, and it may be that the 'Shakespeare mythos' expanded as the demand for it increased. On the other hand, earlier records also need to be taken into account. In 1598, a survey in Stratford named William Shakespeare as the possessor of eighty bushels of corn and barley; many other Stratford men were included in this list, which identified grain-hoarders in a period of grain shortage. The grain, it was suspected, would be used for illegal brewing. Six years later Shakespeare sued Philip Rogers for debt, Rogers having failed to pay him for twenty bushels of malt. In 1614 a preacher was entertained at New Place, Shakespeare's house, and the Stratford chamberlain paid out 'for one quart of sack and one quart of claret wine, given to a preacher at the New Place, xx^{d}'. These could have been perfectly normal transactions for a leading Stratfordian. If, as seems likely, the William Johnson who acted as Shakespeare's trustee in 1613 was the host of the Mermaid tavern, and Shakespeare wrote commemorative verses for Elias James, a member of a prominent brewing family,[2] we begin to wonder whether he had a professional interest in brewing. But professional brewers and their financial backers are not inevitably heavy drinkers, and perhaps the best reason for not repudiating Shakespeare's drinking-exploits as an improbable fiction can be found in the plays – in Falstaff's tavern-haunting exuberance. Or should Hamlet disqualify Falstaff ('They clepe us drunkards, and with swinish phrase / Soil our addition' – I.4.19–20)?

Sometimes we cannot reach a rational verdict, even though we feel strongly tempted to accept or reject an allusion. But there are exceptions, where converging evidence from different sources persuades me that an allusion, albeit one that jars with one's picture of 'gentle Shakespeare', should be taken seriously. The verses on John Combe are a case in point. Is it conceivable that Shakespeare was as tactless as Rowe made out in 1709? The dramatist had a 'particular intimacy' with Mr Combe, an old gentleman noted in Stratford for his wealth and usury; Combe asked for an epitaph for himself, and 'desired it might be done immediately, upon which Shakespeare gave him these four verses'.

Ten in the hundred lies here engraved,
'Tis a hundred to ten his soul is not saved.
If any man ask, 'Who lies in this tomb?'
'O ho!' quoth the Devil, ''tis my John a Combe!'

Earlier memorialists had preserved the same verses, with slight variations, which Shakespeare, put on the spot, could have adapted from an epitaph ascribed to John Hoskins ('Ten in the hundred lies under this stone, / And a hundred to ten to the devil he's gone'). Yet would he do so? Do these hurtful lines accord with our image of Shakespeare as a kindly, a universally popular man?

Why not? Heminge and Condell stated that 'what he thought he uttered, with that easiness that we have scarce received from him a blot in his papers'. Even more pertinently, Ben Jonson said that 'he flowed with that facility that sometime it was necessary he should be stopped . . . . His wit was in his power; would the rule of it had been so too.' These are excellent witnesses, close to the poet for many years. Shakespeare's evident delight in repartee in the plays, and in other reported conversations, confirms that he might have overshot himself when challenged by Combe – not unlike Hamlet when confronted by Polonius.

Although Shakespeare himself seems to have engaged in occasional money-lending,[3] as a side-line, I believe that the epitaph fits in too neatly with all that is known about his character to be easily rejected. And yet it also strikes me as uncharacteristic, contradicting the evidence of the Sonnets, where his exceptional sensitivity to the feelings of others, and willingness to overlook faults, is so unmistakable. Perhaps this ought to serve as a warning: why should Shakespeare's character be wholly consistent, any more than the average man's?

Biographers look for consistency, and must be cautious when they think they find it. A. C. Bradley[4] rightly attached importance to Ben Jonson's posthumous tribute to Shakespeare, that 'he was indeed honest, and of an open and free nature', and noted that 'these words are true also of the great majority of Shakespeare's heroes'. Jonson almost repeated the words of Iago ('The Moor is of a *free and open nature*, / That thinks men *honest* that but seem to be so'), and the same words, Bradley went on, also apply to Hamlet, Brutus, Lear and other tragic heroes, while the sufferings of free and open natures are Shakespeare's favourite tragic subject – 'a decided peculiarity, not found thus in other tragic poets. Here he painted most, one cannot but think, what his own nature was most inclined to feel.' The poet of the Sonnets has the same character, free and open, affectionate, therefore doomed to suffer many disappointments.

Bradley's Shakespeare is attractively consistent, but not necessarily a true likeness. Even if earlier tragic poets preferred quite different heroes, Shakespeare will have been influenced in his plays and Sonnets by contemporary models, particularly by the much-discussed idea of 'the gentleman'. Spenser wrote *The Faerie Queen* to provide a model of 'a gentleman or noble person in virtuous and gentle discipline'. As a follower of the Earl of Southampton, Shakespeare must be seen as a member of the Essex circle;[5] and Essex himself was a living model of a free and open nature, impulsive, undiplomatic in not concealing his dislike of his political opponents, loyal to his friends (including Southampton) even when this could harm his own future. Shakespeare adopted an open-hearted and almost romantic tone in dedicating *The Rape of Lucrece* to the Earl of Southampton ('The love I dedicate to your Lordship is without end. . .') and again, five years later, in alluding to Essex in *Henry V*:

> As, by a lower but *loving likelihood*,
> Were now the General of our gracious Empress –
> As in good time he may – from Ireland coming.
> (V, Prologue, 29–31)

The tone of the Sonnets is similar, and the choice of 'open and free' tragic heroes might have been determined less by the dramatist's own nature than by the literary and living models of his age.

'I believe the sonnets to be, substantially, what they purport to be,' said Bradley. While I agree as to the outlines of the story they tell, I am not so convinced by the characters. The young man is cast in the role of the ideal gentleman, the poet in that of a gentleman of lower rank, an admirer of the young man's beauty and 'worth'.

> For whether beauty, birth, or wealth, or wit,
> Or any of these all, or all, or more,
> *Entitled* in thy parts do crowned sit,
> I make my love engrafted to this store.
> (37.5–8)

It is sometimes said that nothing in the sonnets proves that the young man was more than a gentleman of some note, more than plain 'Mr W.H.' The social and economic gap between two gentlemen could be considerable, yet so many of the Sonnets allude to a princely world in general, to the young man's high

rank, to the almost miraculous bridging of the distance between
poet and friend, that I think he must have been 'entitled'.

> Lord of my love, to whom in vassalage
> Thy merit hath my duty strongly knit . . . .

> Nor thou with public kindness honour me
> Unless thou take that honour from thy name.

> Thy love is better than high birth to me,
> Richer than wealth . . . .
>   (26.1–2; 36.11–12; 91.9–10)

Whether a lord or not, the young man's higher rank seems to me
vitally important, triggering off all those passing references to
honour, wealth, gilded tombs, and so on. The poet, though much
the older, is always respectful, indeed worships him as a remote
sun –

> Full many a glorious morning have I seen
> Flatter the mountain-tops with sovereign eye . . .
> Even so my sun one early morn did shine.
>   (33.1–3)

We need not doubt that the poet was genuinely dazzled – but by
what? Not just by the young man's beauty, though that receives
more emphasis than his intellectual gifts. No: another irresistible
fact is that someone so far above the poet has offered him friendship
and 'love' (that is, affectionate friendship on terms of complete
equality). To be permitted to address a high-ranking friend as
'thou' and 'my love' was clearly exciting – and at the same time
placed both of them in a false position, since the difference in rank
could never be completely forgotten. The poet has to play the part
of a courtier, rather like Queen Elizabeth's Raleigh or Essex, who
paid homage to her wisdom, beauty, virtue, and pretended to be
in love with her. He may genuinely admire his young friend, but
he has to 'dress up' verbally, and in other ways, that being the
courtier's ritual. If the Sonnets are an arm-twisting exercise,
reminding the young man of the poet's high expectations,
perpetually reaffirming a courtly ideal, then the poet is also caught
in his own trap; he, too, must conform to type. The glover's son

from provincial Stratford could have been a very different man.

We can bring this point into sharper focus by comparing the poet of the sonnets with what is known about Shakespeare as a businessman. The Sonnets portray a tender-hearted, inward-looking poet, willing to put up with snubs and treachery – as when the young man encourages the gross flattery of other writers and pays less attention to 'true plain words by thy true-telling friend' (82), or when the young man openly encourages an overbearing rival poet.

> My tongue-tied Muse in manners holds her still,
> While comments of your praise, richly compil'd,
> Reserve their character with golden quill
> And precious phrase by all the Muses fil'd.
> I think good thoughts, whilst other write good words,
> And, like unletter'd clerk, still cry 'Amen'
> To every hymn that able spirit affords
> In polish'd form of well-refined pen.
> Hearing you prais'd, I say, ''Tis so, 'tis true',
> And to the most of praise add something more;
> But that is in my thought . . . .
>
> (85.1–11)

The poet is even more forgiving – and helplessly reproachful – when the young man steals his mistress. 'Take all my loves, my love, yea, taken them all . . . I do forgive thy robb'ry, gentle thief' (40.1, 9).

> That thou hast her, it is not all my grief,
> And yet it may be said I lov'd her dearly;
> That she hath thee is of my wailing chief,
> A loss in love that touches me more nearly.
> Loving offenders, thus I will excuse ye:
> Thou dost love her because thou know'st I love her,
> And for my sake even so doth she abuse me . . . .
>
> (42.1–7)

Here and elsewhere the poet's 'wailing' gives an impression of gentle ineffectiveness ('I all alone beweep my outcast state' – 29.2; 'And weep afresh love's long since cancell'd woe' – 30.7; 'vex'd with watching and with tears' – 148.10): indeed, a talent for silent suffering that seems almost effeminate. We cannot rule out the possibility that his relationship with the young man was homosexual, even though he laughingly dismisses it –

> And for a woman wert thou first created;
> Till Nature, as she wrought thee, fell a-doting,
> And by addition me of thee defeated
> By adding one thing to my purpose nothing.
>   But since she prick'd thee out for women's pleasure,
>   Mine be thy love, and thy love's use their treasure.
>   (20.9–14)

But let us not forget that Shakespeare was a married man and father, wrote scathingly about homosexual practices in his plays (*Troilus*, II.1.110ff.), and that the poet seems to have continued a heterosexual relationship with the dark lady at the very time of the Sonnets; the young man, too, was something of a womaniser (Sonnets 40–2, 133ff.), a characteristic that he shared with William Herbert, the later Lord Pembroke.[6]

The poet's strong affection could also be explained as partly paternal ('As a decrepit father takes delight / To see his active child do deeds of youth' – 37.1–2). Shakespeare had lost Hamnet, his only son, in 1596, at the age of eleven, and probably wrote many of the Sonnets a year or two later, to a son-substitute. What is certain is that the two other principals, the young man and the dark lady, treat him with little respect. He pleads, they scarcely listen; he loves, they betray. Many of the most interesting Sonnets were written, I think, out of frustration – to express what the poet could not bring himself to say face to face. The tender-hearted poet, alas, was not a forceful man.

Now consider the business dealings of the glover's son, very definitely a man to be reckoned with, hard-headed, shrewd, successful. We first see him through the eyes of an embittered rival: 'there is an upstart crow, beautified with our feathers, that with his "tiger's heart wrapped in a player's hide" supposes he is as well able to bombast out a blank verse as the best of you, and, being an absolute *Johannes factotum*, is in his own conceit the only Shake-scene in a country.' Robert Greene misquoted a line from *3 Henry VI* ('O tiger's heart wrapp'd in a woman's hide' – I.4.137) for the sake of that 'tiger's heart', which evidently summed up the man for him – a ruthlessly efficient man who threatened to put all competitors out of business. Greene was prejudiced, yet other witnesses paint a similar picture. In 1598, when a group of Stratfordians needed to raise money, Adrian Quiney wrote, 'If you bargain with Mr Sha. or receive money . . . bring your money home if you may'; and Abraham Sturley, hearing 'that our countryman, Mr Wm. Shak. would procure us money', commented, 'which I will like of as I shall hear when, and where, and how; and I pray let not go that occasion if it may sort to any indifferent conditions.' Those who knew 'Mr Shak.' clearly braced themselves for tough bargaining. At the very end of his life Shakespeare changed his will, on 25 March 1616, to protect his daughter Judith against her husband, Thomas Quiney. Thomas was due to confess publicly on the very next day, 26 March, that he had committed fornication with Margaret Wheeler, and Shakespeare's insertions in his will, rearranging his bequests to Judith, make it embarrassingly obvious that he had no confidence in his son-in-law.[7] The dramatist also sued fellow Stratfordians for the non-payment of smallish debts, 35s. 10d. and £6. Had he been less hard-headed in his business dealings, less determined to stand up for his rights, he would not have died as he did, a very wealthy man.

Again, two totally different pictures present themselves – a forceful businessman and, in the Sonnets, a sensitive poet too yielding for his own good. The two are not necessarily irreconcilable, since one gives an external and the other an internal view. The businessman's character is partly a matter of inference – though Greene's 'tiger's heart', Sturley's letter, the Combe epitaph and other contemporary evidence independently confirm that, now and then, the glover's son could cut up rough. And if the young man of the Sonnets did indeed belong to a much higher social sphere – as would be the case if he was William Herbert (heir to the Earl of Pembroke, born 1580) or Henry Wriothesley (third Earl of Southampton, born 1573), the two most likely candidates – then perhaps the poet's many polite reminders of what he considered owing to him from the 'sweet boy' should count as forceful, coming from a mere glover's son, rather than as excessively yielding. A few Sonnets, also, must be regarded as magnificently self-confident, almost condescending –

Not marble nor the gilded monuments
Of princes shall outlive this powerful rhyme . . . .   (55)

Not mine own fears, nor the prophetic soul
Of the wide world dreaming on things to come
Can yet the lease of my true love control
Suppos'd as forfeit to a confin'd doom . . .
    And thou in this shalt find thy monument
    When tyrants' crests and tombs of brass are spent.
                                                    (107)

Perhaps there is a trace of emotional blackmail here (Horace built
a monument *for himself* in his poetry – *Odes*, 3.30; Shakespeare
keeps reminding the young man of the monument he owes to the
poet); and, to be sure, the relationship described in the Sonnets is
so complicated that an initial impression of the poet's
ineffectiveness may have to be modified. Was his refusal to compete
with the rival poet mere feebleness, or was he 'struck dead' by a
superior understanding of what was going on (85, 86)? Is the
attempt to justify himself in these two Sonnets, after the event, a
triumph or yet another sign of weakness? The relationship is as
psychologically impenetrable as Falstaff's with Hal, and the key
to it, I believe, lies in the social distance between poet and patron.
As for the poet's 'wailing', I see that more straightforwardly as
influenced by poetic convention; to 'beweep' one's outcast state
(29.2) means little more than that one is saddened.

Nevertheless, while we can certainly nudge the images of the
businessman and the poet closer together, we must not pretend
that they are identical. The same is true of the two images with
which I began, the convivial and the more solitary man – which,
be it noted, partially overlap with the two I have just examined. I
now return to the 'solitary' Shakespeare, the private and less
accessible man, who has been neglected by biographers, even
misrepresented, and can too easily slip out of sight altogether.
Once more I have to disagree with Bradley.

Some of Shakespeare's writings [wrote Bradley] point to a strain
of deep reflection and of quasi-metaphysical imagination in his
nature; and a few of them seem to reveal a melancholy, at times
merely sad, at times embittered or profound. . . . Yet nothing
in the contemporary allusions or in the traditions would suggest
that he was notably thoughtful or serious, and much less that

he was melancholy. . . . Shakespeare's writings, on the whole, leave a strong impression that his native disposition was much more gay than grave.[8]

First, consider an anecdote reported by Sir Nicholas L'Estrange, probably between 1629 and 1655.

> Shakespeare was godfather to one of Ben Jonson's children and, after the christening, *being in a deep study, Jonson came to cheer him up and asked him why he was so melancholy.* 'No, faith, Ben,' says he, 'not I. But I have been considering a great while what should be the fittest gift for me to bestow upon my godchild, and I have resolved at last.' 'I prithee, what?' says he. 'I' faith, Ben, I'll e'en give him a dozen good latten spoons, and thou shalt translate them.' [*Latten* was a cheap alloy; godfathers more usually gave *silver* spoons. Perhaps also alluding to *The Alchemist*, and to Jonson's view of Shakespeare's 'small Latin and less Greek'.][9]

Next, the Sonnets, surely the most significant of all of Shakespeare's writings if one wants to know whether his native disposition was merry or grave. How many merry sonnets did he write, and how many of the other sort? Should it be objected that the sonnet tradition favoured unhappiness and solitary musings, we can fall back on the small number that referred to more social occasions.

> Alas, 'tis true I have gone here and there
> And made myself a motley to the view,
> Gor'd mine own thoughts, sold cheap what is most dear,
> Made old offences of affections new . . . .
>
> (110.1–4)

> Your love and pity doth th' impression fill
> Which vulgar scandal stamp'd upon my brow;
> For what care I who calls me well or ill,
> So you o'ergreen my bad, my good allow?
> You are my all the world . . . .
>
> (112.1–5)

Of 110, Beeching said that 'there is no reference to the poet's profession of player. The sonnet gives the confession of a favourite of society', and Bradley agreed.[10] If they are right then the striking

fact is not that Shakespeare could make himself a social favourite –
we know that from other evidence – but that he thought of this as
cheapening. And 112 is one of many Sonnets that express the
poet's sense of a strangely hostile universe, one man against many.
The sonnet tradition regarded Death and Time as man's dreaded
enemies, whereas Shakespeare seems to have been almost equally
uneasy about other men – their mindlessness, destructiveness,
faithlessness: an unease highlighted by his relations with the young
man and the dark lady. If ever anyone took a gloomy view of his
fellow creatures, and thought of himself as sometimes cut off from
them in his deeper being, that man was the poet of the Sonnets –
hence his too hopeful response to the young man's love.

Yet another glimpse of Shakespeare's stand-offish side comes
from John Aubrey (*circa* 1681). 'The more to be admired quia
[because] he was not a company keeper, lived in Shoreditch,
wouldn't be debauched, and if invited to [be debauched], writ he
was in pain.' A 'company keeper' at this time could be a reveller,
as well as 'one who keeps company' (*OED*, company, 10); Aubrey
meant either that Shakespeare avoided revelling or that he preferred
to live quietly, away from company.

One of the very earliest allusions to Shakespeare affirms,
surprisingly, that the writer had not met 'the only Shake-scene in
a country' when he, Henry Chettle, prepared Greene's
posthumously published attack on Shakespeare for the press.
Chettle, a young man with literary ambitions, apologised for not
moderating Greene's anger.

> With neither of them that take offence was I acquainted, and
> with one of them I care not if I never be. The other [Shakespeare],
> whom at that time I did not so much spare as since I wish I had
> . . . I am as sorry as if the original fault had been my fault,
> because myself have seen his demeanour no less civil than he
> excellent in the quality he professes . . . .

When Francis Meres gave his account of the English literary scene
six years later, in *Palladis Tamia* (1598), this literary 'insider', who
knew some of Shakespeare's friends and business associates[11] and
was proud of the fact, did not claim to know Shakespeare personally
but only to be on the fringe of his circle. 'The sweet witty soul of
Ovid lives in mellifluous and honey-tongued Shakespeare, witness
his *Venus and Adonis*, his *Lucrece*, his sugared sonnets among his

private friends, etc.' These allusions suggest that Shakespeare may not have been easy to meet, had any Boswells set out to introduce themselves – and a letter from Lady Pembroke to her son, reported by William Cory but not now traceable, seems to make the same point. Cory visited Wilton House in 1865 and noted,

> The house (Lady Herbert said) is full of interest: above us is Wolsey's room; we have a letter, never printed, from Lady Pembroke to her son, telling him to bring James I from Salisbury to see *As You Like It*; 'we have the man Shakespeare with us'. She wanted to cajole the King in Raleigh's behalf – he came.

'We have the man Shakespeare with us'! Evidently a special treat, even for the master of the King's Men (the official title of Shakespeare's company from 1603). This is one of several indications that the dramatist may have withdrawn from regular acting once he became famous. A veiled attack on a leading player, almost certainly Shakespeare, is another. In *Ratsey's Ghost* (1605), Ratsey ironically advises the chief actor of a touring company, 'when thou feelest thy purse well lined, buy thee some place or lordship in the country, that, growing weary of playing, thy money may there bring thee to dignity and reputation'.[12]

Much positive and some negative evidence suggests that Shakespeare avoided company, at least sometimes, and liked to keep to himself. He impressed his contemporaries as 'our Shakespeare', a nonpareil, a classic, as when John Davies addressed a poem in 1610 'to our English Terence, Mr. Will. Shakespeare' – is it not curious then that not one of the great man's letters has survived? Were there not avid collectors in his day, such as John Weever and Augustine Vincent, who are known to have been admirers of the dramatist? We have the originals or copies of letters by Spenser, Jonson, Donne, and nothing at all from Shakespeare – is that not astonishing? Even if the letters written to Anne Hathaway were not treasured as works of genius, or were destroyed after her death, what of all the other letters written by her husband to, one would think, scores of different correspondents?

Only one explanation seems plausible – that the master dramatist did not trouble to write many letters. Or, rather, that he did not compose the formal letters that other authors sent to their patrons or friends. Shorter, informal notes he must have written often, as we may deduce from Aubrey: 'not a company keeper . . . wouldn't be debauched, and if invited to, writ he was in pain'. The picture we are here given of an author who was sought after but kept his distance is, as I have said, confirmed elsewhere. He neither offered nor asked for complimentary verses. He belonged to no literary clique, and praised very few contemporary writers, though many praised him. Unlike other dramatists he would not write in collaboration, as Leonard Digges observed.

> Nor begs he from each witty friend a scene
> To piece his acts with, all that he doth write
> Is pure his own, plot, language exquisite . . . .

We have not given proper attention to the possibility that Shakespeare was an essentially reserved and private man, perhaps because so many stories circulated about his drinking-habits and wit-combats, which suggest a convivial temperament. These stories, however, were mostly written down or printed long after Shakespeare's death, and need not always imply boon companionship. 'Many were the wit-combats betwixt him and Ben Jonson,' wrote Thomas Fuller in his *Worthies of England* (1662),

> which two I behold like a Spanish great galleon and an English man-of-war; Master Jonson, like the former, was built far higher in learning . . . Shakespeare, with the English man-of-war, lesser in bulk but lighter in sailing, could turn with all tides, tack about and take advantage of all winds, by the quickness of his wit and invention.

Born in 1608, Fuller could scarcely have witnessed such encounters (Shakespeare lived chiefly in Stratford in his last years). One tends to think of the combats as friendly, probably taking place in a tavern, but Fuller did not say so – they could just as well have been the sharp exchanges of professional rivals. The only early allusion intimates an *unfriendly* wit-combat. In Part Two of *The Return from Parnassus* (*circa* 1601) the actor Will Kempe says, 'Why, here's our fellow Shakespeare puts them all down, ay, and Ben Jonson too. O that Ben Jonson is a pestilent fellow, he brought up Horace giving the poets a pill, but our fellow Shakespeare hath given him a purge that made him beray his credit.' Jonson gave the poets a pill to induce vomiting, in *Poetaster*; Shakespeare retaliated by giving Jonson a purge that made him, in vernacular parlance, shit himself (*OED*, beray, 1: 'To disfigure, dirty, defile, befoul (with dirt, filth, ordure)').

The stories about Shakespeare's merry meetings in taverns should not be discounted altogether. Even Milton, after all, permitted himself some gaudy days. I believe, though, that Aubrey's note ('not a company keeper . . . wouldn't be debauched') counts for more than dubious rumours about Shakespeare's drinking-exploits. He was more Hamlet than Falstaff. This image is corroborated by the Sonnets where we likewise find a reserved and private man, one who resented that Fortune forced upon him a life of 'public means which public manners breeds' (111.4). So it was not out of character that he bought himself, at the age of thirty-three, a house in Stratford to retire to and that he abandoned his theatrical career, at any rate as a writer, in his forties.

We must learn to live with two images of Shakespeare. He could have been easy and unconstrained with his friends ('of an open and free nature', as Jonson put it), and at the same time more forbidding to the world at large. The two images come together in Nicholas L'Estrange's delightful anecdote of Shakespeare as a godfather (quoted above, p. 13), but there are so many more amusing stories about his convivial wit than about his silences that biographers have focused too exclusively on one side of his character – a great loss.

The plays, taken on their own, tell us little about their author's character except that he may have possessed some chameleon qualities (visible too in the Sonnets, in the poet's adaptability to courtly extravagance, which the dramatist seems to have disliked). And taken as supporting evidence the plays must be used sparingly. I turn, finally, to the visual evidence – the Stratford bust and the Droeshout engraving. The bust having been repainted and 'restored' more than once, Droeshout's portrayal must be accepted as the more reliable of the two; nevertheless, the bust helps to authenticate the engraving.

When all is said, the outstanding fact remains – that the forms of the [Droeshout] skull, with its perpendicular rise of forehead, correspond with those in the Stratford effigy; and this – the formation of the skull – is the definitive test of all the portraits. The Droeshout and the sculptured effigy show the skull of the same man.[13]

Not everyone likes Droeshout's engraving. Jonson praised it but that means very little, we are told; such verses were commonplace, therefore meaningless –

> This figure, that thou seest here put,
> It was for gentle Shakespeare cut;
> Wherein the graver had a strife
> With Nature, to out-do the life.
> O, could he but have drawn his wit
> As well in brass, as he hath hit
> His face, the print would then surpass
> All that was ever writ in brass.
> But since he cannot, reader, look
> Not on his picture but his book.

More damagingly, the Folio portrait lacks technical skill and looks like the work of a beginner. 'A huge head, placed against a starched ruff, surmounts an absurdly small tunic with oversized shoulder-wings. . . . The mouth is too far to the right, the left eye lower and larger than the right, the hair on the two sides fails to balance. Light comes from several directions simultaneously' – all of which proves 'the artist's ineptitude'. Whether or not we accept Samuel Schoenbaum's view of 'Droeshout's vapid engraving', something has clearly gone wrong with the relationship of the face and the rest of the body, including its clothes. M. H. Spielmann has offered a plausible explanation, 'that Droeshout, working from a limning of the head only, stuck it (and that too high) above the body he so infelicitously invented and so flatteringly attired'.[14] But whose limning? 'It is most unlikely that Droeshout, a Londoner, ever sketched his subject in the flesh', thought Schoenbaum. 'He was only fifteen when the poet died after several years of retirement in Stratford.' And 'Droeshout is depicting a man some years younger than the one portrayed at Stratford'; therefore the limning dates from *circa* 1610 or earlier, when Martin was nine or less.

In point of fact, two Martin Droeshouts lived in London in 1623, an uncle and a nephew. The uncle was granted denization on 20 January 1608, being described as a painter. His brother Michael, the father of Martin the younger, was an engraver who came to London in 1590, so we may assume that Martin the elder had some knowledge of a sister art. Martin the elder lived in London, and would have been old enough between 1600 and 1610 (the years to which we may tentatively assign the postulated limning) to sketch Shakespeare from the life. Moreover, the Droeshouts belonged to London's Protestant immigrant community, and the dramatist lodged with a Huguenot family in London around 1602–4: it seems reasonable to conclude that a member of the Droeshout family sketched or painted Shakespeare's head at about this time.

Why did the Folio syndicate choose an incompetent engraver for the portrait of Shakespeare, the eye-catching centre of their title-page? The answer may well be that there was only one known likeness of Shakespeare as he appeared in his middle years – one limning that Heminge and Condell, and others who remembered 'our fellow Shakespeare' from the time when he wrote his greatest plays, admired as authentic. If the artist who had drawn Shakespeare from the life would only allow the Folio syndicate to use his limning on condition that he himself – or a member of his family – would engrave it, this would explain why an inexperienced engraver had to be given so important a commission.

In short, the technical faults of the Droeshout engraving should not be allowed to interfere unduly with our judgement of the face. Schoenbaum and others dismiss the face as 'vapid', therefore unconvincing. Perhaps it lacks the sparkle we expect from 'witty' Shakespeare. But, as I have argued, the contemporary evidence gives us two images of Shakespeare, and Droeshout's face portrays the less familiar one – thoughtful, reserved, not the tavern-haunting, overflowing poet of popular mythology. Once we recognise that the withdrawn and fastidious features represented by Droeshout are not intrinsically improbable, we may yet learn to be grateful for this glimpse of William Shakespeare, the private man.

Was he himself aware of a difference between the public and the private man?

> O, for my sake do you with Fortune chide,
> The guilty goddess of my harmful deeds,
> That did not better for my life provide
> Than public means which public manners breeds.
> Thence comes it that my name receives a brand,
> And almost thence my nature is subdu'd
> To what it works in, like the dyer's hand.
> Pity me then, and wish I were renew'd;
> Whilst, like a willing patient, I will drink

Potions of eisel, 'gainst my strong infection;
No bitterness that I will bitter think,
Nor double penance, to correct correction.
  Pity me then, dear friend, and I assure ye,
  Even that your pity is enough to cure me.
                                              (111)

2

Politics, rhetoric and will-power in *Julius Caesar*

All of Shakespeare's history-plays and most of his tragedies deal with political problems, yet his critics, until quite recent times, have refused to take his politics seriously. I am particularly irritated by those who assume that in *Julius Caesar* the political implications are obvious, and are exactly the same as the politics in Shakespeare's other works. The dramatist, we have read often enough, supported the 'Elizabethan settlement', a strong central government that promises the best chance of political order in unsettled times, and would have seen Julius Caesar as a regal figure, the Roman equivalent of Queen Elizabeth. To assassinate Queen Elizabeth would be manifestly wicked, we are told, in the eyes of all right-thinking Englishmen, therefore the murder of Julius Caesar is wicked, therefore all the political and moral questions raised by the play admit of straightforward solutions. Brutus and Cassius should not have done it; Rome needed Caesar, as England needed Elizabeth – is that really what Shakespeare thinks in this penetratingly political play?

Two objections immediately suggest themselves. First, the Caesar–Elizabeth, Rome–England parallels are not as clear-cut as has been suggested. True, the Pope had excommunicated Queen Elizabeth, attempts to assassinate her were frequent in her last thirty years, and rumoured and suspected attempts on her life were even more numerous. The two political parties in *Julius Caesar* loosely reflect the division of Shakespeare's England: Queen Elizabeth suppressed the 'old faith', establishing Tudor Protestantism with herself as head of Church and State, and Caesar threatened the old republicanism, replacing it with a new form of government, which he headed as perpetual dictator. In Rome, as in Elizabeth's England, the old 'order' and the new were indeed locked in battle; Caesar, however, is presented in the play as a dangerous innovator, whereas Elizabeth was hailed as her country's innovating saviour. Caesar and Elizabeth stood for entirely different

21

political values, and so, despite superficial similarities, their political positions are not the same. Even if it was wicked to assassinate Queen Elizabeth, the moral and political implications of a plot against a perpetual dictator are not so easily resolved.

Second: is it likely that someone as brilliantly original as was Shakespeare, in his understanding of individual human beings, would have no new ideas when he analyses groups of human beings, in their political relationships? The notion that Shakespeare simply and unquestioningly accepted the politics of his Tudor masters, and had no political ideas of his own, was once wide- spread; T. S. Eliot spoke for many others when he said that Shakespeare, like Dante, adopted the political–intellectual framework of his age. 'I can see no reason', said Eliot, 'for believing that either Dante or Shakespeare did any thinking on his own . . . . Neither Shakespeare nor Dante did any real thinking – that was not their job.'[1] I shall assume, on the contrary, that 'real thinking' *is* the job of a writer, and that one as alert as Shakespeare might also develop in his thinking. The moral and political implications of *Julius Caesar* may resemble those of Shakespeare's other plays, yet must be examined separately, and will probably turn out to be unique – as all important features of a Shakespearian play always prove to be unique, the more closely we look at them.

When Shakespeare set out to write *Julius Caesar*, in 1599, at the age of thirty-five, a new phase began in his writing-career, whether or not he knew it at the time. Hitherto he had specialised in comedy, and in English history-plays; *Julius Caesar* was not only his first mature tragedy, it was also his first mature play with a consciously non-Christian background: which affects the play's treatment of husbands and wives, masters and servants, suicide, the supernatural – and politics. We can be sure, I think, that the decision to move off in these new directions was not taken lightly. In addition, though, there is another reason for regarding *Julius Caesar* as a very special departure. Shakespeare had been publicly chastised, some years earlier, as an 'upstart crow' who dared to compete with his betters – with the 'university wits', Oxford and Cambridge graduates who flaunted their classical know-how in their plays and poetry. Now, for the first time, Shakespeare himself, though not a graduate, undertook to write a play about classical Rome, aware that any theatre-goer who had been to grammar-school would certainly know about the age of Caesar (the age of Livy, Horace, Virgil), whereas his previous historical plays would not have been subjected to the same expert scrutiny (since English history was not on the curriculum in English schools). So it behoved him to be on his guard: a second public attack on him as an upstart, muscling in on classical territory in which he was not really at home, would have been most unfortunate. Moreover, a new young dramatist had recently appeared on the literary scene, a 'pestilent fellow' with a sharply critical tongue, a bricklayer's son (as his enemies alleged) who had studied the classics more intensively than Shakespeare, and was later to refer to Shakespeare's 'small Latin and less Greek'. Ben Jonson, and others, could be expected to look for faults in Shakespeare's play – and indeed we know that Jonson pounced on *Julius Caesar*. Many times, according to Jonson, Shakespeare 'fell into those things [which] could not escape laughter; as when he said, in the person of Caesar, one speaking to him, "Caesar, thou dost me wrong", he replied. "Caesar did never wrong without just cause" – and such like; which were ridiculous.'[2]

Writing a play about Julius Caesar therefore involved several kinds of risk. The man from provincial Stratford, who was rumoured to have been in his younger years a schoolmaster in the country (Jonson once remarked contemptuously that a schoolmaster 'sweeps his living from the posteriors of little children') – the 'upstart crow', it would be said, was trying to get above himself. And Shakespeare must have anticipated this reaction. How, then, did he prepare for it and try to outflank it?

For those who think they know the story of Julius Caesar the play is full of surprises. First and foremost there is the portrait of Caesar himself, falling apart physically and mentally – deaf in one ear, superstitious, childishly proud of his shrewd judgement, easy game for flatterers (weaknesses largely invented by Shakespeare). This in itself is a warning to us that the dramatist was not afraid of pedantic fault-finders, such as Jonson, and interprets and rearranges history freely, as in the English history-plays. Shakespeare's Cicero, Cassius, and Antony are also surprising – for example, Antony's subservient, almost servile, relationship with Caesar in the first half of the play.

CAESAR.   Antonius!
ANTONY. Caesar, my lord!
CAESAR. Forget not in your speed, Antonius,
    To touch Calphurnia; for our elders say

> The barren, touched in this holy chase,
> Shake off their sterile curse.
> ANTONY.   I shall remember.
> When Caesar says 'Do this', it is perform'd.
>
>   (I.2.4)

According to Plutarch, Antony had already reached high political office, second only to Caesar; Shakespeare transforms Antony into something close to a lackey. It follows that he was *not* trying to impress classicists by painting historically unimpeachable portraits of the principal characters.

As many commentators have said, Shakespeare's special effort went into the *language* of *Julius Caesar*. Apart from the poets and prose-writers that I have already mentioned (Livy, Horace, Virgil), the Rome of Julius Caesar bred orators, such as Cicero, trained in the schools – and Shakespeare's unique achievement was that he re-created a world dedicated to speech-making and the arts of persuasion. Deciding to go 'extra-territorial' and to compete with dramatists who could boast a finished classical education, the 'upstart crow' invites his audience to attend to a new rhetoric – loosely based on Latin models in its self-conscious artistry, its sheer professionalism. I suspect that Ben Jonson perceived that this was the special achievement of *Julius Caesar*, and thought he would go one better in his own two Roman plays by offering more authentic speeches – those interminable orations that crush the life out of his *Sejanus* and *Catiline*.

Of course, Shakespeare had written many plays before *Julius Caesar* in which 'speech-making' is important, notably *Henry V*. I am not sure why *Julius Caesar* seems more 'classical' in this respect than its predecessors – partly, no doubt, the feeling is influenced by the high concentration of 'Roman allusions'.

> Wherefore rejoice? What conquest brings he home?
> What tributaries follow him to Rome
> To grace in captive bonds his chariot wheels?
> You blocks, you stones, you worse than senseless things!
> O you hard hearts, you cruel men of Rome,
> Knew you not Pompey?
>
>   (I.1.33)

This, the first 'big speech', centres on Pompey; Cassius's 'Well,

honour is the subject of my story', on Caesar; and Portia's appeal
to Brutus climaxes in another name with historic associations.

> I grant I am a woman; but withal
> A woman well reputed, Cato's daughter.
> Think you I am no stronger than my sex
> Being so father'd and so husbanded?
>   (II.1.294)

Pompey, Caesar, Cato – magic names. These, and the many
allusions to Roman landmarks and customs, help to create the
impression that we are listening to 'Roman' oratory. But the
rhetoric of *Julius Caesar* differs from that of Shakespeare's earlier
plays in at least one other point: again and again the big speeches
exhort stage-listeners to abandon their purposes, to change their
minds. Compare *Henry V*, the nearest rival to *Julius Caesar* in
speech-making, and you find the very opposite: Henry wants to
go to war, and the Archbishop of Canterbury encourages him; his
men are there to fight, at Harfleur and Agincourt, and Henry
cheers them on; at the end, everyone wants peace, and Burgundy
speaks for all. These orations, like the chorus-speeches, lift the
listeners by reinforcing a wish or a mood already present in them.
In *Julius Caesar* the orator swims against the tide, not with it, quells
the mood of his listeners, and changes the course of events. The
tribune Marullus subdues the skylarking of the plebeians in Act I
scene 1, till they creep away, 'tongue-tied in their guiltiness';
Cassius talks to an unwilling Brutus, pushing him in a direction
he had not intended to go; Portia also compels Brutus to do what
he had not wished. These are forensic speeches, moving from
point to point with a professional expertise till they reach an
irresistible conclusion, which is followed, as often as not, by a kind
of surrender from the listener.

> O ye gods,
> Render me worthy of this noble wife!
>   (II.1.302)

This is Brutus's polite way of saying, as many a husband has said
since, 'O God, what a wife!' (He doesn't *quite* say 'O God, she's
got round me again!') And these speeches all lead up to Antony's
'Friends, Romans, countrymen', where, again, the rhetoric totally

changes the mood of the listeners and drives them to actions they
had not contemplated.

It is, therefore, the professionalism of its rhetoric that so sharply
distinguishes *Julius Caesar* from earlier histories and tragedies. The
speakers, when they want to persuade, know exactly how to go
about their business, because they belong to a tradition – a Roman
tradition – of oratory. One senses this professionalism when the
speaker plays his ace-card to maximum effect, as a last resort, as
when Portia suddenly reveals her wound, or Antony at last spells
out the provisions of Caesar's will – namely, that the whole thing
was planned, step by step, by one who anticipated and shaped an
inevitable response. I feel it, too, when the speaker, having
finished, congratulates himself on a job well done –

> Well, Brutus, thou art noble; yet, I see,
> Thy honourable metal may be wrought
> From that it is dispos'd.
>
> (I.2.307)

Similarly, Antony rubs his hands at the end of the Forum-scene.

> Now let it work. Mischief, thou art afoot,
> Take thou what course thou wilt.
>
> (III.2.261)

These, again, are signals to us that the speaker has not drifted
aimlessly but has fulfilled a conscious purpose.

Having observed the technical proficiency of those who resort
to rhetoric in *Julius Caesar*, and how effortlessly men and women
in this Roman world, in public and private situations, switch on
the arts of persuasion, we must next note that a failure to speak
effectively becomes all the more meaningful. Julius Caesar, at home
'*in his night-gown*', is not only superstitious and pompous, he is
positively garrulous – a tendency already visible when he protests
too much that he does not fear Cassius.

> Would he were fatter! But I fear him not.
> Yet *if* my name were liable to fear
> I do not know the man I should avoid
> So soon as that spare Cassius. . . .
> I rather tell thee what is to be fear'd

Than what I fear: for always I am Caesar.
(I.2.198)

Such uncontrolled, 'give-away' speaking is all the more remarkable
set beside the highly wrought rhetoric of this play. Similarly, when
the uncouth Casca explains how Caesar was offered a crown, and
the scene's verse gives way to stumbling prose, a point is made
about the standards one could expect from an educated Roman.

> I can as well be hanged as tell the manner of it: it was mere
> foolery; I did not mark it. I saw Mark Antony offer him a crown –
> yet 'twas not a crown neither, 'twas one of these coronets – and,
> as I told you, he put it by once; but for all that, to my thinking,
> he would fain have had it. Then he offered it to him again; then
> he put it by again . . . .   (I.2.234)

He pours it all out, drawing from Brutus the remark

> What a blunt fellow is this grown to be!
> He was quick mettle when he went to school.
> (294)

Brutus refers disparagingly to one who does not know how to
express himself properly, though he would have been told how in
elegant lectures 'when he went to school'.

Even more significant than the gap between careless and careful
speakers is the contrast between different kinds of competence
exhibited by a single speaker. Brutus's Forum-speech proves him
to be highly skilled in oratory (many critics have condemned it as
weak and ineffective but, as Granville-Barker observed, 'it is
certainly not *meant* to be ineffective, for it attains its end in
convincing the crowd'[3]). When the conspirators meet at his house,
Brutus also speaks fluently. All the more surprising, therefore,
that so practised a speaker seems so helpless when Portia sets
about him, that he wards off her rhetorical flow with short phrases
totally devoid of rhetorical art –

> I am not well in health, and that is all.
> (II.1.257)

She persists –

Brutus is wise, and, were he not in health,
He would embrace the means to come by it.

He shrugs –

Why, so I do. Good Portia, go to bed.

Portia finds her second wind – as wives sometimes do, in these
domestic situations – and sails off into another beautifully measured
speech, and he avoids answering, saying simply, 'Kneel not, gentle
Portia.' Now, when Cassius had appealed to him in Act I with
similar emotionalism, Brutus did not refuse to engage with him
rhetorically – quite the opposite. The turn of his sentences, their
deliberate patterning, matches Cassius's verbal artistry, warding
him off, as it were, with his own weapon – and the same speech,
or one very like it, could have been made to Portia.

That you do love me, I am nothing jealous;
What you would work me to, I have some aim;
How I have thought of this, and of these times,
I shall recount hereafter. For this present
I would not, so with love I might entreat you,
Be any further mov'd.

                                        (I.2.162)

Why does Brutus not silence Portia's pleading with a similar
speech? I believe that, although his short replies to Portia are
sometimes spoken as if he is only half-listening to her (a typical
husband?), a more likely explanation is that he is overwhelmed by
her vehemence. For a while the skilled orator is speechless.

Brutus's feeblest speech, in my view, comes at the end of
the quarrel-scene, when he plucks up courage to address that
'monstrous apparition', the Ghost of Caesar.

BRUTUS. Speak to me what thou art.
GHOST.   Thy evil spirit, Brutus.
BRUTUS.   Why com'st thou?
GHOST.   To tell thee thou shalt see me at Philippi.
BRUTUS. Well; then I shall see thee again?
GHOST.   Ay, at Philippi.

BRUTUS. Why, I will see thee at Philippi then.   [*Exit* GHOST.]
                                                        (IV.3.279)

This is an extraordinary example of not knowing what to say:
'Why, I will see thee at Philippi then – if you say so.' The fact that
in Plutarch almost the same words are used would be no excuse
for such a feeble line – except that feebleness is right at this
moment, expressing Brutus's shock and confusion, which he
admits in the very next line: 'Now I have taken heart thou
vanishest.'

In this play, then, we find a complete rhetorical range, from
formal orations and other long speeches that set out to persuade
down to mumbled excuses and near-helpless echoing of what
another has said. Perpetually switching from speech-making to
talk, from one register to another, Shakespeare draws attention to
rhetoric as a basic fact of Roman life, a mental discipline that he
has woven into the fabric of this studiously Roman play, just as
he very deliberately threads in allusions to Roman history and
topography. I want to give one more example, from the scene that
contemporaries seem to have admired above all – the quarrel-
scene. It is one of the master-strokes of this great scene that it dips
so suddenly from Brutus's high-toned

> Remember March, the ides of March remember:
> Did not great Julius bleed for justice sake?
>   (IV.3.18)

down to exchanges that sound like the wrangling of five-year-olds:

1   – Go to; you are not, Cassius.
    – I am.
    – I say you are not.

2   – Did I say 'better'?
    – If you did, I care not.

3   – I denied you not.
    – You did.
    – I did not.

Lifted out of context, these exchanges sound almost laughable. Yet they are absolutely natural in a quarrel (and intimate, among other things, that Brutus and Cassius, who call each other 'brother', have probably known each other since childhood, and can relapse into the speech-habits of earlier years); and, in addition, they make us all the more conscious of other ups and downs, of the scene's rhetorical texturing.

So far I have argued that in *Julius Caesar* Shakespeare presents a Roman world highly conscious of the powers of rhetoric, one where the skilled orator uses words as weapons that can change the course of events. The tribune Marullus and Cassius in Act I; Portia in Act II, and Decius Brutus, persuading Caesar to go to his death; Mark Antony in Act III – these are some of the prize exhibits of what rhetoric can actually achieve. But Shakespeare was not so naïve as to believe that the best argument, or the best speech, always wins, in a political situation. The very opposite is often true. This very 'political' play shows, again and again, that crucial decisions are made because one person imposes his *will* on others; Shakespeare rewrites history to prove that the man who can dominate others by force of personality, rather than force of argument, must rise to the top. The 'man of destiny', the Napoleonic man, the Thatcher phenomenon, may employ argument, but wins political battles because he or she is the dominant baboon in a wilderness of monkeys – he is 'constant as the northern star' to the conviction that he is always right, 'for always I am Caesar'. As Napoleon put it, 'Wherever I am not, there is chaos' – expressing the supreme self-confidence that is both the strength and the fatal flaw of every Caesar or Thatcher in history.

Shakespeare underlines this point most unmistakably in dramatising Brutus's ascendancy over his fellow conspirators. In Act II, Cassius makes several proposals and Brutus, every time, immediately makes counter-proposals – and anyone who knows the story knows that Brutus's are errors of judgement. If only Cicero had been brought into the conspiracy, as Cassius wished, Cicero – the greatest orator of his generation – could have presented the case for the murder of Caesar so much more convincingly than Brutus that Antony would not have dared to turn the tide of opinion. If only Antony had been killed with Caesar, or had been forbidden to speak at Caesar's funeral, the course of history might have been different. Shakespeare draws attention to the fact that something other than reason prevails when Brutus compels Cassius, against his better judgement, to march to Philippi.

> BRUTUS.   What do you think
>   Of marching to Philippi presently?
> CASSIUS. I do not think it good.
> BRUTUS.   Your reason?
> CASSIUS.   This it is:
>   'Tis better that the enemy seek us;
>   So shall he waste his means, weary his soldiers . . . .
>   (IV.3.194)

But Brutus, having just won the clash of wills in the quarrel-scene, loftily insists that he knows best. 'Good reasons must, of force, give place to better.' Cassius still objects, Brutus remains arrogantly overbearing, and at last Cassius submits. 'Then, with your will, go on.' A curious phrase, 'Then, with your will, go on.' How many times, one wonders, have cabinet ministers, Pyms and Priors, mumbled their submission, against their better judgement, in similar words? 'Then, with your will, go on, Prime Minister.'

Not only in the clashes of Brutus and Cassius but in many other scenes Shakespeare is concerned, in *Julius Caesar*, with the triumph of will over reason. Whatever powers the aging Julius Caesar of the play has lost – and the commentators are agreed that Shakespeare chose to depict the great Roman in decline – we are left in no doubt that Caesar believes himself to be pre-eminent because he sees himself as a man of irresistible will.

> And tell them that I will not come to-day.
> Cannot, is false; and that I dare not, falser;
> I *will* not come to-day. Tell them so, Decius . . . .
> The cause is in my will: I will not come.
>   (II.2.61)

The play shows, of course, that one's strength of will can decline, as do other mental and physical abilities, but Caesar's vision of himself as the man of unshakable purpose, even if grotesquely untrue of the man he has become, reveals what he was, or believed himself to be, when he rose to the top as 'the noblest man / That ever lived in the tide of times'. You may outlive yourself, and lose your decisiveness (as Napoleon did) but you remember what it was that lifted you above the common pack of men.

> I could be well mov'd, if I were as you; ·
> If I could pray to move, prayers would move me;
> But I am constant as the northern star,
> Of whose true-fix'd and resting quality
> There is no fellow in the firmament.
>
> (III.1.58)

Shakespeare shows that a leader of men, whether Caesar or Brutus, may misunderstand people, arguments, and even the very situation in which he finds himself, and yet can dominate others, who see more clearly, by sheer force of will. This shocking political insight – so very different from the dear old 'Elizabethan World Picture' – emerges as the 'philosophy of history' in *Julius Caesar*, if I may use so grand a phrase. For the play undeniably suggests that the *next* 'man of destiny', though neither outstanding as a general nor as a thinker, possesses the one gift that matters.

> ANTONY. Octavius, lead your battle softly on,
>   Upon the left hand of the even field.
> OCTAVIUS. Upon the right hand I: keep thou the left.
> ANTONY. Why do you cross me in this exigent?
> OCTAVIUS. I do not cross you; but I will do so.
>
> (V.1.16)

Shakespeare's thesis, that sheer will-power is the decisive political factor and overcomes almost all opposition, surfaces in many ways.

> Nor stony tower, nor walls of beaten brass,
> Nor airless dungeon, nor strong links of iron,
> Can be retentive to the strength of spirit . . . .
>
> (I.3.93)

Brutus's interview with Portia is another example. It begins as quiet pleading, and ends as a fearful clash of wills, when Portia discloses the 'great gash' in her thigh. The fact that she was able to bide her time, while the blood was flowing beneath her robes, until the psychological moment when the sight of her wound will destroy Brutus's resistance, proves *her* 'strength of spirit', *her* will to succeed. Not her eloquence, but this exercise of pure will, overcomes Brutus. And in *her* case Shakespeare shows, I think, that devotees of will-power may conquer others but, in the end, overthrow themselves as well. The strength that inflicted her 'great gash' must be connected with that even more extraordinary exploit, her suicide by 'swallowing fire'. Caesar's determination also contributes indirectly to his death, in so far as he insists on remaining 'constant as the northern star' when surrounded by opposing wills: his 'constancy' blunts his perception. As for Brutus, whenever he forces Cassius and the rest in a direction they do not wish to follow, we feel each time that his need to dominate blinds his reason and hurries him to his destruction.

A. C. Bradley once remarked that the quarrel-scene in *Julius Caesar* 'can hardly be defended on strictly dramatic grounds'[4]. Perhaps we can defend it by saying that it presents the play's most exciting clash of wills, bringing to a head one of its central interests, which, we may add, explains Shakespeare's rearrangement of some of the incidents of the Forum-scene. In Plutarch's *Life of Marcus Brutus* these are described as follows:

> [The conspirators] came to talk of Caesar's *will and testament*, and of his funerals and tomb. Then Antonius, thinking good his *testament* should be read openly, and also that his body should be honourably buried, . . . Cassius stoutly spake against it. But Brutus went with the motion, and agreed unto it. . . . When Caesar's *testament* was openly read among them, whereby it appeared that he bequeathed unto every citizen of Rome 75 drachmas a man, and that he left his gardens and arbours unto the people. . . . The people then loved him, and were marvellous sorry for him. Afterwards, when Caesar's body was brought into the market-place, Antonius, making his funeral oration in praise of the dead, . . . framed his eloquence to make their hearts yearn the more . . . .

Closely as the play appears to follow this narrative, there is some significant retouching of detail. In Plutarch, the contents of Caesar's *testament* are published *before* Antony's funeral oration; in Shakespeare, we hear almost invariably of Caesar's *will*, and its contents are revealed later, as the climax of Antony's oration; the plebeians are kept dangling, so to speak, to give maximum repetition to an ominous word that has already caught our attention.

- We'll hear the will. Read it, Mark Antony!
- The will, the will! We will hear Caesar's will! . . .
-                     The will! Read the will!
- You will compel me then to read the will? . . .
- Why, friends, you go to do you know not what.
  Wherein hath Caesar thus deserv'd your loves?
  Alas, you know not: I must tell you then.
  You have forgot the will I told you of.
- Most true. The will! Let's stay and hear the will!
                (III.2.139–40, 155–6, 236–40)

Not only has Shakespeare given greater emphasis to 'the will' by making Antony's oration circle round it, and by verbal repetition. He also contrives to suggest that the man who had dominated Rome by his will ('The cause is in my *will*: I *will* not come') somehow wills the mischief and mutiny that follow from the reading of his testament.

Caesar's *will* survives him as a political force, and, like his 'spirit, ranging for revenge', continues to dominate the Roman world – a point also underlined for us by a stage-direction in Act IV: '*Enter the Ghost of Caesar.*' In Plutarch there is no hint that this 'wonderful strange and monstrous shape' appears in the likeness of Caesar; 'I am thy evil spirit, Brutus', it explains (in the Life of Marcus Brutus), or, alternatively, 'I am thy ill angel, Brutus' (in the Life of Caesar). Even without the Folio's stage-direction, though, we might well have guessed that the play's ghost ought to take the shape of Caesar, after what Brutus had said earlier about 'the spirit of Caesar'.

We all stand up against the spirit of Caesar,
And in the spirit of men there is no blood.
O that we then could come by Caesar's spirit,
And not dismember Caesar!

                (II.1.167)

The *spirit* of Caesar and the *will* of Caesar are just about identical in the play: the Ghost appears as a dismembered, menacing will, and does not even have to explain its reason for coming. Brutus *knows* –

> O Julius Caesar, thou art mighty yet!
> Thy spirit walks abroad and turns our swords
> In our own proper entrails!
>
> (V.3.94)

Reading *Julius Caesar* as a political play, in which the author contrasts 'strength of spirit' and rhetoric as mighty opposites, the two political forces that really matter, one wonders about Shakespeare's own assessment of the rights and wrongs of the Roman political situation. It has been said that he 'makes it abundantly clear that the rule of the single master-mind is the only admissible solution' for the problems of Rome.[5] I am not so sure. Shakespeare demonstrates, I think, that the so-called master-mind has outlived itself, and has become a mere husk of itself: the 'master-mind' is a prey to superstition, flattery, a neurotic wife, and megalomania. Under Caesar, the political system appears to work, but does it? The senate is treated by him with contempt, and he himself is manipulated by other men, and is portrayed by Shakespeare as an amalgam of rigid prejudices and an almost unbelievable capacity for dithering. Caesar has in effect destroyed the political institutions of Rome; Antony, a consul at the time of the Feast of Lupercal, actually offers his political master a crown, but he lacks the will to take it; the tribunes 'Marullus and Flavius, for pulling scarfs off Caesar's images, are put to silence' (I.2.280). What does it mean, 'put to silence'? They would know in a police-state, where people are dragged from their homes in the small hours, and are never seen again. Caesar's Rome is a fascist state, which began its rule with the murder of Pompey, where opponents are 'put to silence' or banished, where mob-rule is the ultimate source of power. (We are not told with what honeyed words Antony offered the crown to Caesar, but clearly this was an appeal to the mob, as was Antony's later funeral-oration.) Caesar and his gang have highjacked the government of Rome, much like the generals who have seized power of late in many parts of the world; and Shakespeare seems to me to have very little sympathy with General Caesar's political methods or aspirations.

Antony prophesies that after the death of Caesar

Domestic fury and fierce civil strife
Shall cumber all the parts of Italy.
(III.1.264)

Shakespeare, however, retouched the historical picture in many ways to suggest that the political system had already broken down before Caesar's death, which, I think, makes the conspiracy of Brutus and Cassius more understandable, and perhaps justifiable.

Shakespeare's play presents a political jungle, in which one man has temporarily gained control. Yet the dramatist no more commits himself to the view that Rome needs Caesar than to any other political solution: Caesar simply follows Pompey as the next cowboy who thinks he can ride the political bronco, and gets thrown like Pompey. Shakespeare's attitude is fairly cynical where politicians are concerned, as in most of his other plays. He makes it clear that Caesar has *not* solved Rome's problems, and, accentuating Caesar's weaknesses, more than hints that with such a leader things must fall apart, the centre cannot hold. He also rewrites history to suggest that Caesar's chief opponent, Brutus, lacks the political instinct to be a successful leader of men, turning Brutus into Cassius's dupe, which he was not in Plutarch. The play's Cassius decides

I will this night,
In several hands, in at his windows throw,
As if they came from several citizens,
Writings, all tending to the great opinion
That Rome holds of his name . . . .
(I.2.314)

Plutarch's Brutus receives genuine letters, not fakes, from his 'friends and countrymen'. It is surely significant that, in Shakespeare's account, the two principal figures, Caesar and Brutus, are both intellectually down-graded: both are made the dupes of other men, both suffer from an inflated sense of their own importance, and both speak pompously of themselves, in the third person.

Danger knows full well
That Caesar is more dangerous than he.
We are two lions litter'd in one day

And I the elder and more terrible . . . .
                                        (II.2.44)

It is sheer fantasy. A man who believes that will believe anything –
and Caesar seems to believe it. Brutus, too, fantasises about
himself –

My heart doth joy that yet in all my life
I found no man but he was true to me.
                                        (V.5.34)

After Brutus's treachery to Caesar, his sense of his own honour
and truth becomes less and less plausible, as Antony helps us to
understand: 'For Brutus is an honourable man.' Shakespeare, of
course, invented the special way Caesar and Brutus speak and
fantasise about themselves, and thus intimates that these leading
politicians are dangerously out of touch with reality.

Politics can only be as good as the politicians. Shakespeare seems
to have set out to prove that the supposedly great men of Caesar's
Rome, despite all their talk about high principles, have been
ridiculously overrated – a cynical reappraisal that affects not only
Caesar and Brutus but also secondary figures. Cicero, who battled
courageously against Caesar's ambitions, becomes an ineffectual
bystander in the play. 'Did Cicero say anything?' asks Cassius,
after Caesar was offered the crown. 'Ay, he spoke Greek. . . .Those
that understood him smiled at one another, and shook their
heads' – a glimpse of the man added by Shakespeare that subtly
degrades him. Strange, too, that in a play containing such
memorable orations, Cicero is given nothing memorable to say.

Shakespeare's cynicism about the heroic figures of the classical
past must have astounded his contemporaries, such as Ben Jonson;
at times the play reads like a deliberate exercise in debunking, in
the manner of *Troilus and Cressida*. His cool rewriting of history is
evident not only in his portraits of individuals but in many
incidental touches – for example, the six lines that begin Act IV
scene 1, where Antony and Octavius and Lepidus haggle over the
lives of a brother and nephew.

ANTONY. These many, then, shall die; their names are prick'd.
OCTAVIUS. Your brother too must die. Consent you, Lepidus?
LEPIDUS. I do consent.

OCTAVIUS.   Prick him down, Antony.
LEPIDUS. Upon condition Publius shall not live,
   Who is your sister's son, Mark Antony.
ANTONY. He shall not live; look, with a spot I damn him.

Plutarch thought this proscription quite outrageous. 'In my opinion,' he wrote, 'there was never a more horrible, unnatural, and crueller [ex]change than this was. For thus [ex]changing murder for murder, they did as well kill those whom they did forsake and leave unto others, as those also which others left unto them to kill.' Shakespeare, however, made it an even blacker incident by omitting all signs of reluctance, whereas, according to Plutarch, 'they could hardly agree whom they would put to death: for every one of them would kill their enemies, and save their kinsmen and friends'. Shakespeare turns it into a kind of poker-game, a test of nerves where no one flinches and every man watches the others for signs of weakness. On the surface, all is harmony and restraint – but, introducing slight pauses, the actors can signal to us that this is not a rational discussion at all; it is, quite simply, a clash of wills:

   – Your brother too must die. Consent you, Lepidus?
   – I . . . do consent.

The scene develops in masterly fashion to expose the basest political opportunism. 'Lepidus, go you to Caesar's house', says Antony;

   Fetch the will hither, and we shall determine
   How to cut off some charge in legacies.

Just two lines are needed to demonstrate Antony's total unscrupulousness. The next forty lines continue the poker-game, as Antony tries to persuade Octavius that Lepidus is 'a slight, unmeritable man', and Octavius pretends not to believe him. On the surface they argue about Lepidus; the real issue is different: which one will win an ascendancy over the other? Antony places himself in the weaker position by talking down to Octavius ('Octavius, I have seen more days than you'), only to find that the

younger man turns the tables on him – by giving him permission
to do as he chooses.

> You may do your will;
> But he's a tried and valiant soldier.

Antony then makes the mistake of *appealing* to Octavius –

> So is my horse, Octavius, and for that
> I do appoint him store of provender.

Trying to justify himself when Octavius has already given his
consent, Antony proves himself the weaker man – and such small
verbal advantages can lead to larger victories, as when Octavius
refuses to accept Antony's orders at Philippi; and to the overthrow
of empires.

Julius Caesar is a play that hums with 'political' implications.
Even in private or domestic conversation the participants jockey
for advantage, and Shakespeare expects us to know enough about
Roman history to understand how private clashes can affect the
larger political scene. In the fifth act, however, the play's wonderful
coherence, its simultaneous exploration of the outer and the inner
world, seems to me to be succeeded by writing of a lower order –
a change that has long puzzled me. In the few minutes that remain
I want to consider the purpose of Act V, and how it connects with
what went before.

At one time my simple-minded solution to this problem was that
Shakespeare, exhausted by the Forum-scene and the quarrel-scene,
those twin glories of the play, lost interest in the story and hurried
with indecent haste to the end – perhaps because he was already
pondering his next work, *The Tragedy of Hamlet, Prince of Denmark*.
To accuse Shakespeare of such irresponsibility is always dangerous,
and I have to admit that the loss of power in Act V is less evident
in the theatre than in the study. Nevertheless, the switch to
battle-scenes, the absence of 'big' speeches, the general sense of
diminuendo, demands an explanation. What did Shakespeare think
he was doing in this very strange fifth act?

It may be that we can answer this question by considering the
prominence given to Cassius's birthday.

> Messala,
> This is my birth-day; as this very day
> Was Cassius born. Give me thy hand, Messala.
>
> (V.1.70)

Here Shakespeare dramatises, without comment, a sentence from Plutarch:

> Messala writeth that Cassius, having spoken these last words
> . . . he bade him farewell and willed him to come to supper to
> him the next night following, because it was his birthday.

Shakespeare, however, returned to the fact that Cassius died on his birthday (which, incidentally, seems to have been Shakespeare's own fate as well) – and made Cassius comment as follows:

> This day I breathed first: time is come round,
> And where I did begin, there shall I end;
> My life is run his compass.
>
> (V.3.23)

It suited Shakespeare to make this point about the circularity of life because, when you think about it, the fifth act as a whole seems to make the same point about history, and the events of the play. That is, although the fifth act appears to cobble together the final, confused events in the lives of the principal conspirators, Brutus and Cassius, below the surface it retraverses the ground of the first four acts, and suggests that history keeps on repeating itself. Cassius asks Pindarus to kill him with the very sword that killed Caesar –

> with this good sword.
> That ran through Caesar's bowels, search this bosom.
>
> (V.3.41)

Cassius covers his face before Pindarus stabs him, and no doubt Brutus also does so before *his* death, exactly repeating Caesar's gesture as described by Antony –

> Then burst his mighty heart;
> And in his mantle muffling up his face,

> Even at the base of Pompey's statua,
> Which all the while ran blood, great Caesar fell.
> (III.2.186)

History repeats itself, since Caesar was in effect responsible for Pompey's death, and dies 'at the base of Pompey's statua'; then Brutus and Cassius kill Caesar, and later kill themselves with the same swords, and, it seems, with the very same dying gesture. History also repeats itself in so far as Caesar was hunted to death –

> Here wast thou bay'd, brave hart;
> Here didst thou fall; and here thy hunters stand
> (III.1.205)

– and the 'low alarums' that close in on Brutus in the final scene repeat this image: a pack of pursuers hunting a doomed man to death.

The use of *déjà vu* being so important, we must remember that it could be reinforced by production-methods that have disappeared from the text. As I have already mentioned, Shakespeare remodelled Brutus in the likeness of Caesar, giving him similar speech-habits, and a similar sense of being a very special person; and both men, of course, are similarly hero-worshipped by their followers. The irony that the two men, Caesar and Brutus, who take it upon themselves to set Rome to rights, *both* have to pay the price with their lives, could be underlined choreographically – by making the survivors flow away from, or tip-toe towards, the bodies, so as to remind the audience that it has seen something like it before.

I feel, too, that the unexpected appearance of young Cato, about a hundred lines before the end of the play, needs a similar explanation.

> I am the son of Marcus Cato, ho!
> A foe to tyrants, and my country's friend.
> I am the son of Marcus Cato, ho!
> (V.4.4)

He speaks five lines, and is immediately killed. What is the point of it? Being the son of Cato, he is the brother of Portia – and, since it is stressed that he is young to be a soldier, he might well have been played by the very boy-actor who had taken the part of Portia. Thus, again, the producer can bring out that history repeats itself – that Portia's passionate spirit lives on in another, and again tries to protect Brutus.

The idea that history repeats itself has been present from the beginning of the play. Brutus feels obliged to resist Caesar's ambitions because his 'ancestors did from the streets of Rome / The Tarquin drive, when he was call'd a king' (II.1.53). In the fifth act Shakespeare powerfully reactivates this idea – suggesting that those who *think* they are in control of their own destiny, and who *think* they can control the destiny of nations, are in the grip of invisible forces that bring about Caesar's death 'at the base of Pompey's statua', and Cassius's death on his birthday, with the very sword that killed Caesar, and so on. Despite all the intense political activity of the human actors, a higher force seems to have willed and prearranged the outcome, imposing a beautiful symmetry that, in effect, mocks the efforts of mere mortals to take charge of the world themselves. The confusion and misunderstanding of the battle-scenes mirror the political events of the first four acts, and bring out unmistakably that the leading figures have all misunderstood themselves, and the situations in which they exercised their political talents. Shakespeare's disenchanted comment on the great events of the play is heard, I think, in Titinius's despairing cry when he discovers the body of Cassius –

> Alas! thou hast misconstrued everything!
> (V.3.84)

It is a line that reaches into all parts of the play, wonderfully right about Cassius, and equally relevant to Caesar, Brutus and Antony, the play's leading politicians –

> Alas! thou hast misconstrued everything!

It is a magical if one-sided summing-up line for this cynical play, but, I have to admit it, it is also a slightly unfortunate summing-up line at the end of a lecture.

3

The politics in *Hamlet* and 'the world of the play'

'The constitution of the state of Denmark is vital to our conception of the drama as a whole.' With these words J. Dover Wilson embarked upon one of the most influential studies of *Hamlet* of the present century (*What Happens in 'Hamlet'*, Cambridge, 1935), and within a few pages indicated how the politics of the play strike deep into its moral structure: 'Hamlet was the rightful heir to the throne and Claudius a usurper', and 'usurpation is one of the main factors in the plot'. For, in Wilson's eyes, 'Hamlet is an English prince, the court of Elsinore is modelled upon the English court, and the Danish constitution that of England under the Virgin Queen.'

Behind these far-reaching claims there lies an assumption to which many modern critics still subscribe: that Shakespeare's plays, whatever part of the world they are set in, always portray England and Englishmen:

Nothing is more certain than that Shakespeare has England chiefly in mind in other plays. The scene may be Rome, Venice, Messina, Vienna, Athens, Verona, or what not, and the game of make-believe may be kept alive by a splash of local colour here and there, but the characters, their habits, their outlook, and even generally their costumes are 'mere English'.

A most misleading doctrine, for it reduces the creative imagination to something uncomfortably close to photography. And a doctrine very easily exploded, for who would call Othello, or Shylock, or Ariel and Caliban, 'mere English'? Or, to take a further step, Cleopatra, Iachimo, or Coriolanus? Even if Shakespeare never left the shores of his native England, there existed opportunities in London for meeting Moors and Jews and Indians – and even fairies. Anyone as interested as the author of *Henry V* in the 'foreignness' of foreigners could also interrogate travellers, or dip

43

into the publications of the many predecessors of Hakluyt and Coryate. It is therefore important not to overemphasise the anachronisms and 'Elizabethanisms' in Shakespeare's plays – and of course there are many – at the expense of the often all-pervasive special colouring or foreign flavour which, acting more delicately, will be more easily missed.

At the very time when Wilson laboured at his indispensable books on *Hamlet* a new critical method was being explored, a method which has probably put an end to the once-popular identification of Shakespeare's 'play-worlds' and contemporary England. Wilson Knight described 'the *Lear* Universe' and 'the *Othello* Music', Miss Spurgeon explained 'the influence and presence of the moon' in *A Midsummer Night's Dream*, Charlton concentrated on the special moral qualities of the various tragedies, and innumerable books and articles helped to demonstrate that for every one of his mature plays Shakespeare created a unique 'world' or 'universe' or 'pattern' – through the imagery, the names, the local colour, the 'address to the world', the manipulation of ideas, and in a thousand other ways. The distinctness of each play-world, we now know, is not just a matter of atmosphere: it is an organic principle that extends to the personal relationships of the characters, to social organisation – and even, when the subject comes sufficiently into the foreground, to politics.

According to Wilson – and I think that he is right – the politics in *Hamlet* occupy part of the foreground, since 'The constitution of the state of Denmark is vital to our conception of the drama as a whole.' If so, it seems unlikely that the Danish constitution will simply reproduce that 'of England under the Virgin Queen' – for the form of the play will translate its materials to satisfy its individual needs.

To put it at its simplest, we have to ask whether Hamlet was 'the rightful heir to the throne' after his father's death, or whether an elective system made it possible for Claudius to become king quite legally. A great deal hangs upon this point, as Belleforest's Hamlet explained to his mother:

> if I lay handes upon Fengon [= Claudius], it will neither be fellonie nor treason, hee being neither my king nor my lord, but I shall justly punish him as my subject, that hath disloyaly behaved himselfe against his lord and soveraigne prince.[1]

Belleforest's Hamlet took it for granted not only that he was 'the

rightful heir to the throne' but that he was king *de jure*, and that
Fengon, who occupied the throne, was an impostor. No such
certainty is entertained by Shakespeare's hero, who admits that he
expected an election after his father's death: Claudius, he says,
'Popp'd in between th' election and my hopes' (V.2.65). As I read
it, this means that Hamlet does not regard himself as the only
possible successor to his father. Wilson, on the other hand, held
that 'however it be looked at, the elective throne in Shakespeare's
Denmark is a mirage'.

'There is no question of an elective monarchy in either Saxo or
Belleforest', Wilson assures us, for 'Amleth's father and uncle were
governors or earls of Jutland appointed by the King of Denmark'.
In fact Hamlet's father and uncle, and he himself, are frequently
referred to as kings by Belleforest, and the subject of their *election*
arises at a critical juncture in the story which Shakespeare – unlike
his modern commentators – will hardly have overlooked. Justifying
the violent death of his uncle, Hamlet addressed a lengthy oration
to the Danes (subtitled by Belleforest 'Harangue d'Amleth aux
Danoys') and concluded with the appeal 'chuse me your king, if
you think me worthy of the place' ('meslisez pour Roy, s'il vous
semble que j'en sois digne'). 'This oration of the yong prince so
mooved the harts of the Danes . . . [that] al with one consent
proclaimed him king of Jutie and Chersonnese, at this present the
proper country of Denmarke' (pp. 280–3).

It was a serious misrepresentation to say that 'there is no question
of an elective monarchy' in the sources. In his valuable but, I
believe, misdirected opening chapter Wilson also failed to bring
forward some relevant evidence from within the play. If
'Shakespeare and his audience thought of the constitution of
Denmark in English terms', how did they think of that of Norway?
In Norway, as in Denmark, a king's son was passed over in the
succession in favour of his uncle:[2] is old Norway, 'impotent and
bed-rid', another usurper – and young Fortinbras a second Hamlet,
a prince too 'tender' to seize his own? Admittedly Fortinbras will
have been a child when his father died (Hamlet himself was born
on that very day, and Fortinbras will hardly be much older than
Hamlet[3]) – but in countries where primogeniture is the rule even
the unborn son of a deceased king would take precedence over
his uncle. Clearly in the Scandinavian 'world' of *Hamlet* a son did
not always succeed his father: Fortinbras, who could 'find quarrel
in a straw', would have proceeded with his lawless resolutes

against his uncle, rather than against Denmark and Poland, if he thought himself cheated of his inheritance.

What Fortinbras, a very minor character, would or should have done at a point in the story lying well outside the play will seem to some readers totally irrelevant. Not so: though Bradley and his predecessors have been rebuked for speculating about characters and events 'outside the play', the reaction against conscientious prodding into the darker corners of Shakespeare's dramaturgy has been carried to quite unhealthy extremes. For, as one more recent critic contended, we must often imagine incidents that occur off-stage between scenes:

> some attention to these periods *in absentia* is absolutely necessary to an understanding of the scenes actually shown. We are justified in trying to fill these lacunae in the action so long as our observations have some basis in the play itself; only when we speculate upon possibilities not indicated in the text do we forget the author's intention . . . .[4]

I would extend the range of this counter-argument to include events before the commencement of the play 'so long as our observations have some basis in the play itself' and are 'indicated in the text'. After all, why should events taking place off-stage before Act II be thought more pertinent, and more legitimately discussible, than events taking place off-stage before Act I? Despite all the sarcasms at Bradley's expense he was surely right, and his opponents wrong, to wonder about 'Hamlet as he was just before his father's death', and 'the real Hamlet'.[5] Shakespeare alludes again and again to Hamlet's early life and behaviour because the character of the prince is his centre of interest: the 'real Hamlet', as distinct from the distraught Hamlet presented more directly to our view, is one of the cardinal facts of the play.

I am forced to say a word in defence of Bradley because 'the politics in *Hamlet*' invite Bradley's critical method. Shakespeare 'plants' constitutional ideas which suggest Hamlet's lost opportunities and thus have an obvious bearing on the play's main action – as on its moral texture. What is more, these ideas are worked into a coherent picture, and one which seems to be Shakespeare's invention, not just a straight transference from the sources. Even though some of them lie, in a superficial sense, 'outside the play', we may insist that they 'have some basis in the play itself' and deserve scrutiny.

For a brief example of Shakespeare's adept 'planting' I return to the Norwegian succession. That Old Fortinbras was actually king of Norway emerges only once:

> Such was the very armour he had on
> When he the ambitious Norway combated . . . .
>
> (I.1.60)

'Norway' must refer to the king, especially as Shakespeare immediately reverts to the Norwegian's ambition and challenge:

> Fortinbras of Norway,
> Thereto prick'd on by a most emulate pride . . . .
>
> (I.1.182)

In the next scene we learn that 'Norway', the present sovereign, is 'uncle of young Fortinbras' (I.2.28) – which completes the 'Hamlet parallel'. Shakespeare, however, limned in the Norwegian dynasty as an addition to Belleforest, who, it will be remembered, mentioned the 'battaile' between 'Collere, king of Norway' (= Old Fortinbras) and 'Horvendile' (= Old Hamlet), but gave Collere neither a son nor a brother. In adding these two, Shakespeare, it may seem, also added an inconsistency, in so far as he states (i) that the loser of the Old Fortinbras–Old Hamlet combat should 'forfeit, with his life, all those his lands / Which he stood seiz'd of' (I.1.88); (ii) Old Fortinbras was defeated and in fact Norway was dispossessed of 'those foresaid lands' (103); (iii) yet the kingdom of Norway fell, apparently, not to the crown of Denmark but remained under the rule of the Fortinbras family. Nevertheless, despite his indifference to inconsistencies elsewhere, Shakespeare left none in this case – though he might be convicted of 'ambiguity'. Editors usually gloss 'seiz'd of' (in 'all those his lands / Which he stood seiz'd of') as 'possessed of', yet it appears from Belleforest that a less comprehensive notion may be intended. In the source the Norwegian king envies the Dane's reputation as the greatest pirate of the seas, and for this reason challenges him, 'with conditions, that hee which should be vanquished should loose all the riches he had in his ship' (p. 183). Shakespeare dropped the piracy motif, but his 'seized of' could also refer to lands seized by the two kings in war – and then would not include the whole of Norway.

It suited Shakespeare to build up the 'Fortinbras story', for a number of excellent reasons. The open rivalry between Old Fortinbras and Old Hamlet contrasts with Claudius' secret rivalry; young Fortinbras, like Hamlet, lost his father by violent means, as also lands which he expected to possess, and circumstances compel him to delay taking the law into his own hands; the political issue of the succession is the same in Norway and Denmark.[6] To make so much of the bare mention of the 'battaile' of the two kings Shakespeare had to plan ahead very carefully: his 'plot' hangs together, and therefore we have to take account of it. The possibility of 'electing' a king also receives a bare mention in Belleforest – and similarly becomes something much more important, part of a network of 'political' cross-references woven through the moral fabric of the tragedy. Wilson, of course, denied this. Having missed the crucial passage in Belleforest he argued that the allusions to an 'elective' constitution in Denmark come far too late in the play and cannot mean what to the simple-minded reader or audience they seem to mean:

> it is absurd to suppose that he wished his spectators to imagine quite a different constitution from that familiar to themselves, when he makes no reference to it until the very last scene. It is plain to me that, in using the word 'election' . . . in act 5, scene 2, he was quite unconscious that it denoted any procedure different from that which determined the succession in England.

Shakespeare introduced the audience to 'a different constitution from that familiar to themselves' by means of the parallel of the Norwegian succession, which occupies a considerable amount of space in the first two scenes.

Comparing Shakespeare's Denmark and contemporary England in order to show that in both states a 'succession problem' would be solved according to the same procedure, Wilson then brought forward an 'exact parallel' which would move any lawyer to indignation.

> After all, was not the throne of Elizabeth and James an 'elective' one? The latter monarch, like Claudius, owed his crown to the deliberate choice of the Council, while the Council saw to it that

he had the 'dying voice' of Elizabeth, as Fortinbras has that of Hamlet.

Hankins added the 'not very different' instances of 'the claims of Henry VIII's two daughters', and the abdication of Mary Stuart in favour of her son, enforced by the Scottish lords.[7] But in these three more or less 'contemporary' cases a female heir, or the absence of an indisputable heir, created a situation completely different from that in *Hamlet*, where the deceased sovereign left a son. If we are looking for an 'exact parallel' we should ask, instead, whether there was any question of an 'election' or a 'dying voice' when Charles I followed James I, or when Henry VIII succeeded Henry VII.

To continue on the theme of inheritance, could a Macbeth have been crowned, in early seventeenth-century England, in the lifetime of the legitimate sons of the deceased monarch? This happened during the Wars of the Roses, but never with general consent. Even in 1657, when Cromwell contemplated such a step, he met with implacable opposition and had to draw back: and by then the 'constitution' was far less rigid than in Shakespeare's day. Could Henry VIII have sliced up England among his three children after the manner of King Lear? Much as it has taught us, 'historical criticism' fails when it offers such unsubtle equations of the real world and the imagined.

Unlike later theatrical audiences, peeping through the 'fourth wall' at dramas which are billed up as 'significant' or 'up-to-date' or 'sordid' (all labels that mean merely 'realistic'), Shakespeare's public was not encouraged to think that it eavesdropped upon 'real people'. The vocabulary of the theatre[8] was frequently employed together with other devices to remind the audience that it *was* an audience, a collection of 'Elizabethans' at the Globe watching a play: the unreality of the play was thus emphasised, or, rather, its special reality, its otherness, its unique 'world'.

At the performance of any play of Shakespeare's, and especially of one starting as mysteriously as *Hamlet*, a good audience takes nothing for granted, but feels its way into the story as this unfolds. Actors appear on the stage, yet the audience may not even assume that they represent human beings until told to do so, for they could be fairies, or weird sisters, or even (as in one Stratford production of *The Tempest*) the waves of the sea. Similarly, a good audience will not import into a play contemporary ideas about the laws of inheritance or about politics, but will wait for the dramatist to define these subjects according to his own requirements. Sometimes the definition will be clear-cut from the beginning, sometimes it takes shape only gradually in the course of the play, and sometimes it may remain blurred to the very end – deliberately blurred, for one of the secrets of Shakespeare's wonderfully irradiating art was his mastery of the subordinate art of shadowing.[9]

How, then, is the constitutional problem introduced to the audience? We learn in the second scene that the brother of the late King of Denmark has married 'Th' imperial jointress to this warlike state', and ascended the throne, the 'better wisdoms' of the nobles – presumably the Council[10] – having 'freely gone / With this affair along'. At the same time it transpires that in Norway, as in Denmark, a deceased king's son did not succeed his father, an 'impotent and bed-rid' uncle reigning there; and a little later that Claudius officially recognises Hamlet as 'the most immediate to our throne' (I.2.109). The king himself offers all this information – which, to be sure, Hamlet greets with sour hostility, but challenges neither openly nor in soliloquy for several acts. As Blackstone observed, Hamlet's long silence indicates acquiescence: the prince admits that the king's position is now unassailable.

> I agree with Mr Steevens, that the crown of Denmark (as in most of the Gothick kingdoms) was elective, and not hereditary. . . . Why then do the rest of the commentators so often treat Claudius as an *usurper* . . . ? Hamlet . . . never hints at his being an *usurper*. His discontent arose from his uncle's being preferred before him, not from any legal right which he pretended to set up to the crown . . . .[11]

In fact, Blackstone erred in declaring that Hamlet never hints at Claudius being a usurper. In the closet-scene Hamlet describes Claudius as a 'cutpurse of the empire' who 'stole' the precious diadem (III.4.99–100): to this otherwise unrepeated charge of usurpation I shall return in a moment. Let us note at the same time that Acts II and III are filled with cryptic statements about Hamlet's ambition and thwarted hopes which keep alive the subject of the succession, and the mystery surrounding it: 'O God, I could be bounded in a nutshell and count myself a king of infinite space, were it not that I have bad dreams. GUILDENSTERN. Which dreams indeed are ambition . . .' (II.2.253); 'Beggar that I am, I am even poor in thanks . . .' (271); 'He that plays the king shall be welcome – his Majesty shall have tribute on me . . .' (317); 'their writers do them wrong to make them exclaim against their own succession' (346); 'I am very proud, revengeful, ambitious . . .' (III.1.124); 'I eat the air, promise-cramm'd: you cannot feed capons so' (III.2.92); 'Sir, I lack advancement' (331). Together these innuendoes may be called the second phase in the unfolding of the Danish constitution.

A third phase comes in Act IV, which discloses the part played by the rabble in the king's calculations.

> How dangerous is it that this man goes loose!
> Yet must not we put the strong law on him:
> He's lov'd of the distracted multitude . . . .
> > (IV.3.2)

> > The other motive,
> Why to a public count I might not go,
> Is the great love the general gender bear him;
> Who, dipping all his faults in their affection,
> Would, like the spring that turneth wood to stone,
> Convert his gyves to graces; so that my arrows,
> Too slightly timber'd for so loud a wind,
> Would have reverted to my bow again
> > (IV.7.16)

The fourth and final phase arrives in Act V scene 2, where, for the first time, Shakespeare alludes directly to an 'elective' system:

> He that hath kill'd my king and whor'd my mother;
> Popp'd in between th' election and my hopes . . . .
> > (64)

> But I do prophesy th' election lights
> On Fortinbras; he has my dying voice . . . .
> > (347)

> Of that I shall have also cause to speak,
> And from his mouth whose voice will draw on more.
> > (383)

We can now, I think, retrace Shakespeare's steps and his

'audience-psychology'. In the council-scene (I.2) he conveys the impression that a smooth and plausible Claudius has seized the throne – legally, but not perhaps without some sharp practice. Since, according to the *Oxford English Dictionary*, the word 'jointress' first occurs in *Hamlet*, the audience would not know certainly what was implied by 'Th' imperial jointress to this warlike state' – any more than we do today.[12] It would gather, however, that the new king's swift marriage to his recently widowed 'sometime sister' was, at least in part, a political move; and that the 'better wisdoms' of the council obliged Claudius by bringing 'this affair' to a satisfactory culmination. The disgruntled behaviour of the dead king's son raises further doubts, in so far as the Elizabethans would expect the son to succeed the father in their own 'world': but the 'world of the play' need not correspond to theirs, as the 'Norwegian succession' confirms; therefore the audience will not rush to conclusions. All in all, this second scene continues a process begun in the first, even though superficially contrasting with it. In the first we enter a gloomy region of shadows, a ghost rises, questions are asked but no answers given; in the second a state occasion translates the scene from the shadows to a brilliant public spectacle, and instead of questions there ensue explanations. But the explanations only operate at one level. Claudius intends in his long first speech to present his accession as natural and 'this affair' as closed; yet behind Claudius Shakespeare suggests that 'this affair' is not quite straightforward. Very different as it shows outwardly, the second scene has one important function in common with the first: it mystifies.

Hamlet, of course, consists of a number of interlocking and gradually revealed mysteries. We only become sure of Claudius' guilt in Act III scene 3, and of Gertrude's innocence of murder in Act III scene 4; an end is put to speculation about Hamlet's ability to revenge his father only in the very last scene, while the ghost remains an enigma even after Hamlet decides that he will take its word for a thousand pound.[13] In a play that follows as many threads as expertly as *Hamlet* it should therefore come as no surprise that the mystery of the Danish succession only yields its secret in Act V scene 2, even though Wilson (cf. p. 48) thought such a belated unravelling 'absurd'. Shakespeare kept alive our mild suspense by allowing Hamlet to flash into resentment at his uncle's succession (Acts II and III), and by making Claudius admit the dangers of Hamlet's popular appeal (Act IV). Then, in Act V, he provides a key to the mystery – the 'elective' constitution, which he alludes to three times to ensure that the audience takes it in.

From the vantage-point of Act V most of the earlier references to the succession fall into place. Normally, one assumes, the death of a Danish sovereign leaving a son, a brother and an 'imperial jointress' would lead to an election; Claudius, who dared not risk an election opposed to a rival as popular as Hamlet, managed to by-pass the usual processes by winning over the 'better wisdoms' of the nobility, and by marrying his sister-in-law.[14] When later, on a single occasion, gripped by an agonising passion, Hamlet cries that Claudius *stole* the precious diadem, the audience believes this literally no more than that the king resembles a 'mildew'd ear' and a 'king of shreds and patches' (III.4.64, 102) – for, after all, Claudius has by this time established his dignified and indeed commanding presence in various ceremonial and also private scenes. In determining what weight should be attached to this single charge of an illegal accession we shall do well to bear in mind A. C. Sprague's rule 'that the more dramatic should give place, as evidence, to the less'.[15] Hamlet rants,

A cutpurse of the empire and the rule,
That from a shelf the precious diadem stole
(III.4.99)

at one of the most 'dramatic' climaxes in the play, in one of the two or three passages when we see him at breaking-point – immediately before the reappearance of the Ghost, a possibly self-induced hallucination. Comparably overwrought speeches are found after the Ghost has told its tale (1.5.92ff.), after the king's flight from the play (III.2.265ff.), and, perhaps, in Ophelia's grave (V.1.268ff.: though here Hamlet's 'mouthing' and 'ranting' is partly deliberate). At these times of high tension Hamlet exaggerates, and the audience instinctively distrusts his 'testimony'.

In broad outline Shakespeare's 'Danish constitution' hangs together. None the less, as one would expect, some details are never fully integrated in the general scheme. Who, for instance, voted at the Danish elections? Hardly, one imagines, the 'multitude' – and yet Hamlet's popular support perhaps inclined him to think well of his chances in an election, if only retrospectively, for he seems to have lacked powerful friends at court. Possibly Shakespeare thought of 'the noblest' as the electors, but, if so, he did not bother to make this manifest.[16] Consequently we too need not bother to prod into such 'wingy mysteries' and 'airy subtleties'.

As I have indicated, Shakespeare dwelt on the 'Danish constitution' not only for its own sake but partly to bring into sharper focus the morality of the play; and, similarly, he uses it to direct the play's moods. In the opening scenes uncertainty about Hamlet's and Claudius' rights to the throne links with larger moral uncertainties – for, as C. S. Lewis succinctly phrased it, 'The Hamlet formula, so to speak, is not "a man who has to avenge his father" but "a man who has been given a task by a ghost"' – by a ghost that remains 'permanently ambiguous'.[17] The ghost is not only a doubtful quantity in itself but, to adapt Falstaff, the cause that doubt creeps into men, and into all the familiar appearances of life: doubt becomes a generalised mood in this part of the play.

Likewise the references to Hamlet's popularity in Act IV connect with an atmospheric presence. Not just the 'distracted multitude's' love of Hamlet (IV.3.4, IV.7.18) but also the distraction of the multitude now interests Shakespeare.

> 'Twere good she were spoken with; for she may strew
> Dangerous conjectures in ill-breeding minds.
>
> (IV.5.14)

> the people muddied,
> Thick and unwholesome in their thoughts and whispers
> For good Polonius' death . . . .
>
> (78)

> The rabble call him lord;
> And, as the world were now but to begin,
> Antiquity forgot, custom not known,
> The ratifiers and props of every word,
> They cry 'Choose we; Laertes shall be king.'
>
> (99)

True, earlier parts of the play also animadvert upon the foolishness of 'the million . . . the general' (II.2.430) and the 'groundlings' (III.2.10) – through Hamlet and, by the bye, quite unlovingly – but without political implications. In Act IV the 'general gender' loses its head, to the extent of making a completely 'unconstitutional' attempt to dethrone Claudius. This casts doubt retrospectively upon the absolute legality of his succession, and at the same time distends the act's over-all mood of 'distraction', a growing force in the play which spreads from Hamlet to engulf Ophelia, Laertes (in his ill-considered uprising), the 'multitude' – and even assails the king himself (IV.5.73ff.).

The references to Hamlet's popularity in Act IV connect with still another emergent force.[18] After the moment of truth in Act III, when Hamlet finds proof of Claudius' guilt and Claudius discovers that he must strike or be struck, the law and legal form suddenly become important as instruments of policy. Claudius writes to England to order the legalised murder of his nephew (IV.3.55ff.); he offers to submit Laertes' grievances to arbitration (IV.5.198ff.); he plans to get rid of Hamlet in a duel, a perfectly 'legal' way of despatching one's enemies; and both his allusions to Hamlet's popularity lead to the reflection that it prohibits resort to 'the strong law' (IV.3.3) and 'a public count' (IV.7.17). We get a clear indication of the way his mind works in his soliloquy, when he reflects that in this world, if not in the next, one can 'buy out the law' (III.3.60). As the pressures build up against him, his desire to operate within the bounds of law and, where possible, to make the law his tool, gives further substance to the impression that Claudius did not boggle to take advantage of the law in seizing the crown – an impression that helps to define the special rottenness of Denmark. (Later, in V.1, Shakespeare demonstrates at some length how the court wrests the law: as the grave-digger says, 'the more pity that great folk should have count'nance in this world to drown or hang themselves, more than their even Christen', or, more plainly, in the words of the priest, 'great command o'ersways the order'.) Claudius knows exactly how far he may push the law, yet before the end he becomes a prisoner to his respect for 'the appearance of legality', just as Hamlet is a prisoner of his 'morality', and thus the law defeats him.

Similarly, the 'elective constitution' reinforces generalised thoughts upon which Shakespeare wishes to fix attention in Act V.[19] All through the play the difficulties of 'election' or moral choice are kept in mind, yet in the last act there comes a shift in emphasis – conveniently illustrated by the two main discussions of suicide. The first (III.1.56ff.) puts the question 'To be, or not to be' on a purely personal level, the very possibility of an after-life being seen initially merely in terms of the individual ('To die, to sleep:/To sleep, perchance to dream'); and even as Hamlet's mind plays on the theme it never rises above the personal, or to the truly religious, in 'The undiscover'd country, from whose bourn/No traveller returns'. When the two grave-diggers resume the subject, however, it is in the language of 'crowner's quest law' and with a three-fold iteration of the phrase 'Christian burial', a phrase instantly placed before the audience in that pregnant first speech: 'Is she to be buried in Christian burial *when she wilfully seeks her own salvation?*' Shakespeare now looks at suicide and other 'elections' from a social and religious view-point, underlining time and again the fallibility of the individual:

> Rashly,
> And prais'd be rashness for it – let us know,
> Our indiscretion sometime serves us well,
> When our deep plots do pall; and that should learn us
> There's a divinity that shapes our ends,
> Rough-hew them how we will . . . .
>
> (V.2.6)

Not a whit, we defy augury: there's a special providence in the fall of a sparrow. If it be now, 'tis not to come; if it be not to come, it will be now; if it be not now, yet it will come – the readiness is all.   (211)

> So shall you hear
> Of carnal, bloody, and unnatural acts;
> Of accidental judgments, casual slaughters;
> Of deaths put on by cunning and forc'd cause,
> And, in this upshot, purposes mistook
> Fall'n on th' inventors' heads . . . .
>
> (372)[20]

It enlarges the area of fallibility to suggest that Claudius 'popp'd in' before Denmark, or the Danish nobles, could exercise the right of election, for thus the state is placed in much the same position as Hamlet, who also found it difficult to 'elect' his future. Shakespeare, in fact, mirrors the moral confusion of his hero in the public mind, a confusion mentioned in the first scene (where the 'romage in the land' puzzles ordinary men such as Marcellus), but rising to the proportions of a rebellion in Act IV, and in the final scene to the extraordinary behaviour of the courtiers, who cry 'Treason! treason!' when Hamlet stabs the king but, apparently, do nothing thereafter to prevent him from forcing Claudius to drink the poison. One might almost say that through the momentary indecision of the courtiers the audience glimpses 'the Danish election', for they hold back partly because in doubt as to who is or should be king.

As soon as it grew fashionable to analyse Shakespeare's play-worlds, the 'world' of *Hamlet* became, as one would expect, all things to all men. One held that 'the idea of an ulcer or tumour, as descriptive of the unwholesome condition of Denmark morally, is, on the whole, the dominating one' of its atmosphere; another found in the tragedy a 'central reality of pain', yet sketched in 'the *Hamlet* universe' as 'one of healthy and robust life, good-nature, humour, romantic strength, and welfare'; a third, Mack, submitted that 'the world of *Hamlet*' has as its attributes 'mysteriousness', uncertainty about appearance and reality, and 'mortality'; a fourth, Foakes, that the 'court of Elsinore is . . . at the same time a place of nobility, chivalry, dignity, religion, and a prison, a place of treachery, spying and, underlying this, corruption'.[21] Still another possibility, and a very popular one, is to compare the 'two worlds' of a play, court *versus* country in *As You Like It*, nature and nurture in *The Tempest*, Egypt and Rome in *Antony and Cleopatra*, or Wittenberg face to face with the heroic past in *Hamlet*.[22] The overlap in the five important studies of *Hamlet* which I have cited will be less apparent in my all-too-brief summaries than is actually the case, but one common feature must strike every reader: whether it goes under the name of 'atmosphere' or 'mood' or 'imaginative environment' or 'values', nowadays we tend to consider the 'world of the play' principally as an ambience rather than as a 'reality' that is a 'system of things'.

Looked at as a system of things the world of *Hamlet* reveals a court that differs in essentials from the English court (for example, in its dearth of great noblemen), a constitution nowise resembling that of England, a Christianity neither Roman Catholic nor Protestant, though the imagined world shades into the 'real' one of Shakespeare's England, more or less, in some of its social

structures such as universities, burial rites, dramatic
entertainments. On a different level the system of things in the
play resolves itself into scene after scene of 'policy' or 'diplomacy'.[23]
The king in council, in consultation with Polonius or Laertes, and
even at prayer, pursues the devious paths of policy, sifts, weighs,
bargains, glides over embarrassing obstacles; against him stands
Hamlet, whose 'crafty policy' and 'politike inventions' Belleforest
lauded at every opportunity;[24] against them both, as a foil, stands
Polonius, the politician gone to seed, whose brain 'Hunts not the
trail of policy so sure / As it hath us'd to do' (II.2.47), so that before
long 'a certain convocation of politic worms are e'en at him'
(IV.3.20); and also those shallow vessels, Rosencrantz,
Guildenstern and Osric, would-be politicians who 'did make love
to this employment'. The queen, too, tries her hand, wins Hamlet
to her will (1.2.68ff.), or briefs Rosencrantz and Guildenstern
(II.2.19ff.), while such innocents as Ophelia and Laertes become
the tragic pawns of policy. Three formal embassies enter upon the
stage (to Norway; to England; from England), and diplomatic
letters and messengers bustle in the background from the second
scene to the last. Shakespeare also borrows from Belleforest the
politic notions of the antic disposition, of the employment of
Ophelia as a decoy, and so on, and throws in such further politic
inventions as the play within the play entitled 'The Mouse-trap'.
In private as in public life 'policy' and 'diplomacy' rule all: Polonius
forgets his daughter's feelings, and the king has to hide behind
'painted word[s]' (III.1.53) even with his closest allies, Polonius
and Gertrude. When Hamlet throws aside 'policy' in the queen's
closet (III.4) and speaks daggers the result is a scene of such
intensity that, atmospherically, we re-enter the 'world' of the
soliloquies. No wonder, then, that Horatio's summary of the story
of the play ends with an image inspired by 'the engineer / Hoist
with his own petar' (III.4.206), an image that reflects as in a
raindrop the 'world' of policy and gives us Shakespeare's tersest
formula for the play as a whole:

> And, in this upshot, *purposes mistook*
> *Fall'n on the inventors' heads*: all this can I
> Truly deliver.
>
> (V.2.376)

Of course, the Danish court and constitution and the 'purposes' and 'policy' in *Hamlet* do not even add up to '*Hamlet* without the prince'. The legal and social and visible system of things in a play-world grows into an organism, but no simple formula really explains the life of that organism – partly because it cannot be removed from its medium, or 'ambience'. Unlike some of his modern critics, Bradley knew this: in his *Shakespearean Tragedy* he concentrated, as everyone remembers, on the system of things, and sometimes too hastily identified dramatic characters with 'real people'; nevertheless, he also wrote some splendid pages on the atmospheres of individual plays.[25]

The politics of Shakespeare's Denmark afford a useful example of the complex of elements in the 'world' of a play, and of their osmotic relationship. No one can tell whether Shakespeare planned from the start to make use of the distracted multitude and the elective constitution in the fourth and fifth acts, so that the unfolding of the political and general system of things helped to determine changes of 'imaginative environment' – or whether, at times, Shakespeare paid attention primarily to the moods of his play and fabricated correlatives such as the elective constitution (or a new character or location or the like) in response to the mood's requirements. The constitutional issue is laid before the audience at first vaguely, then more and more definitively, yet the mystifying indications and counter-suggestions of the first act serve an immediate purpose and in no sense commit Shakespeare in advance to an elective Denmark. We *can* tell, however, that the 'mood' and the 'system' grow out of one another, or, perhaps, flash into existence simultaneously, and consequently we may guess that the life-principle of a play is intimately bound up with their organic unity.

4

Trends in the discussion of Shakespeare's characters: *Othello*

I start with a quotation. 'Modern criticism, by and large, has relegated the treatment of character to the periphery of its attention, has at best given it a polite and perfunctory nod and has regarded it more often as a misguided and misleading abstraction.' It *could* be a statement about modern Shakespeare criticism, but in fact it comes from W. J. Harvey's *Character and the Novel*[1] and refers to what is called 'the retreat from character' in discussions of the novel. Professor Harvey found that modern commentators grew shy of 'character-criticism' because of several converging forces, which included the influence of the 'New Criticism', with its commitment to close verbal scrutiny, and of Shakespeare criticism, which had veered in the same general direction a little earlier.

It is useful to remember that the 'attack on character', as Professor Harvey called it, is not an isolated phenomenon in Shakespeare studies, but forms part of a larger critical movement. And it is significant that the reaction that has now begun also straddles traditional critical boundaries. For, just as Professor Harvey decided that 'great novels are chiefly memorable for the characters they portray', and attempted to reinstate character-criticism, at least two voices have independently protested against the fashionable preoccupation of modern Shakespeare criticism with words and poetry, at the expense of character, by citing the same sentence from Ezra Pound: 'The medium of drama is not words, but persons moving about on a stage using words'.[2]

Perhaps, then, it may occur to us belatedly, Bradley was right to devote so much space in a book called *Shakespearean Tragedy* to 'character-criticism'. Certainly, if Shakespeare was admired in the seventeenth century for one pre-eminent gift, it was as a creator of dramatic characters – and, despite all the efforts of historical critics and students of imagery, who tried with art and artifice and with wheels of fire to drag Shakespeare criticism away from nineteenth-century attitudes, the good, old-fashioned interest in character has survived. I want to ask, today, whether it has survived undamaged – or whether, better still, it has mellowed and matured, and is now ready again for public consumption.

As time is short I shall confine myself to one play, *Othello*, in which psychology has a special importance. Shakespeare himself seems to have recognised that this play raised questions about motives which it left unanswered, for he made Othello ask, near the end,

> Will you, I pray, demand that demi-devil
> *Why* he hath thus ensnar'd my soul and body?
> (V.2.304)

Later in the seventeenth century Thomas Rymer fussed more verbosely about the play's psychological mysteries, arguing that it was 'the most absurd maggot that ever bred from any poet's addle brain' to have a lord general, a Venetian lady and an honest soldier behave as they do in Shakespeare. And Coleridge, in effect, made the same point when he coined his famous phrase 'the motive-hunting of motiveless malignity', since Iago, if he was truly motiveless, becomes non-human, a psychological monster.

Throughout the nineteenth century the humanity of Shakespeare's characters nevertheless grew into an article of faith, until another Darwin arrived to challenge faith with scientific method. 'O Shakespeare and Nature', Hazlitt had said, adapting a famous quotation, 'which of you copied from the other?' The Darwin of Shakespeare criticism arrived late, after Bradley's *Shakespearean Tragedy*, in the person of Elmer Edgar Stoll, whose 'historical criticism' repudiated not only Bradley but, by implication, all of his most admired predecessors. In brief, Stoll held that Shakespeare was interested in *story*, not in *character*, and that Shakespeare willingly sacrificed consistency of characterisation whenever this made possible a fine dramatic effect.

Without Stoll's attack upon character there might have been no general critical rebound from character to poetry (as instanced in imagery studies, and the work of L. C. Knights). Yet, though Stoll preached for several decades against the inadequacies of 'character-criticism', his own explanations of Shakespeare failed to carry conviction. Writing of *Othello*, he urged that 'in life' the hero would not 'really have done what he did', that his conduct in the play is 'not in keeping with his essential nature' (which I find perplexing, for, if Stoll feels conscious of an 'essential nature', doesn't that presuppose 'character'?) Be that as it may, Stoll accounted for the miraculous speed of the temptation-scene by detecting a cleverly disguised convention, that of 'the slanderer believed'. Othello succumbs to Iago's lies, Stoll held, because Shakespeare resorted to the age-old story-teller's trick that a slanderer's allegations are not tested but simply believed, a convenient short-cut when a writer is more interested in fine dramatic effects than in psychology.[3]

That there is some dramatic foreshortening in the temptation-scene would be hard to deny. In *Othello*, where fast time and slow time are made to coexist amicably, the convention of 'the slanderer believed' (which is as old as the biblical story of Joseph and Potiphar's wife) may be seen as a time-accelerator, though one that does not inevitably destroy the hero's psychological credibility. After all, clock-time and dramatic time often diverge in drama, and we find it possible to make the necessary mental adjustment. The historical critic, therefore, identifying a convention that probably exerts *some* pressure in the temptation-scene, has not really explained the scene's central mystery, for which most of us would still like to find a psychological explanation.

One is tempted to give an equally half-hearted welcome to the better 'historical' work that followed Stoll. Miss Bradbrook, in *Themes and Conventions of Elizabethan Tragedy* (1935, 1960), proposed a 'historical' explanation of Iago that may have a bearing on his apparent motivelessness, without convincing me that she has solved the problem.

> A character who is behaving 'according to type' will need no motivation at all. In the same way, the 'motiveless malignity' of Iago is not proof that he was a monster. The Elizabethans did not expect every character to produce one rational explanation for every given action. . . . [Iago] is plainly a villain, as he is at pains to expound in soliloquy. Villains are villains; there is no need to ask why.[4]

No need to ask why – and yet Othello (and, through him, Shakespeare) asked precisely this question! Miss Bradbrook's explanation may help us to understand the villains in inferior Elizabethan plays, but fails to acknowledge the insistent life-likeness of Shakespeare's characters in their elusive complexity. Iago is not just *any* villain; and indeed the 'slanderer believed' in

Othello has only the remotest resemblance to Potiphar's wife. To give a name to a 'convention' is not even to begin to explain how it works, since life itself is full of conventions, and 'conventional behaviour' in no sense contradicts the laws of psychology, whether inside the theatre or outside.

Turning back, disappointed, from historical criticism to psychology, we might expect that Freud and his successors would rejuvenate 'character-criticism', since they became respectable just when Stoll began to arouse misgivings (at least in England). Yet the new psychology has never really caught on in Shakespeare studies, and I think that we can see why when we look at a Freudian explanation of Iago, first proposed, I believe, by Dr Ernest Jones (a close associate of Freud).

> *Othello* like *The Winter's Tale* turns upon sexual inversion, there being no possible motive for Iago's behaviour in destroying Othello and Desdemona except the rancour of the rejected and jealous lover of the Moor. . . . This reading . . . explains . . . Iago's baseless suspicions about Othello and Emilia: Iago, like Leontes, projects upon his wife desires in himself the conscious knowledge of which he would avoid.[5]

Though F. L. Lucas made the same suggestion a couple of years later and, it seems, quite independently,[6] I cannot take it seriously – for it assumes that a dramatic character can be placed on the psychologist's couch, and that his forgotten past can be brought back like Eurydice from the grave. A dramatic character, we have to insist, has no forgotten past (unless the play positively gives it a local habitation and a name, whereupon it ceases to be forgotten). As there is not the slightest shred of evidence for Iago's past love of the Moor, we are no more entitled to bring 'sexual inversion' into our explication than to drag in Iago's unmentioned father and mother. Indeed, we ought to ask whether the psychologists' description of what happens *in* the play, let alone what happened before it began, tallies with our experience. Is it correct to speak of Iago's rancour and malignity? I have always thought that the most terrifying fact about Iago is that, despite all his efforts, he cannot really feel hatred for Othello and Desdemona. (He says he does, in passing, without making his malignity much more convincing than his other alleged motives.) He is a moral defective partly because he is without feeling for others, who are merely objects in

the fantasies he weaves for himself – all his passion being reserved
for himself, and for his art as a manipulator of men.

It may be, then, that professional psychologists have failed to
unlock Shakespeare's secrets because they fail to do justice to the
plays at the purely descriptive level, and because they do not
distinguish between the mode of existence of a patient and a literary
fabrication. And yet the 'psychological' interest in Shakespeare
continues. Indeed, it would be fair to say that the most talked-
about reinterpretation of *Othello* of our century reverted to a purely
'psychological' approach. I refer, of course, to F. R. Leavis's
'Diabolic intellect and the noble hero',[7] an essay too well-known
to require a detailed summary, which, despite all the sarcasms
about Bradley's resolute fidelity in wearing his blinkers, strikes me
as, in essence, precisely the same kind of criticism as Bradley's.
(And none the worse for that, though the two reached very
different conclusions). Leavis, you will remember, rejected the
traditional Coleridge–Bradley view of Othello as 'purely noble,
strong, generous and trusting', and merely the victim of Iago's
devilishness, urging instead that 'we should see in Iago's prompt
success . . . not so much [his] diabolic intellect as Othello's
readiness to respond. Iago's power . . . in the temptation-scene is
that he represents something that is in Othello . . . the essential
traitor is within the gates.' In short, Othello does not really love
Desdemona (according to Mr Leavis), and therefore he succumbs
so readily to Iago's lies. Othello's supposed love is rather 'a matter
of self-centred and self-regarding satisfactions – pride, sensual
possessiveness, appetite, love of loving'.

Anyone who now rereads Bradley and Leavis, after a lapse of
time, 'all passion spent', is bound to wonder whether the case of
'the noble Moor' versus 'the brutal egotist' is really an either/or
argument, or something more complicated. To take one short
quotation, which has been pressed into service against Leavis, can
we really disregard Iago's own opinion that Othello has a noble
nature?

> The Moor, howbeit that I endure him not
> Is of a constant, loving, noble nature.
>   (II.1.282)

This, the grudging testimony of a hostile witness, may not be
brushed aside lightly – but, on the other hand, can we dispose of

Leavis's clever essay by simply asserting that Desdemona and Cassio and even Iago think of Othello as the 'noble' Moor?

Before I try to salvage what is most worthwhile in Bradley's reading *and* Leavis's I should like to mention that this particular critical battle had been fought before, and is not as new as Leavis made it appear. Bernard Shaw, in the Preface to *Getting Married* (1908), already voiced disbelief in a nobly loving Othello:

> Othello's worst agony is the thought of 'keeping a corner in the thing he loves for others' uses'. But this is not what a man feels about the thing he *loves*, but about the thing he *owns*. I never understood the full significance of Othello's outburst until I one day heard a lady, in the course of a private discussion as to the feasibility of 'group marriage', say with cold disgust that she would as soon think of lending her toothbrush to another woman as her husband. The sense of outraged manhood with which I felt myself and all other husbands thus reduced to the rank of a toilet appliance gave me a very unpleasant taste.

Isn't this Leavis's point about Othello's possessive, sensual love? A generation earlier Dostoevsky took the opposite view:

> 'Othello was not jealous, he was trustful', observed Pushkin. And that remark alone is enough to show the deep insight of our great poet. Othello's soul was shattered and his whole outlook clouded simply because his ideal was destroyed. But Othello did not begin hiding, spying, peeping; he was trustful. On the contrary, he had to be led up, pushed on, excited with great difficulty before he could entertain the idea of deceit. The truly jealous man is not like that.[8]

Othello's trustfulness, though it may not by itself prove Leavis to be in the wrong, seems to me sufficiently important to deserve a further comment. Othello, I would add, not only trusts Desdemona but has a generally trusting nature. When his confidence in Desdemona is undermined his trust attaches itself to Iago, it clings to him with an almost child-like surrender of intelligence. So, too, his trust in Venice, in the state to which he dedicated his life, seems ill-considered (from Othello's point of view), for it was a total trust and dangerously romantic. And his attitude to the magic handkerchief also seems trusting, not to say superstitious, placed as it is *after* Brabantio's talk of spells and witchcraft, which was given such a cool reception in Act I.

It will be clear that I am reluctant to abandon entirely the traditional view of Othello as a trusting, loving, noble nature; and yet I am disturbed by Leavis's essay, and think that it would be wrong to refuse to learn from it. In this dilemma we may turn for help to sociology, following other 'psychological' critics of Shakespeare who have turned hopefully to an El Dorado called 'character and role'.

Though I have suggested that Leavis adopted essentially the same critical method as Bradley, which we may describe as 'amateur psychology', and that both marshalled their evidence in much the same way, the critics each made a different and disabling decision about Othello's character and role (before these terms were made fashionable by sociologists). Both Bradley and Leavis recognised *two* Othellos in the play, the 'real Othello' and another; Bradley assumed that we meet the 'real Othello' first, at the beginning of the play, and Leavis thought that the essential man emerged in the temptation-scene. Leavis was aware of Othello's 'role-playing', (or 'ideal conception of himself'), and that it has a confusing effect, but took for granted too readily that character and role *can* be distinguished.

The notion that a man's 'inner timbers' and true personality disclose themselves under stress is superficially attractive. We certainly come into more psychologically revealing contact with the stranger who sits next to us in a bus when the bus skids, or crashes. Yet it is also possible that stress *depersonalises* behaviour, that fear, jealousy, revengefulness do not so much reveal the 'inner self' as destroy individuality in a common, human melting-pot. In Shakespeare's tragedy I feel particularly reluctant to accept that the 'real Othello' only finds himself under stress in Act III in so far as he then adopts a way of thinking (in obscene suggestions and animal images) that has been powerfully established as Iago's. In short, it seems at least a possibility that instead of shedding a 'role' and finding his 'character' Othello in Act III merely takes on a new role, reflecting Iago's character more than his own.

Notice that as soon as we begin to speak about 'role-playing' in drama, the character, the 'ghost in the machine', becomes more ghost-like, and is in danger of disappearing altogether. As Peer Gynt discovered, when we shed all of our *roles* there may be no *self* underneath: the 'Emperor of Self' could be an onion, without a heart. In the end *all* behaviour may appear to be role-playing of one kind or another: the more 'role-conscious' we grow the more difficult is it to locate that poor, bare, forked animal, 'unaccommodated man'. Recognising this difficulty, we have to admit that the character-criticism of Shakespeare has, in the past, confused *character* not only with *role* but with *mood*, with *inclination*, and no doubt with other ill-assorted inner processes. Nevertheless, though I dare not *define* character, and I am not at all certain that 'character' or the 'inner self' is sufficiently visible in Shakespearian drama to bear detailed analysis, I would suggest that Shakespeare occasionally allows us to glimpse the inner mystery, and that he gives us just enough information to make it possible to arbitrate between Bradley and Leavis.

We can never quite trust the testimony of those close to the tragic hero who think they understand him, whether a Iago or a Desdemona, since they speak from a definite *parti pris*; and the same is true of the hero himself, especially when he describes himself in moments of tension (for example, as 'one that loved not wisely but too well') – for we sense instinctively that no man thinks dispassionately of himself, least of all just before he commits suicide. Consciously or unconsciously we distrust all of the play's simplistic statements about character, evaluating whatever is said, weighing it against all the conflicting evidence. Yet there are moments when we glimpse the ghost in the machine – and, though we cannot drag it to the light of day, we are left with a conviction that we have encountered the ghost: that is, that beneath Othello's many roles there lurks a definite *character*. The character is partly screened from our gaze by Othello's roles, but we can see it reflected, as the lady of Shalott saw the world in her mirror, when he responds spontaneously to whatever moves him deeply:

> She lov'd me for the dangers I had pass'd,
> And I lov'd her that she did pity them.
>   (I.3.167)

In this and other passages where the Moor responds to moral beauty we feel that he *shares* this beauty, and that deep answers unto deep. The 'real Othello', I suggest, is reflected through his feeling for Desdemona and other intensely held ideals, and flashes upon us in occasional exclamations torn from the very centre of his being, when all the posturing has stopped: 'If she be false, O,

then heaven mocks itself!' (III.3.282); 'But yet the pity of it, Iago!
O, Iago, the pity of it, Iago!' (IV.1.191); 'Be thus when thou art
dead, and I will kill thee / And love thee after' (V.2.18).

Having decided against Leavis as regards Othello's character,
we may still believe that Leavis has enriched our understanding
by pointing to Othello's 'habit of self-approving self-dramatization',
or role-playing. How can we reconcile this with the 'noble Moor'?
Though I worship Bradley 'on this side idolatry', I am dismayed
that he was aware of a theory rather like Leavis's, and rejected it
totally. Others had said, even more bluntly than Leavis, that 'the
play is primarily a study of a noble barbarian, who has become a
Christian and has imbibed some of the civilisation of his employers,
but who retains beneath the surface the savage passions of his
Moorish blood'. Bradley disagreed[9] – but was he right? Othello
surely differs from Shakespeare's other tragic heroes in suffering
from an ethnic and cultural split – the only other example being
Cleopatra's Antony, who, however, embraces his two cultures
more comfortably, without strain. We can see what is distinctively
'ethnic' in Othello when we compare his cry 'O blood, blood,
blood!' (III.3.455) with Lear's 'kill, kill, kill!' In Othello's case, a
primitive blood-lust is supported by other barbaric desires: 'I'll tear
her all to pieces!' (435); 'O, I see that nose of yours, but not the
dog I shall throw't to!' (IV.1.140); 'I will chop her into messes!'
(196). The desire to rip and slash and mutilate, combined with
Othello's monumental dignity in other scenes, sets him apart from
Lear and the rest, but reminds us of portraits of the noble savage –
such as Melville's Queequeg – and helps to identify him as,
inalienably, a Moor.

And yet, though Bradley understressed the Moorish elements,
we do not have to equate Othello's Moorish behaviour-pattern
with his 'inner self'. It should occur to us that, though he may
never have played the part of the savage Moore before, the role
lay to hand in his past, as the prescribed response of one of his
race whose wife has deceived him; that is, the role was 'culturally
available', and tells us little more about the man than his self-
dramatising speech-habits in Venice. I make this reservation
because Othello plays the 'savage' role so very imperfectly,
repeatedly thrusting it aside as he feels the power of Desdemona's
beauty (at which point he ceases to be the 'brutal egotist'):

Ay, let her rot, and perish, and be damn'd to-night; for she

shall not live . . . . O, the world hath not a sweeter creature
. . . .   (IV.1.177)

> O thou weed
> Who art so lovely fair, and smell'st so sweet
> That the sense aches at thee!
>   (IV.2.68)

> O balmy breath, that dost almost persuade
> Justice to break her sword!
>   (V.2.16)

In these and other speeches a 'split' in Othello is made manifest.
He pulls away from the savage role he has adopted, for he cannot
free himself from his instinctive response to Desdemona's physical
and moral beauty – which is still lingeringly that of a lover. The
same speeches suggest that the noble and the savage Moor are
much more intimately one than either Bradley or Leavis was willing
to allow – and that we misread the play when we put all our
money on one or the other.

If we now look back from criticism to the play's stage-history we
find that the relationship of the noble and the savage Moor has
always caused trouble. In the earlier eighteenth century the play's
most 'primitive' episode, Othello's fit, was simply omitted. When
Garrick brought it back it was said that 'in the records of the
theatre' this 'shameful' scene had 'never been acted'. Predictably,
the nineteenth century moved in the other direction, and its most
admired Othello, Tommaso Salvini, took every opportunity to
accentuate the 'primitive', sometimes justifiably, sometimes not.
One of his most striking effects was 'when he seized Iago by the
throat and threw him down as if to trample the life out of him:
then suddenly remembering himself, he gave him his hand and
helped him to his feet',[10] which seems to me an inspired addition,
since it makes an emblematic moment of the split in the Moor. On
the other hand, Salvini also tried excessively to alienate and disgust:
'Most offensive of all was the shockingly realistic manner of the
suicide. With a short scimitar he literally cut or hacked at his throat,
and fell to the ground gasping and gurgling.'[11]

Both the stage tradition and Leavis's essay seem to have
influenced Laurence Olivier's interpretation in its quite excessive
primitivism. Olivier's Moor, with his sudden changes of mood and

expression, his unexpected chuckling and sniggering to himself, his deliberately slurred speech, suggested a barbarian who had scarcely begun to acclimatise to Europe. His Moor's dignity often degenerated into an African swagger. His fit became a focal episode, more prolonged and more unbearably physical than is usual in the theatre; and there were moments in later scenes when his eyes glazed over and one feared that he would fall again. When, enraged, he tore the crucifix from his breast, and kneeling to make his vow 'by yond marble heaven', he put his forehead to the ground in the Mohammedan manner, it became all-too-clear that *this* Othello's Christianity had been the thinnest of veneers. What was lost in this reading was Othello's desperate need to be *assimilated* in Venice, to be something other than a Moor (witnessed in his final pathetic appeal to Desdemona's uncle: 'Uncle, I must come forth!' – V.2.257): what was lost was the pluralism, the complex oneness, of Othello.

A different kind of split was indicated by Paul Robeson's performance at Stratford in 1959. The famous bass spluttered and gasped out the less important dialogue, and more or less sang the great set speeches. This reminded me of T. S. Eliot's comment on Othello's suicide-speech: 'What Othello seems to me to be doing . . . is, cheering himself up. He is endeavouring to escape reality; he has ceased to think about Desdemona, and is thinking about himself.'[12] The 'Othello music', indeed, has this same function throughout the play: whenever Othello feels a sense of racial insecurity he intones it, speaking of his royal ancestors, his services as a soldier, his success as a lover — to cheer himself up. We have all known those who hum to themselves from nervous habit: Othello *sings* to himself, and sings always the same cheering, invigorating song — the 'song of myself'. The defensiveness of the Moor's great arias came across well in Paul Robeson's delivery – and yet the sharp contrast when spluttering speech is suddenly replaced by musical fluency again damaged the essential unity of the Moor's character.

Is it so very surprising that in modern times critics and actors have favoured the notion of *two* Othellos, and have usually found that one is the 'real Othello' and the other a defensive disguise? 'Character and role' criticism, which is only in its infancy, may well encourage this kind of approach – and so it is worth mentioning that Shakespeare's contemporaries were familiar with this way of thinking, though they used different terms. 'All the world's a stage' said Shakespeare, echoing a commonplace that was expounded in a completely modern spirit by Montaigne:

> All the world doth practise stage-playing. We must play our parts duly, but as the part of a borrowed personage. Of a visard and appearance we should not make a real essence. . . . We cannot distinguish the skin from the shirt. It is sufficient to disguise the face, without deforming the breast.[13]

Though Shakespeare and his contemporaries discussed character and role, in their own way, I am not entirely happy about this (to us) new critical game, as we are still inclined to talk too glibly about 'character', as if we know exactly what it is. Unhampered by modern, post-Freudian theories Shakespeare seems to have anticipated eighteenth- and nineteenth-century writers who took a pluralistic view of personality, as did Diderot in *Le Neveu de Rameau*, and Walt Whitman, who declared,

> Of every hue and caste am I, of every rank and religion . . .
> I resist any thing better than my own diversity.[14]

Strindberg's famous Preface to *Miss Julie* illustrates the emerging, modern point of view – one that seems far removed from the psychology of 'humours' but very relevant to Shakespearian tragedy:

> In the course of time the word *character* has been given many meanings. Originally it no doubt denoted the dominant trait in the soul-complex and was confused with temperament. With time it became the middle-class term for an automaton, an individual who had become . . . fixed in his nature. . . . This bourgeois notion of the fixed state of the soul was transmitted to the stage. . . . *My* souls are conglomerates of a past stage of civilisation and our present one, scraps from books and newspapers, pieces of humanity, torn-off tatters of holiday clothes that have disintegrated and become rags — exactly as the soul is patched together.

Without equating Shakespeare's views with Strindberg's, or any other man's, we can see that he too repudiated 'the fixed state of the soul', and that his Othello may be more easily understood as a 'conglomerate' than as an 'automaton'.

What, then, is the relationship of the 'noble Moor' and the savagely jealous Othello who takes over in Act III? Not so long ago the commentators might have said that Othello's character grows or changes, but the notion that dramatic characters develop has now been questioned, and it is sometimes urged that they do not so much develop as gradually reveal themselves. One might argue, for example, that Othello's ferocity does not surprise us when it appears since it had been glimpsed before: his earlier display of calm and nervelessness was potentially menacing. Conversely, as I mentioned earlier, the 'savage Othello' relapses every so often into tenderness and nobility, and seemingly incompatible moods exist together quite convincingly.

It appears, then, that, rather than separate the 'two Othellos' with Bradley, Stoll, Leavis, Olivier, Robeson and the rest, we should recognise that Shakespeare 'stretched' the idea of character to the limits, without *entirely* 'splitting' his Moor. It would be as well, too, to admit that, though we find it convenient to chatter about character and role, or to postulate an 'inner self' or 'deep centre', the inner principle is bound to be more elusive than a simple formula such as either the 'noble Moor' or the 'brutal egotist'. Bernard Beckerman, whose valuable book *Dynamics of Drama* probed some of these mysteries, suggested that in analysing character 'we need to locate the distance from the surface where the true inner life of a character resides'.[15] Admirable advice – except that, for better or worse, Shakespeare's complex characters are so life-like that they keep their 'true inner life' to themselves. I conclude, therefore on a defeated note: modern discussions of Shakespeare's characters have explored his art in new and rewarding ways, and yet we have to admit that we still cannot explain Hamlet and Lear and Othello. Shakespeare's poetry persuades us that they are life-like, but we lack the critical vocabulary to prove it.

5

The uniqueness of *King Lear*: genre and production problems

Thirty years ago it was not a punishable offence to talk about 'Shakespearian tragedy'. Literary critics even dared to discuss 'Shakespeare's tragic period' and 'Shakespeare's tragic vision' in that golden age, that age of innocence, which has passed away like a dream. The fashionable thing now is that you analyse a single work – sorry, you deconstruct a text; you put it against a wall, frisk it, remove all its explosive devices, and ensure that it looks exactly like every other beaten-up text to which you have applied your theory.

We have travelled a long way since the appearance of the most perceptive of all Shakespeare critics, A. C. Bradley. Bradley has been accused of many crimes, almost always unfairly, but it is true that he sanctified the 'Shakespearian tragedy' approach in his well-known chapters on 'the substance of Shakespearian tragedy' and 'construction'. Those who clamour for due recognition of the single text, and therefore 'the death of the author', would be surprised by the many similarities in the substance and construction of Shakespeare's tragedies, as described by Bradley – similarities that point back to a not entirely unnecessary factor, the humble author. But, Bradley discovered, there is an important exception. One play does not really fit in with his account of the essential sameness of Shakespearian tragedy. That difficult old man, King Lear, refuses to play the game.

We all remember Bradley's problem. '*King Lear* alone among these plays', he said, 'has a distinct double action.' More awkwardly, Lear himself cannot be the 'leading figure', since he does not 'initiate action' after Act I. It is impossible, Bradley thought,

> from the point of view of construction, to regard the hero as the leading figure. If we attempt to do so, we must either find the crisis in the First Act (for after it Lear's course is downward), and this is absurd; or else we must say that the usual movement

is present but its direction is reversed, the hero's cause first
sinking to the lowest point (in the Storm-scenes), and then rising
again. But this also will not do. . . . The truth is, that after the
First Act . . . Lear suffers but hardly initiates action at all; and
the right way to look at the matter, *from the point of view of
construction*, is to regard Goneril, Regan and Edmund as the
leading characters.[1]

That is the sort of tangle you get into if, again, you commit yourself
too enthusiastically to a theory, and it helps to explain why some
recent critics have abandoned 'Shakespearian tragedy', and prefer
to hack their way through less difficult territory, the single text.

I had better say clearly, at the start, that I am not opposed to a
genre approach to Shakespeare – quite the contrary. The 'genre
approach' remains valuable, even if we have been strangely careless
in identifying genre. One could plead, in our excuse, that Heminge
and Condell, in the First Folio, were content with rough and ready
labels, *comedy, history, tragedy*, so our willingness to put up with
them is historically justified. On the other hand, Shakespeare
himself signals that the old genre-boundaries are breaking down,
when Polonius announces 'the best actors in the world, either for
tragedy, comedy, history, pastoral, pastoral-comical, historical-
pastoral, tragical-historical, tragical-comical-historical-pastoral',
and so on. A play first published as the 'true chronicle history of
the life and death of King Lear and his three daughters' may seem,
on reflection, to have some claim to be called a tragedy – but what
kind of tragedy? I am going to argue that *King Lear* is fundamentally
different from Shakespeare's other tragedies, and that, following
this trail, we are led to a new understanding of the uniqueness of
Shakespeare's masterpiece.

First, let us list some of the superficial differences. I have already
referred to two – a fully developed double plot, and a tragic hero
who suffers but scarcely initiates action after Act I. In addition
King Lear includes a more prominent Fool (there is a clown in
Othello, another in *Antony and Cleopatra*, two in *Hamlet*, and a Porter
in *Macbeth* – but all restricted to one or two scenes). Physical disguise
is much more prominently used, and involves 'disguised speech'
(both Edgar and Kent). These two features, the Fool and disguise,
are merely the two most obvious ones borrowed by this tragedy
from comedy, a cross-fertilisation that several recent critics have
dwelt upon.[2] To continue: the storm-scenes are much more

protracted, and imaginatively potent, than in the other tragedies. Madness plays a much bigger part, as does stage-violence (the blinding of Gloucester); *King Lear* is the only mature tragedy to resemble *Titus Andronicus* in these two respects, hang-overs from the 'tragedy of blood'. Lear's age, as I have argued elsewhere, also sharply distinguishes him: being so much older than the other tragic heroes, his relationships with secondary characters are different. He never interests us as a husband or lover; he alone comes to life, emotionally speaking, through his children. Because of his aggressiveness, verbalised in his tendency to threaten and curse, and because of his madness and age, the audience responds to him at a certain distance; our 'over-view' of the play is therefore more distanced – an effect also achieved by the neat parallelism of the double plot.

I called them superficial differences, but I take it back. Any one of these factors – the Fool, disguise, the storm, madness, violence, double plot, over-view – significantly affects the total impression. When it is revealed that they are all related, we become conscious of a qualitative difference in the play's very fabric, compared with Shakespeare's other tragedies.

How soon do we notice this in the theatre? The play visibly slows down after the opening scenes, instead of gathering momentum. This is partly disguised by Lear's rising passion, though not for long. It becomes obvious that Lear has nowhere to go, and no plans for the future.

> I will do such things –
> What they are yet I know not; but they shall be
> The terrors of the earth.
>
> (II.4.279)

The hero is given no task to perform, as are Brutus, Hamlet, Macbeth; equally, the villains have no clearly defined intentions, such as Iago's – so the play points forward to no 'promised end', through the normal channels of expectation. True, Lear refers several times to the possibility of revenge, but again without clearly knowing what he wants –

> I will have such revenges on you both
> That all the world shall – I will do such things . . . .
>
> (278)

How, indeed, can one revenge oneself on one's own children?

> Is it not as this mouth should tear this hand . . . ?
>
>   (III.4.15)

Later, Lear's fantasy suggests

> To have a thousand with red burning spits
> Come hizzing in upon 'em
>
>   (III.6.15)

and

> It were a delicate stratagem, to shoe
> A troop of horse with felt; I'll put't in proof,
> And when I have stol'n upon these son-in-laws,
> Then kill, kill, kill, kill, kill, kill!
>
>   (IV.6.185)

These, though, are the ravings of a madman, not options seriously proposed by the play; their very improbability underlines the fact that Lear's situation defeats him – that he cannot imagine an appropriate course of action. And this failure of the hero and of the villains to 'look forward', to fix the audience's attention on a task or plot, deprives the play itself of forward-looking suspense, a characteristic strength of the other tragedies.

Not content with a tragic hero marooned in purposelessness, Shakespeare daringly added Gloucester, a second father with nowhere to go. 'I have no way,' he says 'and therefore want no eyes' (IV.1.19). Two fathers cast adrift, with little or nothing to do: they appear to work loose from the plot and just 'hang around'. As Lady Bracknell almost said, 'to lose one father may be regarded as a misfortune, to lose two looks like carelessness'. But of course there is Edgar as well, a third drifter whose most positive forward-thinking can be summed up in the words 'Lurk, lurk' (III.6.115), meaning 'hang around, and hope for the best'. Not really the most exciting recipe, you may think, for a grand tragedy.

When Jan Kott wrote so interestingly about *King Lear* and Beckett's *Endgame* it was the drifting talk of the middle scenes that he had in mind, particularly Lear's meeting with Gloucester. Peter Brook's subsequent production of *Lear* pushed the whole play towards Beckett – too much so, since there is much more to *King Lear* than drifting talk. Nevertheless, Kott has identified another genre that we must keep in mind, one that specialises in characters who 'hang around' and talk rather than act. *Endgame*, however, is best seen as a sub-genre, part of a larger tradition that goes back to the Greeks and is found in many later literatures – the drama of the man who wants to understand the universe. The hero tries to understand the injustice of the gods, man's inhumanity to man, and sometimes embarks on a journey leading to redemption, or self-knowledge. I am thinking of *Oedipus, Faust, Peer Gynt*, Beckett, and, particularly, of a pre-Shakespearian English variant, the morality-play concerned with man's moral education, such as *Magnificence* and *Everyman*.

In what I shall call 'the Oedipus–Everyman play' the hero is, characteristically, a sinner who becomes a thinker; in the course of the play he suffers rather than initiates action. (Goethe's *Faust* does not conform exactly; nor does *King Lear* – the greatest works of art inevitably burst the bonds of tradition.) Now, since the thrust of these plays is towards understanding, not action, we see that all the 'hanging around' in the middle scenes of *King Lear* is not due to carelessness after all; it is artfully contrived, to create opportunities for thinking, for intellectual discovery, the real business of the play.

> O, reason not the need! our basest beggars
> Are in the poorest thing superfluous.
> Allow not nature more than nature needs,
> Man's life is cheap as beast's.
>
> (II.4.263)

Here, and in the many speeches about man and nature, and in all the 'mad scenes' (the mock trial, the speeches on female sexuality or the rascal beadle), Shakespeare could be said to 'slow down' the play, since the 'outer action' does not move forward; yet, as every theatre-goer instinctively feels, these speeches are not digressions but the very life-blood of the tragedy.

In *King Lear* this inner action competes with the outer one of domestic and political intrigue, and our attention is fixed more and more on mental events, Lear's state of mind and the 'visions' he sees and describes in those apocalyptic speeches – speeches that the other characters partly ignore, or dismiss as the ravings of a madman. It is all managed so naturally: for what do you do if you're a poor lost soul, rejected by the young and regarded as useless? You go around giving lectures – and those lectures, of course, are terribly exciting – to yourself – even if no one listens. Lear becomes a kind of lecturer, with urgent messages for the betterment of mankind, and he has to learn a discouraging lesson: a lecturer is a man who usually talks in someone else's sleep.

I have reached my first production-problem. It is a normal courtesy on-stage that when another actor addresses you, you pretend to listen; if your company's leading actor addresses you, you listen. *King Lear*, however, is different. After Lear has abdicated people pay less attention to him, a point immediately visualised in Act I scene 4, when the steward Oswald, crossing the stage, does not answer him properly. 'You, you, sirrah, where's my daughter?' In a hurry, Oswald slips past him, saying 'So please you –', and disappears, enraging the King. As Lear's rage gradually takes possession of him, others regard him less and less – rage, after all, is one way of demanding attention, and the king's rage mounts partly because he senses that others fail to listen. The producer's problem is that while the theatre-audience finds everything Lear says fascinating, the *dramatis personae* or 'stage-audience' in a sense lose interest in him. First Goneril and Regan treat his complaints as dotage, only half-attending to him; later, in the storm-scenes, his faithful attendants are anxious about his well-being without always heeding his rambling words. More and more, Lear turns into a man talking to himself. The common stage practice that the other actors 'freeze' attentively during Lear's great speeches is therefore, in my view, a mistake; indeed, it is arguable that those speeches will affect us more powerfully if in some cases – not all – the other characters pointedly busy themselves with other things (whispering privately, eating a sandwich) so that Lear's most passionate words fall on indifferent ears.

I want to pursue these introductory thoughts by looking more closely at some of the special features of *King Lear*. And, first, the storm-scenes. Now you may think that there is nothing very special about the storm in *King Lear*, except that it does not know where to stop. Are there not storms in *Julius Caesar* and *Othello*, thunder and lightning in *Macbeth*, not to mention *Pericles*, *The Winter's Tale*, *The Tempest*? You may say that dear old William simply enjoyed a good rumble. One might reply, more seriously, that no two things that look alike in Shakespeare are undifferentiated; the storm in *King Lear* differs in many important ways from those in other plays and, given some attention, leads to the very heart of this tragedy. It is not just that it continues through so many scenes, but that it seems to be intimately connected with Lear's mental and emotional states, the 'inner action'.

How and when does the storm begin? As Lear's 'rage' gathers within him it *suggests* a storm to his imagination:

> You nimble lightnings, dart your blinding flames
> Into her scornful eyes.
>
> (II.4.163)

The first clear sign of a storm in the text comes more than a hundred lines later, when Cornwall says 'Let us withdraw; 'twill be a storm' (II.4.286); editors normally insert a stage direction, *'Storm and tempest'*, at about this point – misleadingly, I think, since "twill be a storm' only implies preliminary winds. Sometimes, though, producers call for preliminary noises somewhat earlier, making the storm gather momentum more gradually, and this can have a bearing on interpretation. For, if preliminary winds are audible before Lear addresses the 'nimble lightnings', the image comes to him quite naturally, triggered off by what he hears; on the other hand, if Lear's white-hot imagination thinks of 'nimble lightnings', and he then appeals to the gods –

> O heavens,
> If you do love old men, if your sweet sway
> Allow obedience, if you yourselves are old,
> Make it your cause; send down, and take my part!
>
> (II.4.188)

– and *then*, shortly after, the first rumblings are heard, something quite different is intimated; namely, that the storm is somehow connected with Lear's condition, or even comes in answer to his appeal. Notice that there are at least two possibilities; when the gods respond too unmistakably, as if answering on the telephone, the effect is not the same (there is a good example of this in *The Revenger's Tragedy*, V.3). Shakespeare, never committing his play to the view that the gods actually exist and hear our prayers, manages to suggest that, just possibly, the outer storm is *willed* by King Lear, is, so to say, an extension of his rage, an impression that is reinforced when Lear himself speaks in the same breath of 'this contentious storm' and 'this tempest in my mind' (III.4.6ff.), as if the two are connected.

I feel that it can be no accident that the storm is pretty well coextensive with Lear's madness – or rather, let us say, with his enraged madness. He is in *high rage* when the *high winds* begin to ruffle (II.4.295); later we hear of his *ungovern'd rage* (IV.4.18), and finally that his *great rage* is killed (IV.7.78). If, instead of talking of Lear's madness, we think of his madness as a *great rage*, as Shakespeare encourages us to do, we shall begin to understand the significance of the outer storm:

> Blow, winds, and crack your cheeks; *rage*, blow. . . .
>   (III.2.1)

But, of course, when Shakespeare's imagination fastens on to a good multi-purpose symbol, there is no end to the different uses he may find for it. The storm in *King Lear* is connected with another highly original technique in the play, the way human beings talk past one another, as if insulated from one another – as if they cannot hear properly. I have already mentioned that other characters do not always listen to the king, when he loses his grip on things; the emphasis upon 'not hearing properly' is, however, much more pervasive. Cordelia seems unable to hear what her father tries to say to her in the 'love-test'; she shuts him out, mentally, very much as her sisters later shut the gates on him physically; Lear cannot hear what she and Kent say to him, and fails to hear the danger, the 'glib and oily art' (I.1.223), in Goneril and Regan's words. When the Fool appears, and Lear literally does not listen to him, his attention switching on and off, the play's concern with 'not hearing properly' is unmistakable; the climax comes in the encounters of Lear, the Fool and Poor Tom (III.4 and 6), where each of the three seems to speak from inside a private world. 'What, has his daughters brought him to this pass?'; 'Take heed o' th' foul fiend!' 'Prithee, nuncle, tell me whether a madman be a gentleman or a yeoman?' They all talk to themselves. During these scenes, the central storm-scenes, the speakers are further insulated from each other by the sheer noise of wind and thunder; each of them struggles, almost drowns, in a chaos of sound. A related technique is Shakespeare's use of disguise (a special feature of this tragedy, as I have already said): Kent and Edgar, disguised, may not utter their true feelings, cannot make themselves heard (hence the special use of asides in *King Lear*). The blinded Gloucester, groping on his own or clinging to Poor Tom, also exists in a self-enclosed world, and reinforces the play's emphasis upon individuals locked away from others. Not hearing and not seeing therefore have a similar function in *King Lear*.

Among other things, the storm-scenes press home the view that every man is an island. After the storm is over this view persists for a while, until Lear and Cordelia are reunited. When Lear and Gloucester meet in Act IV scene 6, each is still locked away in a private world, but the play prepares for the Lear–Cordelia scene by focusing on man's struggle to reach out to others. Having been totally self-absorbed, in his blindness, Gloucester now tries to 'get through' to Lear:

> I know that voice. . . .
> The trick of that voice I do well remember.
> Is't not the king? . . .
> O, let me kiss that hand!
>
> (IV.6.95)

But Lear is almost unreachable, wrapped away in visions. And those visions, significantly, also dwell on man's inability to 'get through' to others.

> When I do stare, see how the subject quakes . . . .
> Down from the waist they are centaurs . . . .
> Thou rascal beadle, hold thy bloody hand.
>
> (108)

These visions are still generated by Lear's *great rage*, which began before the 'outer' storm and continues vibrating after it.

By the next scene (IV.7) the outer and the inner storm have passed away, and the king for the first time opens himself to human contact, for the first time genuinely *hears*. It is a gradual process, artfully prolonged by Shakespeare because it is the climactic 'recognition-scene', one of a series in which Lear grapples with the same problem, truly identifying other people –

So young and so untender?
    (I.1.105, to Cordelia)

Your name, fair gentlewoman?
    (I.4.235, to Goneril)

I'll talk a word with this same learned Theban
    (III.4.153, of Poor Tom)

Ha! Goneril, with a white beard!
    (IV.6.96, to Gloucester)

In these earlier attempts to identify others we are conscious of
grotesque, almost wilful, misunderstanding – a habit that has not
left him when he wakes from his sleep and identifies Cordelia as
an angel ('Thou art a soul in bliss' – IV.7.46). But Lear's imperious
need to impose false identities upon others, to make others conform
to *his* view of the world, melts away in Cordelia's presence. Please
observe that the scene requires several tensely expectant silences
(and how much more effective they are after the earlier storm-
scenes!), electrically charged silences during which we see the
king reaching out to 'get through' to Cordelia, reaching out to
understand the here and now. Superficially this 'recognition-scene'
presents a father identifying his daughter; in addition, though, we
sense that everything in the play climaxes here, as the old man
struggles to identify and understand – Cordelia, love, forgiveness,
the moral nature of the universe.

> Methinks I should *know* you, and *know* this man;
> Yet I am doubtful; for I am mainly ignorant
> What place this is; and all the skill I have
> Remembers not these garments; nor I *know* not
> Where I did lodge last night. Do not laugh at me;
> For, as I am a man, I *think* this lady
> To be my child, Cordelia.
> CORDELIA.   And so I am, I am!
> LEAR. Be your tears wet? Yes, faith. I pray, weep not;
>   If you have poison for me I will drink it.
>   (IV.7.64)

This is the most intimate human contact in the play, traditionally brought to its flash-point as the father touches his daughter's cheek, to make sure of her tears. The touch, first introduced by Garrick, is as implication-packed as Michelangelo's God the Father transmitting life to Adam – and yet I have seen this traditional stage-business improved. The actor of King Lear touched Cordelia's tears, and then, scarcely knowing what he was doing, put his finger to his mouth to taste their saltiness, another wonderfully suggestive moment. The tasting, it was later discovered, had been thought of before, by Henry Irving, but was not what the actor had been told to do in rehearsal: it came to him, instinctively, during performance, surprising him as much as the audience, and was felt to belong there, to be right. Why? Well, it reinforces Lear's wondering incredulity, his need to make absolutely certain that he is not dreaming (he sees, touches and tastes the tears); it gives a further hint of something dimly visible in Lear's faltering helplessness, that the old man becomes Cordelia's child (children suck their fingers); also, the tasting, a physical mingle, the finger between the lips, hints at sexual overtones, and adds to the mystery of the intimate contact here.

The storm, therefore, has an extraordinary number of interlocking functions, and, in addition, prepares for the 'resonant' silences of the Lear–Cordelia scene, where, again, so much is said *without words*. The 'outer' storm seems to emerge from Lear's 'inner' storm – or, perhaps, to be the response of sympathetic gods. It insulates Lear from human contact (others cannot hear him, he has to shout); indeed, from all contact (the thunder and the gods seem not to hear). It symbolises the chaos of the moral universe that Lear tries to understand. And of course it is a threatening physical presence, a major character in the play's central scenes – and, accordingly, its 'voice' must be as carefully controlled as that of any human character. How often, though, do producers 'block in' off-stage noises as meticulously as stage-movement, or the intonations of the human voice? The storm in *King Lear* needs to be scored like music, with split-second timing for every thunder-clap, the storm-noise swallowing up only those spoken words that are of secondary importance. 'Rumble thy bellyful. Spit, fire; spout, rain' Lear cries to the elements (III.2.14), probably just after a rumbling thunder-blast – which, however, must not drown Lear's own poetry. Shakespeare therefore inserted the Fool's speech ('O nuncle, court holy water in a dry house is better than this rain-water . . . '). The Fool's high-pitched voice can pierce through the sound of thunder more easily than the Lear-actor's baritone; and if we miss some of the Fool's wisdom it does not matter so much. I am not suggesting that every reference to thunder or wind synchronises exactly with what the audience hears, but only that it must sometimes be so, intimating a mysterious connection, not a cause-and-effect relationship; and, consequently, that every single sound-effect must be perfectly timed.

Having argued that the orchestration of the storm is so important, I had better confess that we do not know precisely how it was done. Modern producers, so much cleverer than the 'Elizabethans', may use recordings or electronic devices; not so long ago they would have called for the 'thunder-sheet', a sheet of metal that generates a prodigious noise, the sort of gadget every lecturer needs to wake up a drowsy audience. Who invented this delicate musical instrument, and when? The infallible *Oxford English Dictionary* tells us – very little. It does not record 'thunder-sheet', but mentions that in the late sixteenth century 'sheet' was used quasi-adjectivally, meaning 'rolled out in a sheet; especially of metals' (sb. 13). Perhaps then, just as Haydn's clock-symphony was inspired by the metronome, and the Pastoral Symphony by the cuckoo-clock, we owe the magnificent bravura of *King Lear* to the humble, newly invented thunder-sheet? But, as Dr Johnson said, of such idle fancies enough! Our only clear-cut evidence as to storms in Shakespeare's theatre occurs in the Prologue to *Every Man in his Humour*:

> Nor nimble squib is seen, to make afeard
> The gentlewomen; nor roll'd bullet heard
> To say, it thunders; nor tempestuous drum
> Rumbles, to tell you when the storm doth come.

Bullets (that is, cannon-balls) rolled in metal containers, explosive devices, kettle-drums (and probably other percussion instruments) were all available for stage-storms. The drums would be played by professional musicians; and other sound-effects, I believe, would be executed with equal precision. Professional actors who could perfectly imitate a cock-crow, as in *Hamlet*, will have known how to apply split-second timing to the storm in *King Lear*.

Recent critics have rightly emphasised the 'resonances' in *King*

Lear – the play's meaningful repetitions and suggestiveness. Such resonances can be found in the other tragedies, but not as an end in themselves, displacing the outer action. In *King Lear* they often demand our chief attention, whereas in the other tragedies they support a story; and in this respect *King Lear* resembles the Last Plays, where symbolism and mythic resonances also compete with the 'story interest'. The storm in *King Lear*, indeed, has more in common with Prospero's tempest, which expresses his fury against those who have wronged him, than with any storm in the tragedies – for both Prospero's tempest and the storm in *King Lear* 'resonate' with implications that point beyond mere story.

Such comparisons are helpful because they can reveal what is unique in a play. 'Honour' and 'honourable' in *Julius Caesar* resemble the repeated 'honest' in *Othello*; once we identify a similarity, we quickly perceive how uniquely each word functions. Lear's waking up to the sound of music resembles a scene in *Pericles*, where Marina sings to her father, and he returns to life; in *Pericles*, however, the dramatic effect is thinner, the resonances being less potent. Let us look again at this climactic scene in *King Lear*, and try to understand the demands the play makes upon us, over and above its 'story interest'. Why is Lear's awakening so different from that of Pericles, despite the superficial similarities?

I have already suggested one reason for the special magic of Lear's slow awakening: the scene counterpoints the frantic bustle and noise of the storm-scenes. Another is that here for the first time the old king, who could not make others listen to him, has the total attention of Cordelia, who hangs breathlessly on his every word – so that every word becomes precious, a jewel tremulously offered to an angel.

> You do me wrong to take me out o'th' grave.
> Thou art a soul in bliss; but I am bound
> Upon a wheel of fire . . . .
>
> (IV.7.45)

'You do me wrong' had been Lear's refrain to all three daughters, to the gods, the storm, the world; now this 'resonating' thought swims to the surface again. The effect depends partly on our awareness that, while Lear's tone has changed, deep down he remains the man he was.

I know you do not love me; for your sisters
Have, as I do remember, done me wrong:
You have some cause, they have not.

(73)

He remains the man he was, for 'I know you do not love me'
makes the same pathetic appeal as the love-test – 'say you love
me!'

Lear's madness gives Shakespeare many opportunities for
meaningful repetition, particularly in Lear's fixed ideas. Repetition
being so important where Lear's own thoughts and actions are
concerned, we see that Shakespeare's decision to echo the main
plot in the sub-plot could not have been taken lightly – for it makes
'resonance' a life-principle of the play. Two fathers and their
children, nature, ingratitude, patience, blindness in the main plot
and sub-plot: it is almost too obvious. And most readers see that
Shakespeare connects the two plots at the outset: 'Nothing, my
lord. – Nothing! – Nothing. – Nothing will come of nothing. Speak
again' (I.1.86). 'Nothing, my lord. – . . . The quality of nothing
hath not such need to hide itself. . . . Come, if it be nothing, I
shall not need spectacles' (I.2.31). Not everyone realises, though,
that the mysterious connection established here between the
two plots resembles others that follow, such as the undefined
connection between Lear and the storm.

The interconnections of the two plots are infinitely suggestive –
let me give another example from Lear's reunion with Cordelia.
Lear at first thinks that he wakes up in the other world, and only
gradually accepts that he is still alive. In the previous scene
Gloucester steels himself for death, leaps, as he thinks, from Dover
cliff, and also has to be painfully persuaded by his own child that
he is still alive. Both men, to adapt Keats's phrase, 'die into life';
as they cross-question their child and learn what has happened,
each finds himself in the same predicament, in the same kind of
'recognition-scene'. Gloucester and Lear both have to 'recognise
themselves' – that is the whole point of the Oedipus–Everyman
play, understanding oneself being the most difficult part of
'understanding the universe'. We should be reminded, as Lear
grapples with the problem and kneels to Cordelia, of his earlier
mock-kneeling to Goneril –

'Dear daughter, I confess that I am old;
Age is unnecessary; on my knees I beg
That you'll vouchsafe me raiment, bed, and food.'

(II.4.152)

But when Lear kneels to Cordelia, theatre-goers should perhaps be reminded of another 'resonance', Gloucester's kneeling to Edgar.

Here is another production-problem. *Should* Gloucester kneel to Edgar? After his 'death-leap' Gloucester does not stand on his feet until twenty-five lines of dialogue have passed (Shakespeare takes some trouble to pin-point the exact moment when he rises, in Edgar's speech. 'Give me your arm. / Up – so. How is't? Feel you your legs? You stand.') Should Gloucester simply lie there, like a dying animal, for twenty-five lines? I believe that it would be natural for Gloucester to struggle first of all into a kneeling position, before he stands up, and that Edgar hovers breathlessly above him, exactly anticipating Lear and Cordelia in the next scene – a tableau that makes its point in an instant: the father kneels, the son stands.

Producers, I have to admit, do not always allow Lear to kneel to Cordelia, perhaps because she does not want him to – but can Cordelia know what he so strangely intends, until he is actually on his knees? It seems to me psychologically right that the king, who had refused to kneel to Goneril, now kneels before Cordelia, and symbolically right that, just as Gloucester is taught by Edgar, Lear learns to 'know himself' mothered by his child.

CORDELIA. No, sir, you must not kneel.
LEAR.   Pray, do not mock me:
    I am a very foolish fond old man,
    Fourscore and upward, not an hour more nor less;
    And, to deal plainly,
    I fear I am not in my perfect mind.

(IV.7.59)[3]

The resonances in *King Lear* add to the play's suggestive uncertainties in plot and theme echoes that are deliberately left undefined. It is a characteristic Shakespearian touch that we are not told *why* the king kneels. Could it be that he simply imitates Cordelia, who has just knelt for his blessing? Or that he wants to ask for her pardon? If the latter, he only says so in his exit-line, almost an afterthought. 'Pray you now, forget and forgive; I am old and foolish.' Between his awakening and his kneel, he seems disoriented – and exactly how much he understands is not clear. Because we are uncertain about his mental state, the effect is all the more wonderful when at last he does understand.

> Pray, do not mock me:
> I am a very foolish fond old man.

It may be that this *understanding* brings him to his knees – the sacramental moment when he finally recognises Cordelia and, in the same instant, the immensity of all that he has done.

I have emphasised the difficulties we have in following Lear's mental processes (they begin before his madness, in the love-test scene, and continue to the very end of the play); and similar difficulties are multiplied by the 'resonances' of the two plots, and by other repetitions that manifestly demand our attention, pulling us away from the 'outer story'. Another trick of the play with a similar effect is its habit of bringing the story close to folk-tale, myth, parable or emblem, without ever superimposing this other image exactly upon the play's realism (as happens when Hamlet meditates with Yorick's skull in his hand, that familiar emblem of the melancholy man). In *King Lear* we are frequently reminded of emblems and the like, but the 'story' and this other image come uneasily together, so that we cannot be sure of our bearings. Producers who strongly suggest, at the beginning, that *King Lear* is to be the story of Cinderella and her two ugly sisters deprive the play of some of its magic, for it works at least as well when Goneril and Regan are glitteringly beautiful; and perhaps the 'other image' here should remind us, though not too obviously, of the judgement of Paris, and of the three goddesses who bid for his favour. At the other end of the play, when Lear cradles the dead Cordelia in his arms, Shakespeare creates a tableau very like a *pietà*, even though he stops short of identifying Cordelia as a 'Christ figure'. An emblem recommending *patience* in the *storms* and *tempests* of life also has its relevance, as has one that claims that 'the wealth of the tyrant is the poverty of his subjects', which reminds me of Lear's prayer for 'Poor naked wretches' (III.4.28ff.). Shakespeare's poetry, however, transcends all such two-dimensional emblems.

The critic who has done more than anyone else to explain the resonances of *King Lear*, Maynard Mack, has not I think gone far enough in writing of the play's distinctive 'combination of parable and parable situations with acute realism'.[4] As I have tried to argue, *King Lear* pulls away from 'acute realism' at many points, and for this and other reasons differs so profoundly from *Hamlet*, *Othello* and *Macbeth*. When Gloucester bids farewell to Edgar and casts himself down, as he thinks, from Dover cliff, producers who are unwilling to disengage from realism meet their nemesis. How far, they wonder, should Gloucester fall to make the leap 'realistic' and convincing? Should the blind man inch to the edge of an overhang, and fall down two or three feet into a conveniently placed sand-pit? Marvin Rosenberg rightly rejects 'an actual fall from some height', and also another 'realistic' expedient. 'Theatre Edgars', he tells us, 'have sometimes circled to catch Gloster as he falls, to make clear to audiences that the scenery described is wholly illusory.'[5] Gloucester's leap is, surely, as decisive a moment in the play as is the statue that stirs and breathes at the end of *The Winter's Tale*; when Gloucester so improbably thumps down on the stage, like a sack of coal, an instantaneous physical impact, and Edgar persuades him that he fell like 'gossamer, feathers, air', we are at the farthest possible remove from acute realism, and can only explain what we see as a wonder, exactly as Shakespeare asks us to understand the awakening of Pericles, and the return to life of the statue in *The Winter's Tale*. Gloucester and Lear think themselves dead, and then are miraculously reborn.

The 'rebirth' of Gloucester and Lear creates two more production-problems that are related. Those who know the story *expect* Gloucester to rise and Lear to wake up cured; Shakespeare, however, asks us to be prepared for other possibilities. Gloucester's leap, though not in fact from Dover cliff, may still destroy him with shock, as Edgar acknowledges –

> I know not how conceit may rob
> The treasury of life. . . .
>
> (IV.6.42)

When Edgar asks 'Alive or dead?' the answer should not be a foregone conclusion. Similarly, there are several warnings that Lear may be permanently deranged (III.6.97ff.; IV.4.11ff.) if 'repose' is withheld; he continues to wander without repose, and at the end of Act IV scene 6 we are told, with seeming finality, 'The King is mad.' Lear's coma-like sleep, his slow awakening and initial confusion, all point forward to the possibility that he may not be cured after all, despite the doctor's hopeful reassurances. Shakespeare wants us to believe that Gloucester may be dead after his leap, and that Lear may be incurably mad – because the magic of their 'rebirth' is so important to the play.

And of course their rebirth is intimately connected with Lear's last entry – '*Enter Lear, with Cordelia dead in his arms.*' So we read it in just about every modern text, although the Quarto and Folio stage-direction, '*Enter Lear, with Cordelia in his arms*', by no means assures us that she is dead; on the contrary, it leaves open the possibility of another return to life – a miracle we long for with Lear, just as in *The Winter's Tale* we identify with Leontes' yearning that the statue should move, and live. This possibility has been prepared for by the 'rebirth' of Gloucester and Lear in Act IV, and by the repentance of Edmund, another miraculous 'rebirth':

> I pant for life. Some good I mean to do,
> Despite of mine own nature.
>
> (V.3.242)

These 'resonances' suggest that in the world of *King Lear* miracles are possible, and that Cordelia may after all be saved in time. Yet in all the productions that I have seen one felt that Albany, Kent and Edgar had enjoyed the doubtful privilege of learning their parts from a modern text; they accepted that Lear enters with Cordelia '*dead in his arms*', and displayed little interest in what they took to be a corpse.

Let us examine the credentials of this stage-direction, which so crucially influences our reading of Shakespeare's most powerful tragic ending. The word 'dead' was first inserted by Nicholas Rowe in 1709 (i.e. '*Enter Lear, with Cordelia* dead *in his arms*'); and Rowe could not have followed a stage-tradition here, since Tate's adaptation was the only version of the play acted in the theatre from 1681, and in Tate's version Cordelia did not die. In 1681 Rowe was only seven years old – so his stage-direction, '*Cordelia* dead *in his arms*', can only be a guess, and, like some of Rowe's other editorial decisions, may be a bad guess. It has no textual authority whatsoever.

Could it be that when one actor carries on another 'in his arms' the second one must be presumed dead? Certainly not. In *Titus Andronicus* Aaron enters *'with his child in his arms'* (V.1.19), and the child is alive. A stage-direction in *Cymbeline* (IV.2.196) is even more revealing: *'Enter Aruiragus, with Imogen dead, bearing her in his Armes'* (Folio). Imogen only seems to be dead at this point, and Cordelia, who is not described as dead in the Quarto or Folio, may equally be alive when Lear carries her on *'in his arms'*. Since the familiar stage-direction, *'with Cordelia dead in his arms'*, has absolutely no authority, let us consider the alternative. I do not wish to propose that Shakespeare merely copied the master-stroke from his previous tragedy, *Othello*, where Desdemona, seemingly dead, revives, speaks a few broken words, and then really dies. Shakespeare never repeated himself so obviously, and Cordelia is not asked to 'do a Desdemona'. If Cordelia returns to consciousness and then dies, as I would suggest, the final twist of the knife is that she is unable to speak. (Lear found her 'hanging'; perhaps her neck is broken.) She opens her eyes; now it is the father who hangs breathlessly over his child. She wants to speak, but the words do not come; father and daughter are locked together in a look – again, so much has to be said *without words*; again, as Lear gazes into his dying daughter's eyes, the mystery of the universe, the need to *understand*.

Could it be done in the theatre? An eye-witness of a production of *Othello*, in 1610, wrote in Latin that 'Desdemona, killed by her husband, although she always acted her part excellently, moved us still more in her death; when lying in her bed she invoked the pity of the spectators merely by her facial expression.'[6] The boy-actor's speaking look, just before death, could evidently hold the audience spell-bound; and that audience, of course, was more familiar than we are with public executions and would know that criminals were frequently taken down from the gallows alive – were hung, drawn and quartered alive – and therefore would not assume automatically that Cordelia must be dead when Lear enters *'with Cordelia in his arms'*.

This, then, is a very different way of explaining the tragic ending. It has exactly the same authority as Rowe's guess that Cordelia is already dead – neither more, nor less – but in my opinion it has some intrinsic advantages. It recapitulates the father's and daughter's earlier attempts to 'get through' to one another, and repeats the tragic message that we are all 'locked away' within ourselves. It could be seen as the climax of this 'Oedipus–Everyman play', the tragic hero's last opportunity to understand, a 'resonance' that sums up all that has gone before. Indeed, the interpretation of *King Lear* that I have proposed, emphasising the mystery of the storm, the mysterious interconnections of the two plots, and a tragic hero who exists not to 'initiate action' but to understand, leads quite naturally to this ending – a silent communion, appropriate in a play that reaches beyond words for so many of its finest effects.

And how relevant are these speculations to the production of *King Lear* that we all look forward to this evening? I hope that I have convinced you that it is our duty to look beyond the story. *King Lear* differs so markedly from the other tragedies because Shakespeare is here less concerned with an exciting 'outer action' than with intellectual and emotional insight: and of course not only the tragic hero but also the audience is asked to understand, and to wrestle with mysteries. I realise that a lecturer cannot hope to convince his listeners in every detail – but, if some seemingly dead Cordelias in this audience would now miraculously open their eyes, I would find that very encouraging.[7]

6

Past, present and future in *Macbeth* and *Antony and Cleopatra*

All of Shakespeare's plays advance through time in their own way, at various speeds, and some – notably *Othello* and *Hamlet* – even have 'double time schemes', simultaneous fast and slow time. In addition all the plays refer to the recent past and imminent future, and some to the remote past or future, a constant zig-zag through time that deserves critical attention no less than Shakespeare's imagery, being equally important in determining the imaginative texture of the play. The interaction of past, present and future can be seen as related to the treatment of cause and effect, and of probability, two other factors that powerfully influence the nature of a play. In comedies such as *As You Like It* time ambles along carelessly, there is little concern for the future, except that we assume that 'journeys end in lovers' meeting', and the author's attitude may be illustrated from the usurping duke's unexpected conversion. Having set out to put his brother to the sword, the usurper came 'to the skirts of this wild wood' and, 'meeting with an old religious man,/After some question with him, was converted' (V.4.153). Why was he converted at the edge of 'this wild wood', at this particular time? Shakespeare had his reasons, but critics have not worried about them. The Forest of Arden is not Birnam Wood.

In the tragedies the treatment of time is more meaningful, and some time-threads twist into time-knots which, invisibly, hold the story together. When the Weird Sisters chant 'All hail, Macbeth! Hail to thee, Thane of Cawdor!' (I.3.49) *we* know that Duncan has already assigned this title to Macbeth in the past, whereas *he* thinks it refers to a possible future; we cannot explain how the Sisters came to hear that he is already Thane of Cawdor, before the age of telephones, but we perceive that by a curious time-warp the past has overleapt the present. (In Holinshed the Weird Sisters hail Macbeth as thane of Cawdor *before* the thane loses his title.) Similarly, when Macbeth thinks that 'present fears/Are less than horrible imaginings . . . . And nothing is but what is not' (137), the future seems more present than the here and now, another time-warp. The prophecies, of course and the speculations they arouse, drag the future into the present with quite exceptional dramatic consequences – totally different from Hamlet's ghost-given duty to revenge, which (in revenge-tragedy) is itself a kind of prophecy. Lady Macbeth's sleep-walking, her 'To bed, to bed, to bed' (V.2.66), looking forward to a future that is already in the past, has a similar effect, as has Banquo's ghost, a time-frozen corpse catapulted into the present, and the special travel-arrangements of the Weird Sisters, 'Posters of the sea and land' (I.3.33). Time-tangles and time-warps go far beyond the prophecies, and need to be seen as a generalised technique in *Macbeth*.

Every one of Shakespeare's works includes some references to the past. In *Macbeth* there are comparatively few to events outside the play, the 'bleeding sergeant speech' being an important exception. This epic speech, and Ross's continuation of it, tells us little about Macbeth personally (compared with Othello's account of the wooing of Desdemona, or Hamlet's soliloquy about his father's death and his mother's second marriage). Nevertheless, though events prior to the play receive little notice, events that happen in the course of the play are frequently recapitulated, so the past is not simply forgotten. When the Weird Sisters vanish, Banquo and Macbeth echo their words; later, Lady Macbeth reads the letter that so vividly describes them. Having murdered Duncan, Macbeth relives the murder and his reaction to it, and Lady Macbeth's sleepwalking relives this reaction. He and she react a second time when Macduff announces Duncan's death; he reacts twice to the ghost of Banquo. There is often a shift of focus the second time round, so that we become unsure about the past and what precisely happened. Macbeth's letter stands back from the Weird Sisters in time, and switches from verse to prose. Did he really hear a voice cry 'Sleep no more'? These uncertainties about the past connect with other backward-looking speeches that have a similar effect. 'What beast was't then', cries Lady Macbeth, 'That made you break this enterprise to me?' (I.7.47). In a husband-baiting scene one wonders whether she bends the truth to make him feel more guilty. One wonders whether she fainted, or merely pretended to. I also ask myself whether she genuinely loves her husband, or loves him only for her own purposes, as her instrument. There is a hint in

> The raven himself is hoarse
> That croaks the fatal entrance of Duncan
> Under *my* battlements
>
> (I.5.35)

and in

> you shall put
> This night's great business into *my* dispatch.
>
> (64)

Uncertainty about the past, heightened by recapitulations that slightly adjust the focus, must be linked with uncertainties about the present and, thanks partly to the equivocation of the fiend, with the play's special preoccupation with an uncertain future. For, more than any other Shakespearian tragedy, this one is forward- rather than backward-looking. The two scenes of prophecies may seem to be responsible, but could turn out to be not so much a cause as a symptom. The signs of future bias are many, and of many kinds. Whereas the other mature tragedies begin with a present or past tense, *Macbeth* immediately points to the future – 'When shall we three meet again?' Compare 'Who's there? – Nay, answer me. Stand and unfold yourself', or 'I thought the King had more affected the Duke of Albany than Cornwall.' An insignificant difference? Consider, then, some of the other evidence. Macbeth scrutinises the future more intently in his soliloquies than any other tragic hero – not excluding Hamlet, whose thinking in soliloquy leaps to the past or to self-analysis, whose forward-planning often appears to be almost an afterthought.

> I'll have these players
> Play something like the murder of my father . . . .
>
> O, from this time forth
> My thoughts be bloody, or be nothing worth!
>
> (*Hamlet*, II.2.590, IV.4.64)

A typical example is 'To be or not to be'; here, whether Hamlet thinks about his own suicide or not, he quickly turns to general questions, unlike Macbeth, whose self-concern always remains uppermost. Iago, I suppose, resembles Macbeth in his habit of forward-looking, but differs from him in being more concerned with practicalities, and with cheering himself up; Macbeth has a very special gift – he feels the moral pressure of the future, and he foresees *alternative* futures.

Though concentrated upon the hero, the future bias in *Macbeth* expresses itself through other characters and produces many of the play's most memorable lines, often dwelling on hypothetical or uncertain futures, or futures no longer possible. 'I'll do, I'll do, and I'll do' (I.3.10); 'To-morrow – as he purposes' (I.5.57); 'He that's coming / Must be provided for' (63); 'And pity, like a naked new-born babe, / Striding the blast . . . Shall blow the horrid deed in every eye' (I.7.21); 'Bring forth men-children only!' (72); 'No; this my hand will rather / The multitudinous seas incarnadine' (II.2.61); 'A little water clears us of this deed' (67); 'What, will the line stretch out to th' crack of doom?' (IV.1.117); 'All the perfumes of Arabia will not sweeten this little hand' (V.1.48); 'She should have died hereafter' (V.5.17); 'To-morrow, and to-morrow, and to-morrow . . . ' (19). Appropriately, almost all the memorable lines about the future are spoken by Macbeth, by Lady Macbeth or by the Weird Sisters.

The tragedy of Macbeth, as conceived by Shakespeare, deals with a man who tries to control the future – which, ironically, invades his imagination and turns the tables on him. Greek tragedy had partly anticipated this idea, and recent criticism has shown that Shakespeare was not as ignorant of Greek tragedy as was once assumed. *King Lear*, for example, seems to be related to the Oedipus story. Oedipus blinds himself and lives as an outcast, having killed his father and married his own mother; he has a loving, courageous daughter, Antigone (compare Cordelia), and curses his ungrateful sons, who kill each other (compare Goneril and Regan); he seems to linger aimlessly in this world, and, like Lear, he meditates about the gods and the state of mankind. Not long after *King Lear* Shakespeare wrote *Macbeth*, which has been called his most Senecan tragedy. There are good reasons for thinking that it echoes Seneca's *Hercules Furens* and *Medea*,[1] and I believe that Seneca's *Oedipus* could have directed Shakespeare back to the Greek Oedipus story, a ghostly influence in *King Lear* and, dramatising as it does an attempt to cheat the future, in *Macbeth*. Shakespeare, however, created a supernatural frame-work of Weird Sisters, spirits, apparitions, fiends, 'couriers of the air', the 'grace of grace', which

I find more mysterious than their Greek counterparts; and 'the future' in *Macbeth* seems to me correspondingly less defined than Greek 'fate' or 'destiny', and altogether a more potent presence in the play.

One of the special tricks in *Macbeth* is that some possible futures appear to be held back, as are the prophecies – they are 'here' and not yet completely here – whereas other possible futures annihilate time-boundaries by coexisting with the present. The hand that will 'the multitudinous seas incarnadine, / Making the green one red' (II.2.62), seems to do so in an instant, now. A naked new-born babe cannot sit or stand without help, but Macbeth's imagination sees it as 'striding the blast', simultaneously helpless and all-powerful. As Lady Macbeth puts it, 'I feel now / The future in the instant' (I.5.54).

While much more could be said about the special role of the future in *Macbeth*, I now turn to 'the present'. The quality of the present depends, in a play, on the state of mind of the characters who experience it, and comment on it. In *King Lear* the three 'fools' who come together in the heath scene are connected with pervasive features of the play – Lear's rage and madness, the storm – because the play revolves around Lear's mental confusion. Lear's failure to understand simple things, such as Cordelia's love or the deprivations of 'poor naked wretches', leads inevitably to love-tests, and other tests and trials, where he stubbornly seeks for clarity but we observe confusion. His characteristic mode of relating to 'the present' persists to his dying moments, even though the tragic heroes in general learn to see more clearly at the end. As we shall discover, Macbeth too has his characteristic mode of relating to the present.

All of Shakespeare's tragic heroes are endowed with heightened awareness in their central scenes, and it is always heightened in different ways. Some are driven to the verge of madness, or beyond it; the moral pressures experienced by Macbeth seem to me as intense as those that torture Othello and Lear, yet Macbeth never falls in a fit or loses his wits, and rarely even rages. Macbeth differs from Lear in understanding clearly – he only chooses badly – and at the same time he resembles Lear in being repeatedly lifted out of himself, as it were, to a level of consciousness that cannot be called normal. I am thinking of his hallucinations – the dagger, the voice that cried 'Sleep no more', Banquo's ghost – as well as his mentally maimed condition when he enters after murdering

Duncan, or reacts to the apparitions. It scarcely matters whether
or not the dagger and ghost are false creations 'Proceeding from
the heat-oppressed brain' (II.1.39): however we wish to explain
them, Macbeth's mental state is one of hypertension collapsing
into trance. The dagger and ghost, indeed, resemble other visions
that seem to acquire a physical reality as Macbeth describes them –

> pity, like a naked new-born babe,
> Striding the blast, or heaven's cherubin hors'd
> Upon the sightless couriers of the air . . . .

> The multitudinous seas incarnadine,
> Making the green one red . . . .

In a state of heightened awareness Macbeth sees images that
displace the present, an alternative reality that has the same effect
as the play's future-gazing, an effect rather like double vision.
Here, again, *Macbeth* resembles *King Lear*, except that Lear
characteristically sees and describes authority-figures (Nature, the
gods, the storm, the rascal beadle), and Lear's imagination more
often fastens on the human body and its functions ('Into her womb
convey sterility', 'Rumble thy bellyful', 'Poor naked wretches',
'Down from the waist they are centaurs'). Macbeth, on the other
hand, sees a great variety of images sparked off by his personal
sense of guilt ('*this my hand* will rather / The multitudinous seas
incarnadine'; 'honour, love, obedience, troops of friends / *I must
not look to have*' – V.3.25). In their most intense moments both Lear
and Macbeth appear to disengage from the present, but they do
so in their own distinctive ways.

In *Macbeth*, as in *King Lear*, the hero's special mode of perception is
reflected in other characters. Lady Macbeth disengages completely
from the present in her sleepwalking. The Porter's tipsiness induces
another kind of double vision, detaching him from the knocking.
The grave-diggers in *Hamlet* are less far gone in drink than the
Porter, and do not talk to themselves as he does (in this he resembles
Macbeth and Lady Macbeth). After murdering Duncan, Macbeth
seems not to hear some of Lady Macbeth's interruptions, transfixed
by his own thoughts; he soliloquises aloud, as it were, Lady
Macbeth overhearing him – and this prepares for the Porter's
speech, which I take to be not soliloquy but true tavern mumble,
audible words provoked by drink. Macbeth's self-intoxicating

tendency is also repeated in the Weird Sisters, who wind themselves up by chanting and dancing, and perhaps by inhaling the fumes of their delicious ragout.

Since the self-intoxicating habit is so pronounced in *Macbeth*, keeping it in mind may help us when considering production-problems. '*Enter Lady Macbeth, reading a letter*': I have heard her stumble through the letter as if she has just received it – but as she omits the beginning we are free to assume that this is not a first reading, and that she returns to a passage that particularly excites her. Instead of coming on-stage 'reading', she could enter in a state of high tension, make sure that she is alone, then read the letter, which she already knows almost by heart. And the stage-direction? In the Folio it is '*Enter Macbeth's wife, alone with a letter*' (in modern spelling). There is no suggestion that she reads as she enters.

As others have observed, Lady Macbeth's invocation to spirits that 'tend on mortal thoughts' calls on the powers of darkness, rather like Dr Faustus conjuring up his devils.

> Come to my woman's breasts
> And take my milk for gall, you murd'ring ministers,
> Wherever in your sightless substances
> You wait on nature's mischief.
>
> (I.6.47)

Whether or not the spirits actually enter into and 'possess' her, she behaves like one possessed as she comes close to hypnotising Macbeth, and herself. Her exaltation in these early scenes, disengaging her from her normal self, and from the immediate, visible present, is resumed in her sleep-walking, in a different key.

Macbeth's own special way of disengaging from the here and now already shows in the conversation-stopping asides in his first scene, and in Banquo's unusual references to them. 'Look how our partner's rapt!', 'Worthy Macbeth, we stay upon your leisure' (I.3.143,148). These asides are connected with his later visions and hallucinations, and it may be that only a man who can switch himself off, so to speak, is capable of committing a murder. One almost feels that an invisible current floods into the Macbeths at certain points, and drains out again, an external grid-system partly controlled by the good and bad 'couriers of the air.'

Double vision is an important technical trick at many moments that everyone remembers, because they are so obviously special – the prophecies, the Porter speech, asides, the visionary soliloquies, hallucinations, the sleepwalking. I think that the same term could be applied to less obviously arresting episodes, which depend for their effect on different kinds of double vision. Lady Macduff's prattle with her son juxtaposes an adult and a child's view, one more far-reaching than the other, and this repeats a contrast in the preceding scene, where the apparitions see further into the future than Macbeth. Another curious factor in this cauldron-scene is that Macbeth assumes that he is in command, that he can compel the spirits to answer him, whereas we sense that *they* are in charge; he gives orders, they appear to obey, but for undisclosed reasons. His view of the present falls short of the truth no less than his peering into the future. Malcolm's long dialogue with Macduff is an example of sequential rather than simultaneous double vision: first Malcolm elaborately paints one picture of himself, then he unpaints it; first black, then white. Even the virtuous equivocate in the world of *Macbeth*. In the second half of the scene Ross goes through the same motions with Macduff, a series of white lies before he risks the black truth.

MACDUFF.   How does my wife?
ROSS. Why, well.
MACDUFF.   And all my children?
ROSS.   Well too.
MACDUFF. The tyrant has not batter'd at their peace?
ROSS. No, they were well at peace when I did leave 'em.
                                             (IV.3.176)

The play resorts to yet another kind of double vision when Birnam Wood moves to Dunsinane. Producers sometimes try to introduce 'realism' by making the soldiers daub their faces, with twigs of green stuck in their clothes – an early exercise in khaki camouflage; or they go in the opposite direction, elaborately marching and counter-marching, a symbolic mime. Shakespeare foresaw the difficulties, and decided to report the wonder before attempting to show it. I think that it is a mistake to equip Malcolm's army instantaneously with boughs as soon as the order is given, (in V.4), as if his soldiers are all over-zealous assistant stage-managers. We see Macbeth reacting to the messenger's news –

MESSENGER. I look'd toward Birnam, and anon methought
  The wood began to move.
MACBETH.   Liar and slave!

(V.5.34)

– and only then are we allowed to see the wonder:

Enter Malcolm, Siward, Macduff, and their army with boughs.
MALCOLM. Now near enough; your leavy screens throw down,
  And show like those you are.

What Shakespeare chose to show was not the wood's moving, but
the future unmasking itself – and I think it adds to the effect if the
principal agents of the future, unaware of the prophecy, do not
even understand the momentousness of their action.

A final example of double vision, again unparalleled in the
mature tragedies, comes with our last glimpse of Macbeth. '*Enter
Macduff, with Macbeth's head.*' Disfigured in death, like the blood-
boltered Banquo, the head must be recognisably Macbeth's, yet
the face is frozen, the voice is stilled: the same head, and not the
same.

Macbeth differs from the other tragedies, it has been said, in its
extensive use of dramatic irony. Some of the examples I have given
of 'double vision' could also be called dramatic irony, but by no
means all: double vision seems to be the superior principle – among
other things, in redefining the mutual interpenetration of past,
present and future, which must be connected with other boundary
changes in this play ('Fair is foul, and foul is fair' – I.1.10). Even
though Shakespeare was certainly interested in the past, present
and future, and in double vision, in his other plays, where else do
we find a spirit-world so intricately meshing into the human,
confounding the outer and inner experience, hallucinations, sleep-
walking, a tipsy Porter, a severed head? It is the interconnections
of all of these and other special features that suggest that in this
play myriad-minded Shakespeare wrestled consciously, like St
Augustine, with the related problems of perception and reality and
time. Especially *time*. After Macbeth has been killed by Macduff,
who was 'from his mother's womb/Untimely ripp'd' (V.8.15; the
word 'untimely' is Shakespeare's here, not Holinshed's) – after this
final juggling with time, Macduff proclaims that 'The time is
free' (55). Strangely resonant words, but what do they mean?

Apparently – that time has slipped away from the control of hostile powers, and is free to go back to normal.

After *Macbeth*, Shakespeare seems to have paused for a year or more before producing what was probably his next play, *Antony and Cleopatra*. After his most concentrated tragedy came the one that has been called his most expansive, yet they both employ the same basic material – adapted, now, to different purposes. Shakespeare's mastery of his medium has become instinctive and apparently effortless, as we see in examining the treatment of past, present and future in a play that is, in so many respects, the very opposite of *Macbeth*.

Consider, first, that the Roman story belongs to the historical world, whereas Macbeth's – even though taken from Holinshed's *Chronicles* – offers only the flimsiest pretence of history. Shakespeare assumes that the spectator brings to the Roman play an awareness of what lies behind it, and of what follows; the future, though, receives less attention than the past. In *Macbeth*, as I have said, we hear next to nothing about the earlier life of any character. Macbeth and Banquo performed bravely in a recent battle. We also hear that Duncan has 'borne his faculties so meek, hath been / So clear in his great office' (I.7.17), that Lady Macbeth had a father and, perhaps, a child – Shakespeare touched in a few such details in passing, barely hinting at historical continuity. In *Antony and Cleopatra* the backward-looking is all-pervasive, operates on many levels, and, if not technically as innovative as the future-gazing in *Macbeth*, has a similar importance. Pompey and Caesar, the two giants of the immediate past, are frequently named, without any attempt to explain their place in history (in *Julius Caesar* a major speech, 'Wherefore rejoice?' [I.1.33ff], has precisely that function). References to other Roman heroes of the recent past are peppered here and there – Brutus, Cassius, Crassus – quite casually, as if they need no introduction. The past is quite simply *there*, a part of the present. Like the play's references to Rome's frontiers, to armies and emissaries in Parthia, Spain, Sardinia, the Alps, Athens, and so on; like the perpetual repetition of place-names and shifting of scenes – these references to recently deceased Romans help to create the play's expansiveness. In addition, they force us to measure the living: compared with the heroic achievements of the

past, Antony's indecisiveness and Octavius' failures of manliness
seem all the more unRoman.

The two principal characters, Antony and Cleopatra, are also
measured against their own personal past, much to their
disadvantage.

> Antony,
> Leave thy lascivious wassails. When thou once
> Was beaten from Modena, where thou slew'st
> Hirtius and Pansa, consuls, at thy heel
> Did famine follow; whom thou fought'st against
> Though daintily brought up, with patience more
> Than savages could suffer. Thou didst drink
> The stale of horses . . . .
>
> (I.4.55)

This sounds like the testimony of a hostile witness, intent upon
belittling the later Antony; behind Octavius, however, there
stands a dramatist who chose to include this speech. Antony
himself says,

> He at Philippi kept
> His sword e'en like a dancer, while I struck
> The lean and wrinkled Cassius; and 'twas I
> That the mad Brutus ended . . . .
>
> (III.11.35)

The glories of the past are no more. A similar point is made by the
great 'Cydnus' speech (II.2.195ff.), despite the fact that it appears
to glamorise Cleopatra. In the past, great and small flocked to see
her, and acknowledged her power (the people, Antony, Caesar).
Now, on the contrary, she has to write to Antony ('He shall have
every day a several greeting, / Or I'll unpeople Egypt' – I.5.77), she
depends on messengers for news (II.5), she feels neglected. She
and Antony try to bring back the glorious past, most poignantly
when her thoughts go back to Cydnus in her death-scene ('Go
fetch / My best attires. I am again for Cydnus . . . Give me my
robe, put on my crown . . . ' – V.2.226, 278). Many references to
the personal past of Antony and Cleopatra have the same double
effect: magnifying them, and at the same time scaling them down
in the diminished present.

Another special feature of the play is that we hear so much about the previous sexual partners of the two principals.

> You were half blasted ere I knew you. Ha!
> Have I my pillow left unpress'd in Rome . . . ?
> I found you as a morsel cold upon
> Dead Caesar's trencher. Nay, you were a fragment
> Of Cneius Pompey's, besides what hotter hours
> Unregist'red in vulgar fame, you have
> Luxuriously pick'd out . . . .   (III.13.105)

Since the play makes a point of asking 'If it be love indeed' (I.1.14), these references to other sexual partners complicate the issue, suggesting cool opportunism. Antony's marriage with Octavia can be nothing else, and his previous marriage to ungovernable Fulvia must have had an advantage-seeking motive as well.[2] Knowing what they do about themselves, Antony and Cleopatra therefore find it difficult to trust each other's love. In the love-relationship of hero and heroine, as in the general historical situation, the past is massively and disquietingly present, implicitly questioning the values of the here and now.

The quality of 'the present', as I have said, depends on the minds that experience it. In *Antony and Cleopatra* the most original mind is Cleopatra's. She deliberately destabilises the present by being forever unpredictable: she switches her moods, or pretends to, defeats expectations, making the present appear infinitely adjustable, and less and less believable.

>   If you find him sad,
> Say I am dancing; if in mirth, report
> That I am sudden sick.
>   (I.3.3)

>   Cut my lace, Charmian, come!
> But let it be; I am quickly ill and well . . . .
>   (71)

> Let him for ever go – let him not, Charmian . . . .
>   (II.5.115)

As Enobarbus intimates, her 'infinite variety' (II.2.240) is one of the sources of her power. She knows it, and pretends that others play similar games.

> I prithee turn aside and weep for her;
> Then bid adieu to me, and say the tears
> Belong to Egypt.
>
> (I.3.76)

She uses her destabilising power more laboriously when she bullies the messenger, persuades herself that Octavia is 'Dull of tongue and dwarfish!' (III.3.16), and then goes back on a previous judgement, since the messenger tells her what she wants: 'I find thee / Most fit for business' (35). Here and elsewhere one wonders whether she can possibly believe what she says, or expect others to believe her. She strains to destabilise Antony's understanding, feeding 'most delicious poison' (I.5.27) to him and to herself by exercising her fascinating talents – which Antony comes close to calling her talents for lying. 'You have been a boggler ever' (III.13.110).

Several of Shakespeare's tragic heroes appear to lose their grip on reality. Macbeth's imagination intoxicates him; in Antony's case, Cleopatra's poison has a similar effect, as has plain old-fashioned drinking. The scene on Pompey's galley may be the most dramatic drinking-scene in the play, and perhaps in the whole of Shakespeare, but there are many others, reported or enacted. In Egypt, says Enobarbus, 'we did sleep day out of countenance and made the night light with drinking' (II.2.181); after making a fool of Antony with a salt fish, Cleopatra 'laugh'd him out of patience', then 'laugh'd him into patience', then 'Ere the ninth hour, I drunk him to his bed' (II.5.19ff.). Even when it is not called for by clear-cut stage-directions,[3] drinking should play a part in several scenes, being one of Antony's delights, one of the elements he lived in. 'Bring in the banquet quickly; wine enough . . . . Mine, and most of our fortunes, to-night, shall be – drunk to bed,' cries Enobarbus in Act I scene 2, where Charmian and Iras may speak as they do, a little greasily, because already tipsy. 'Fill our bowls once more', cries Antony, and promises to 'drink carouses to the next day's fate' (III.13.184; IV.8.34). In the course of the play he should swagger about not infrequently with a cup or drinking-bowl, or somewhat the worse for drink,

particularly in scenes where he too switches mood unexpectedly.
Cleopatra destabilises the present by forever changing her
performance; Antony, by surrendering to her 'poison' and to drink.
In Egypt, unlike Rome, it is not the fashion to talk or walk straight.

In most of the tragedies we are shown the instability of the
present, always in different ways. In *Antony and Cleopatra*
Shakespeare made much of excessive drinking and Cleopatra's
cultivated unpredictability, with this end in view. The instability
of the play's 'present', as I have tried to describe it, perhaps also
explains some of its other distinctive features: its many short
scenes; its vague handling of time, and of battles that are said to
be lost, then appear not to be lost; above all, the relationship of
Antony and Cleopatra, the very identity of such seemingly fluid
personalities, the interest in perception itself.

> ANTONY. That which is now a horse, even with a thought
>   The rack dislimns, and makes it indistinct,
>   As water is in water.
> EROS.   It does, my lord.
> ANTONY. My good knave Eros, now thy captain is
>   Even such a body. Here I am Antony;
>   Yet cannot hold this visible shape, my knave.
>   (IV.14.9)

In one production by the Royal Shakespeare Company the
'destabilised present' of the play was brilliantly caught in the scene
on Pompey's galley, where the actors swayed from the effects of
drink and simultaneously swayed with the rocking of the boat in
water.

The treatment of the future in a play also depends, in part, on
the minds of the principal characters. Antony wants to ignore the
future, and reacts impatiently when a messenger arrives, knowing
that he will have to respond to news and plan ahead (I.1.18); he
'hardly gave audience' to the messenger, and pocketed Octavius'
letters without reading them (I.4.7, II.2.75ff.). How unlike Octavius'
own efficiency ('I have eyes upon him / And his affairs come to me
on the wind' – III.6.62)! Antony thinks only of the immediate
future, of tonight and tomorrow; at the play's beginning he can
still look farther ahead but, significantly, what lies in the distance
remains blurred.

I must from this enchanting queen break off.
Ten thousand harms, more than the ills I know,
My idleness doth hatch.

(I.2.125)

More and more, others have to beg or bully him to think ahead, even comparative strangers such as the soothsayer (II.3), Canidius (III.7) or a common soldier ('O noble emperor, do not fight by sea' – III.7.61). As I shall show, Enobarbus can read the future with striking accuracy, so Antony's failures in forward-looking become all the more noticeable. The messages he sends to Octavius after Actium envisage impossible futures, mere wishful thinking. He

Requires to live in Egypt; which not granted
He lessens his requests and to thee sues
To let him breathe between the heavens and earth,
A private man in Athens.

(III.12.12)

Sliding so readily into that 'which not granted', the ambassador shows that he expected nothing else. And when Antony challenges Octavius to single combat, Enobarbus and Octavius instantly see that he has lost his judgement.

As Antony's fortunes decline he learns, at least, to think of the futures of his followers: 'I have a ship / Laden with gold; take that; divide it. Fly . . . ' (III.11.4). He hears of Enobarbus' defection, and feels no anger.

Go, Eros, send his treasure after; do it;
Detain no jot, I charge thee. Write to him –
I will subscribe – gentle adieus and greetings . . . .

(IV.5.12)

His speaking as he does brings out that he failed to think of their futures earlier; and perhaps we should see the ship and treasure as intended tear-jerkers, grand gestures. Yet Shakespeare, having established Antony's inability to engage seriously with the future, suddenly sweeps away this carelessness as his hero lies dying.

ANTONY.   One word, sweet queen:
  Of Caesar seek your honour with your safety. O!
CLEOPATRA. They do not go together.
ANTONY.   Gentle, hear me:
  None about Caesar trust but Proculeius.

                                        (IV.14.45)

In fact, Antony misreads the future (Proculeius talks soothingly to
Cleopatra in her monument until he can surprise and seize her,
exactly as in Plutarch); Antony's error, though, counts for less than
his genuine anxiety for her future, which comes tragically too late.
Not long before, he had bitterly resented the possibility that she
might make her peace with Octavius (III.13.15f., 110ff.).
  Cleopatra, the very opposite of Antony, foresees the future
consequences of every word and deed – and even anticipates what
is about to be said, often comically.

  I know by that same eye, there's some good news. . . .
  You can do better yet; but this is meetly.

                                        (I.3.19,81)

Skilled as she is in anticipation, she can win round Antony when
he is most incensed against her (III.12, III.13). Her mind darts
ahead of others, and reads the future so instinctively that Antony
refuses to believe her denials of this gift.

  Forgive my fearful sails! I little thought
  You would have followed.
ANTONY.   Egypt, thou knew'st too well
  My heart was to thy rudder tied by th'strings,
  And thou shouldst tow me after. O'er my spirit
  Thy full supremacy thou knew'st . . . .

                                        (III.11.55)

Towards the end, her imagination excels itself in vividly painting
the two futures she must choose between. Either alive in Rome –

            Shall they hoist me up,
  And show me to the shouting varletry

Of censuring Rome? Rather a ditch in Egypt . . . .
                              (V.2.55)

– or dead in Egypt:

Show me, my women, like a queen. Go fetch
My best attires . . . .
                              (226)

Octavius remarks on her habitual future-gazing in his final speech:
her physician reported that 'She hath pursu'd conclusions
infinite / Of easy ways to die' (352). That being so, one marvels at
her silence when her children are threatened with death, if she
commits suicide (130ff.) – a threat to which she never reacts. The
thought of it is not allowed to spoil her satisfaction in her own
spectacular death, and this drives home the point that she has
more than once refused to face up to the consequences of her own
actions, even though she must have foreseen them. The point can
be made visually by bringing the children on-stage in some earlier
scenes – they are mentioned, after all – and having them cling to
Cleopatra as Octavius spells out his intentions.

'Foreknowing the future' has a central importance in *Antony
and Cleopatra*, especially in differentiating between the hero and
heroine. Prophecy and the supernatural also have a part to play,
but there are few signs that Shakespeare wished to repeat the
triumphs of *Macbeth*. A soothsayer appears twice; we also hear of
augury in passing (II.1.10), then more arrestingly –

                    The augurers
Say they know not, they cannot tell; look grimly,
And dare not speak their knowledge.
                              (IV.12.4)

Only in one scene does the supernatural appear to intervene more
directly: when Antony's soldiers hear music 'under the stage', and
one guesses that ''Tis the god Hercules, whom Antony lov'd, / Now
leaves him' (IV.3.16). Shakespeare also invents for Enobarbus a
future-knowing capacity, a sharp perception of the inevitable, as a
serial device which becomes more convincingly prophetic the more
often he proves to be right. For example:

MAECENAS. Now Antony must leave her utterly.
ENOBARBUS. Never! He will not.

(II.2.37)

ENOBARBUS. Then, world, thou hast a pair of chaps – no more;
    And throw between them all the food thou hast,
    They'll grind the one the other.

(III.5.13)

ENOBARBUS. Yes, like enough high-battled Caesar will
    Unstate his happiness, and be stag'd to th' show
    Against a sworder!

(III.13.29)[4]

All of these various forms of prophecy and the supernatural lead to one conclusion: that the model for *Antony and Cleopatra* was not *Macbeth* but *Julius Caesar*. In the later play, however, the soothsayer first appears in a comic scene, and his most ominous remark ('Your fortunes are alike' [I.2.51] to Charmian and Iras, who do indeed die together) lacks the force of 'Beware the ides of March!' The music heard by Antony's soldiers, again, is less terrifying than the Ghost of Caesar. And, while Enobarbus repeats Cassius in foreknowing what will happen and being powerless to stop it, they differ as well. Cassius collides repeatedly with Brutus; Enobarbus usually talks to himself or to bystanders, not to Antony, when he foresees unpleasant consequences. It appears that Shakespeare sought for powerful dramatic effects in *Julius Caesar*, and deliberately softened or avoided them in parts of *Antony and Cleopatra*. How oddly he sometimes copied from himself! Brutus tells Cassius that 'Portia is dead'; Cassius mishears, and has to be told again: 'Ha! Portia? – She is dead' (*Julius Caesar*, IV.3.145). Compare Antony and Enobarbus: 'Fulvia is dead. – Sir? – Fulvia is dead' (I.2.151). It was Shakespeare's idea that the husband, in both plays, should tell a friend of his wife's death (not so in Plutarch); in *Julius Caesar*, again, this leads to an emotional crescendo, which is avoided in *Antony and Cleopatra*. 'How scap'd I killing when I cross'd you so?' (*Julius Caesar*); 'Why, sir, give the gods a thankful sacrifice' (*Antony and Cleopatra*).

For obvious reasons Shakespeare's mind went back to *Julius Caesar* when he wrote *Antony and Cleopatra*; there are many signs of this, not only the treatment of time. No one will argue that the later play as a whole lacks power, compared with the earlier, but locally it seems to, in the instances I have mentioned, where Shakespeare reuses the same dramatic materials. Or should we say that he *appears* to use the same dramatic materials, while in fact he reshapes them, as might a jeweller, to suit their new setting? The past, present and future can be considered 'dramatic materials', and, analysed separately, as in this chapter, can be shown to have their own inner logic in every play. But Shakespeare himself, as he wrote every play, must have imagined its past, present and future not separately but in relation to many interlocking variables (developing character and plot and ideas, language rhythms and patterns, etc.). It is this creative mastery, reaching out in all directions at once, that I think of as one of the most precious gifts of 'myriad-minded Shakespeare'.[5]

7

Shakespeare suppressed: the unfortunate history of *Troilus and Cressida*

More than any other play by Shakespeare, *Troilus and Cressida* needs a 'myriad-minded' approach, one that sees the many problems of this problem comedy together, not separately. I begin with the cancelled title-page of the Quarto and the inserted 'epistle to the reader', oddities that we find in no other Shakespearian text, which will lead us directly to related problems – the play's date, stage-history, textual transmission, genre, ending, and general interpretation.

Originally, the first Quarto of the play, dated 1609, announced on its title-page 'The Historie of Troylus and Cresseida. As it was acted by the Kings Maiesties seruants at the Globe. Written by William Shakespeare.' This title-page was removed, and replaced by one that read 'The Famous Historie of Troylus and Cresseid. Excellently expressing the beginning of their loues, with the conceited wooing of Pandarus Prince of Licia. Written by William Shakespeare.' Why did the printer or publisher go to the trouble and expense of changing the title page? The anonymous epistle that was added in the second issue of the Quarto, together with the new title-page, offers an answer (I modernise the spelling).

> A never writer, to an ever
> reader. News.

> Eternal reader, you have here a new play, never staled with the stage, never clapper-clawed with the palms of the vulgar, and yet passing full of the palm comical; for it is a birth of your brain that never undertook anything comical vainly. . . . At the peril of your pleasure's loss, and judgement's, refuse not, nor like this the less for not being sullied with the smoky breath of the multitude; but thank fortune for the 'scape it hath made amongst you. Since by the grand possessors' wills I believe you should

have prayed for them [Shakespeare's comedies] rather than been prayed . . . .

Whatever the precise meaning of 'clapper-claw' (compare *Troilus*, V.4.1: 'Now they are clapper-clawing one another'), the writer of the epistle seems to be saying that 'the vulgar' have not yet seen the play, and he makes the point a second time: the play has not been 'sullied with the smoky breath of the multitude'. This would explain why the revised title-page dropped the claim, so prominently placed on the first one – 'As it was acted by the Kings Maiesties seruants of the Globe.' But does the writer of the epistle really know what he is talking about? He seems to be wrong on at least two counts. James Roberts had entered *Troilus and Cressida* in the Stationers' Register in 1603 – 'The book of *Troilus and Cressida* as it is acted by my Lord Chamberlain's Men.' So it could not have been 'a new play' in 1609, as the epistle asserted; and, if the Lord Chamberlain's Men acted it, where would this be except at the Globe? One explanation that gets round some of these problems has won support in the last half-century: the play was not acted 'at the Globe', but was written for private performance, perhaps for one of the Inns of Court; it could be called 'new' in 1609 because newly published, though written long before.

Now young law-students might well have savoured some of the play's special features, such as its skilful debating, its scabrous humour, or Troilus' sexual initiation. The 'private performance' theory, however, creates its own problems. It simply does not make economic sense to write and produce a play for a special occasion, unless the same play can be performed publicly thereafter, to a wider audience. *A Midsummer Night's Dream* seems to have been commissioned for an important wedding, probably one attended by the queen in person, yet the Quarto title-page proclaims that 'it hath been sundry times publicly acted'. The *Troilus* epistle makes it clear that this play had a very different stage-history: when it was at least six years old, in 1609, it still had not been acted in public. The 'private performance' theory fails to account for this anomaly.[1]

I want to leave the play's stage-history for a moment, and turn to its date. The 'armed prologue', said E. K. Chambers, 'clearly refers to that of Jonson's *Poetaster*, produced in 1601. Such a reference would have little point after an interval, and I incline to put the play in 1602.' True, the gibe that Shakespeare's prologue is armed, 'but not in confidence', glances at the armed prologue in *Poetaster*, who begs not to be accused of arrogance; if, though, this would have little point after an interval, it is surely relevant that we can give a fairly precise date to *Poetaster*, not later than the early autumn of 1601, perhaps not later than May–June 1601.[2] We know from Henslowe's *Diary* that plays could be written in six to eight weeks; Heminge and Condell, and also Ben Jonson, assure us of Shakespeare's exceptional fluency as a writer – consequently, accepting that *Troilus* will have followed soon after *Poetaster*, 1601 rather than 1602 would seem to be the date for Shakespeare's play. And, since prologues are normally written after the play (that, at least, was the practice in the later seventeenth and eighteenth centuries), Shakespeare probably composed the play in the later or middle months of 1601.

It was a critical year for England, and for Shakespeare's company. The Earl of Essex, hailed in *Henry V* as 'the general of our gracious empress', and likened, implicitly, to 'the mirror of all Christian kings', had been outmanoeuvred by his political enemies in 1600, and was plotting with his friends how to remove the Queen's evil counsellors, as he thought them, a powerful clique that included Sir Robert Cecil and the Lord Admiral – and finally, driven to desperation, attempted to do so by force. The Essex 'rebellion' took place on 8 February 1601, he was on trial for High Treason on 19 February, and executed on the 25th. This must have been an anxious time for Shakespeare, since the Earl of Southampton, to whom he had dedicated *Venus and Adonis* and *The Rape of Lucrece*, was Essex's principal supporter, and was tried and convicted with him; furthermore, other friends of Essex had paid Shakespeare's company to perform *Richard II* the day before the Essex rebellion, presumably to persuade Londoners that a reigning sovereign could be successfully deposed. According to Chambers, 'little blame seems to have fallen upon the Chamberlain's men. . . . They were at court a few days after the trial of Essex.'[3] The company's position was nevertheless a delicate one, for the play of *Richard II* was more embarrassingly topical than Chambers allowed. It was not just that the Queen recognised 'I am Richard II. Know ye not that?'; the Earl of Essex also held the title 'Viscount of Hereford', and Bolingbroke in the play is 'Harry of Hereford, Lancaster and Derby' (I.3); moreover, as was explained in an official sermon at Paul's Cross in March 1601, Essex's 'pretence' was 'all one with that of *Henry* Duke of Lancaster against *Richard* the second, *remoouing certaine* [counsellors] which misled the King'.[4] The company may not have known what was intended by Essex's friends, but they played a part in the uprising, one of them was examined 'upon his oath', they came under suspicion – so they had to be particularly careful.

At about this time or a little later Shakespeare seems to have been at work on *Troilus and Cressida*. Long ago, G. B. Harrison made the case that the play is connected with the Essex rebellion but, I think, understated it. Chapman had dedicated his translation of the *Iliad* 'To the most honored now living Instance of the Achilleian vertues . . . the Earle of Essexe' and, said Harrison, 'contemporary readers were thus encouraged to visualise the Greek hero as Essex.' And Essex, 'like Achilles, was over prone to sulk in his tent'; after the astonishing episode, in 1598, 'when he insulted Queen Elizabeth and received a box on the ears for his answer . . . he sulked at home, refusing to be reconciled.' Later, when the Queen failed to renew Essex's grant of the taxes on sweet wines, a major source of his income, 'Essex House became the meeting-place for malcontents who openly sneered at the Queen and her chief ministers.'[5]

Harrison's argument can be strengthened in several ways. First, Chapman called Essex 'Achilles' in two books, not one; and he was not the first to do so. Hugh Platt anticipated him in 1594; and Saviolo called Essex 'the English Achilles' in 1595.[6] It was an almost inevitable comparison, since Essex was a general who personally led the assault at Cadiz and elsewhere, and, over and above his undoubted courage, resembled 'The large Achilles' (I.3.162) in being exceptionally tall and well-made.[7] Second, it was the view of the Essex faction that their impulsive hero, who excelled on the battle-field, was opposed by goose-quilled gentlemen, politicians, plotters, foxes,[8] who outmanoeuvred him at court. Now Lord Burghley, in his last years, was described as England's 'Nestor',[9] and in the play Ulysses and 'father Nestor' (II.3.247) work as a team, as Sir Robert Cecil and his father had seemed to do.[10] Achilles and his opponents in the play, therefore, resemble Essex and his opponents: the 'policy' of 'that stale old mouse-eaten dry cheese, Nestor, and that . . . dog-fox, Ulysses' is emphasised (V.4.8); Ulysses complains, 'They tax our policy and call it cowardice. . . . They call this bed-work, mapp'ry, closet-war' (I.3.197).[11] And, when Ulysses explains that

> The providence that's in a watchful state
> Knows almost every grain of Plutus' gold
>   (III.3.196)

and is almost god-like in unveiling thoughts 'in their dumb cradles' (200), how could one *not* think of Sir Robert Cecil, whose information network, to give it no worse a name, was an open secret?

I am not suggesting, please observe, that Shakespeare introduced topical allusions in *Troilus and Cressida* to defend Essex and mock the Cecil faction. That would have been foolhardy in 1601, when Essex was down and out, Southampton condemned to death, and the other side had triumphed. Also, Achilles is not an entirely flattering portrait; and, if he *were* meant for Essex, would not Southampton have to be – Patroclus? What I do suggest is that the play was written shortly after the Essex crisis, and that its dangerous resemblance to recent events was not appreciated, or not fully appreciated, until it was ready for performance – at which point, when Shakespeare and his fellows asked themselves whether they might give offence, it was deemed prudent not to proceed. Indeed, once the possibility of such an allusion is recognised, more and more Essex resemblances suggest themselves. The earl did not merely 'sulk' before his uprising; when summoned to court he more than once feigned illness. The French envoy reported in 1597, 'According to report he was feigning illness, and had been in disgrace with the Queen since returning from his voyage'; again, an observer from Bruges described Essex's dilemma in February 1601: 'On being summoned he feigned illness; they insist none the less that he attend in person. . . . Being fully aware that the conspiracy was known, he agreed to comply if his safety were assured.'[12] So transparent a feigned illness could not have been a common political expedient. Yet in the play Achilles is said to be 'ill-dispos'd' (II.3.73): Ulysses knows it is a sham ('We saw him at the opening of his tent. / He is not sick' – (80)); Agamemnon calls it an 'evasion' (110). Another unfortunate coincidence is that Achilles had secret communications with Troy, as Essex was accused of secretly corresponding with Spain and Scotland about the English succession.[13] Perhaps Shakespeare could have deleted these lines. Other possible 'allusions', however, are threaded into the very fabric of the play, and could not be easily removed: for example, the many references to the pride and arrogance of Achilles, and the lecture Ulysses reads him about honour, an important theme-carrier, climaxing in the reminder that 'Perseverance, dear my lord, / Keeps honour bright' (III.3.150). (Essex's motto was *Basis virtutum constantia*.[14]) At his trial Essex was taxed with his inordinate pride, and he himself said 'several times that he had not come there to save his life, but to defend his honour'.[15] Admirers defended Essex's actions as dictated by honour, as in R. Pricket's *Honors Fame in Triumph Riding. Or, The Life and Death of the late honorable Earle of Essex* (1604) – so it is another unfortunate coincidence that Achilles and Essex, devoted to their sense of honour, are both charged with betraying it and are both accused of monstrous pride.

Having seen that, once the suspicion of an 'Essex allusion' is aroused, *Troilus and Cressida* gives us every excuse for playing the allusion-game, we must note that other writers either destroyed their own work or abandoned it, in 1601, because they feared that allusions to Essex would be read into it. Fulke Greville destroyed his *Antony and Cleopatra*, a tragedy 'apt enough', he said, 'to be construed, or strained, to a personating' of contemporary affairs: 'seeing the like instance not poetically, but really fashioned in the Earle of *Essex* then falling. . . . This sudden descent of such greatnesse . . . stir'd up the Authors second thoughts, to bee carefull (in his owne case).'[16] In May 1601, Abraham Colfe, an Oxford BA, wrote to Cecil to explain how he had 'darkly' alluded to Essex's fall – 'I thought to praise the virtues of the Earl, and darkly to point at his death under the history of Cicero. . . . I confess I said he had enemies some of whom I called Piso, Cataline (*sic*), and Anthony, who were enemies of Cicero. Pray pardon this offence . . . .'[17] Even before Essex's rebellion, the Bishop of Worcester, preaching at court, 'made many proffers and glances in [Essex's] behalf, as he was understood by the whole auditory, and by the Queen herself, who presently calling him to a reckoning for it, he flatly foreswore that he had any such meaning'.[18] As late as 1605, when Samuel Daniel published *The Tragedy of Philotas*, he was called before the Privy Council and accused of reflecting on the Essex affair; he added an Apology to the printed version, claiming that he started to write *Philotas* 'neere halfe a yeare before the late Tragedy of ours [that is, of Essex], (whereunto this is now most ignorantly resembled)'; at this point he stopped writing, then resumed some years later. Dramatists and preachers alluded 'darkly' to Essex[19] and got into trouble for doing so, while others suppressed their own work since it might be 'ignorantly' thought to refer to a political crisis about which the authorities were so very sensitive. *Troilus and Cressida* is not an isolated case, as it would be if it was the only play written by Shakespeare for a private audience; on the contrary, it fits in as one of several texts that suffered in much the same way, for political reasons, at this time. Moreover, since Shakespeare's colleagues had already been asked to explain why they had performed *Richard II* in support of Essex's rebellion, as it seemed, it would have been madness to run the risk of repeating the offence by performing *Troilus and Cressida*.

Why, then, did *Troilus and Cressida* remain unclapper-clawed until 1609, the year of the Quarto? One of the first actions of James I on arriving in London in 1603 was to revoke the Attainder on Essex and Southampton;[20] the men who partly engineered Essex's downfall, however, Sir Robert Cecil and the Lord Admiral, became more influential, and Cecil, soon promoted to the earldom of Salisbury, was particularly touchy about slanders and lampoons.[21] That explains, I think, why the 'grand possessors' refused to publish *and to perform* a play hailed in the Quarto epistle as a masterpiece: in Cecil's life-time it was too dangerous. (Cecil died in 1612, so the Quarto *was* published in his life-time – but not by the 'grand possessors'.)

The argument so far, it will be observed, avails itself not ungenerously of conjecture. In self-defence I would point out that I have indulged myself in very little new conjecture, but have followed up other men's ideas, and have tried to relate them more fully to the events of 1601. I would like, next, to test the argument by asking how it squares with another theory – that the Cambridge *Parnassus* play, usually dated 1601, refers to *Poetaster* and *Troilus and Cressida*: 'O that Ben Jonson is a pestilent fellow, he brought up Horace giving the poets a pill, but our fellow Shakespeare hath given him a purge that made him beray [that is, foul] his credit.' If Shakespeare's 'purge' was *Troilus and Cressida*, and he satirised Jonson in the figure of Ajax, as has been suggested, ridiculing his pride, his 'humours', his erudition and his insatiable appetite for praise,[22] then *Troilus and Cressida* must have been performed at Cambridge. Why not? The first Quarto of *Hamlet*, a play written a year or so before *Troilus and Cressida*, claimed on its title-page performances 'in the two universities of Cambridge and Oxford', and Shakespeare's special popularity in the universities is borne out by contemporary records. Some of his earliest and most enthusiastic admirers were Cambridge men (William Covell, Francis Meres, John Weever, and the authors of two *Parnassus* plays); the impersonations of Kempe and Burbage in the third *Parnassus* play of 1601 surely prove that Shakespeare's colleagues were no strangers, were probably recent visitors – so they might well have put on their newest play. Not, I hasten to add, because it was written for private performance; but as a 'try-out', before launching it at the Globe. (Shakespeare must have written (a) the prologue, which alludes to a recent production of *Poetaster*, and (b) the epilogue-speech, which promises a sequel *here* in two months – 'my will shall here be made' – for a projected performance (a) in London, and (b) at the Globe.) That would mean that the play's unintended echoing of the Essex affair dawned on the company during or just after the Cambridge visit; perhaps, even, that those sharp Cambridge men were the first to notice it, and introduced Shakespeare to the delights of 'close reading' and 'practical criticism'. The Earl of Essex had been a very popular Chancellor of Cambridge University from 1598; two days before the Essex trial a letter to his chief antagonist, Sir Robert Cecil, informed him that the university had now chosen *him* as Chancellor,[23] which shows that the university must have followed the contest between these two leading figures, both Cambridge men, with particular interest.

Let us move on, to the play's genre. I believe that at one stage it was planned as a tragedy. What is the evidence? In other plays, just before the death of the tragic hero, Shakespeare makes it an almost standard device that he receives warning, or has a sense of foreboding, that the end is near – a device that also signals the imminent deaths of Hector *and Troilus* in our play. I am thinking of the dream of Richard III before Bosworth, the Ghost of Caesar that comes to Brutus 'To tell thee thou shalt see me at Philippi' (*Julius Caesar*, IV.3.281), and Hamlet's 'thou wouldst not think how ill all's here about my heart' (*Hamlet*, V.2.204), to name just three instances. In *Troilus* Hector is warned by Priam,

> Thy wife hath dreamt; thy mother hath had visions;
> Cassandra doth foresee; and I myself
> Am like a prophet suddenly enrapt
> To tell thee that this day is ominous.
>
> (V.3.63)

Predictably, after so many warnings, Hector has to die. And in this very scene Troilus, too, is repeatedly warned not to fight: 'tempt not yet the brushes of the war. Unarm thee, go'; 'Troilus, I would not have you fight to-day.' A little later, on the battle-field, just before Hector is surrounded by the Myrmidons and killed by Achilles (which is actually how Achilles killed *Troilus*, in Shakespeare's source), Troilus exclaims, rather like Hamlet,

> Fate, hear me what I say:
> I reck not though thou end my life to-day.
>   (V.6.25)

These in themselves are suggestive indications, warning the audience what to expect. And this evidence is confirmed by a textual muddle in the Folio. Here Troilus repudiates Pandar twice, in almost identical words – in the final scene, and also at the end of Act V scene 3.

> (a) *Pand.* But heare you? heare you?
>   *Troy.* Hence broker lackie, ignomy, and shame
>   Pursue thy life, and liue aye with thy name.
>   (V.10,F)

As others have noted, these lines are more appropriate in a palace-scene, than in a battle-scene – since Pandar nowhere else appears on a battle-field, or wears armour. So it seems that the lines were first written for V.3, the last opportunity for Troilus to renounce Pandar, if Troilus was to die in battle; then, when it was decided not to kill off Troilus, the lines were moved to V.10, thus creating an opening for Pandar and his 'epilogue', where a sequel is promised.

> Brethren and sisters of the hold-door trade,
> Some two months hence my will shall here be made.
>   (V.10.50)

This is an appetiser rather like the one offered at the end of 2 *Henry IV*: 'If you be not too much cloyed with fat meat, our humble author will continue the story with Sir John in it' (another promise of a sequel that could not be kept, it is believed, for fear of giving offence).

Next, a second textual tangle in the Folio. When Ulysses describes Troilus in Act IV scene 5, the Folio repeats 'they call him Troilus'.

(b) *Aga.* What Troian is that same that lookes so heauy?
    Vlis. The yongest Sonne of *Priam;*
        A true Knight; they call him *Troylus;*
        Not yet mature, yet matchlesse, firme of word,
        Speaking in deedes, and deedelesse in his tongue;
        Not soone prouok't, nor being prouok't, soone calm'd;
        His heart and hand both open, and both free:
        For what he has, he giues; what thinkes, he shewes;
        Yet giues he not till iudgement guide his bounty,
        Nor dignifies an impaire thought with breath:
        Manly as *Hector*, but more dangerous;
        For *Hector* in his blaze of wrath subscribes
        To tender obiects; but he, in heate of action,
        Is more vindecatiue then iealous loue.
        They call him *Troylus*; and on him erect,
        A second hope, as fairely built as *Hector*.

                                                    (IV.5.95, F)

In the Quarto Ulysses replies, 'The yongest sonne of *Priam*, a true knight, / Not yet mature, yet matchlesse firme of word', etc. As the first 'they call him *Troylus*' is extra-metrical in the Folio, these four words are sometimes described as a 'first thought', discarded by Shakespeare but not adequately crossed out, therefore printed in error.[24] What this textual gloss fails to explain is why so elaborate a character-sketch, conventional enough when a character appears for the first time, should be given near the end of the play, when Troilus needs no further introduction. The answer is, I think, that the eleven lines between the first 'They call him Troilus' and the second were a later insertion, added to point forward to the sequel, where Troilus would naturally figure more as a warrior than as a lover; Shakespeare, that is, having made Troilus declare at his first entrance that he has no zest for war, having had him overshadowed as a fighter by Hector, now tells us how he will develop the story after Hector's death, with a hero 'Manly as Hector, but more dangerous'. Pointing forward, this insertion would seem to be contemporary with Troilus' second repudiation of Pandar, two adjustments made specifically to prepare for a sequel.

How do these explanations of (a) and (b) square with more general accounts of the textual origins of the Quarto and Folio? In the present century the conviction has steadily grown that both versions of *Troilus and Cressida* are Shakespearian – that is, derive from two different manuscripts in Shakespeare's hand, or, if not that, from manuscripts that transmit (1) the author's 'foul papers' or first draft, and (2) his afterthoughts or revisions.[25] The Folio text, it was said, was printed from foul papers, or from a copy of the Quarto corrected by someone who wrote in readings from the foul papers, and the Quarto itself from an authorial fair copy. Just as this once unthinkable theory was hardening into a new orthodoxy, an alternative theory challenged it: the Quarto (not the Folio) was printed from foul papers, it was now said, and the Folio from a theatrical manuscript incorporating 'the author's own verbal revisions'.[26] For our present purposes it is not essential to decide between these two revision-theories: all that matters is that, authorial revision being a corner-stone of both, (a) and (b) may be interpreted as indications that Shakespeare had second thoughts about the play's ending as he composed Acts IV and V.

Shakespeare, I have suggested, wanted to keep open the possibility of a sequel, therefore did not kill off his hero as he had originally planned. The sequel itself, or something very like it, may actually have existed already, before *Troilus and Cressida*, for does Hamlet not allude to a play about the later history of Troy?

> I heard thee speak me a speech once, but it was never acted; or, if it was, not above once; for the play, I remember, pleas'd not the million; 'twas caviary to the general. But it was – as I received it, and others whose judgments in such matters cried in the top of mine – an excellent play, well digested in the scenes, set down with as much modesty as cunning. I remember one said there were no sallets in the lines to make the matter savoury, nor no matter in the phrase that might indict the author of affectation; but call'd it an honest method, as wholesome as sweet, and by very much more handsome than fine. One speech in it I chiefly lov'd: 'twas Æneas' tale to Dido . . . .　　(*Hamlet*, II.2.428)

This has always seemed to me a curiously defensive speech. The prince 'doth protest too much' – why go on for so long about someone else's failed play? Is it really necessary, for our understanding of Hamlet, to make so big a point of saying that he loved a play that 'pleased not the million'? We learn that Hamlet thinks for himself – which we knew before – but the real reason for insisting on the excellence of a play that 'was never acted; or, if it was, not above once' appears to lie elsewhere: someone was displeased that the play had failed. And, since *Hamlet* goes on to quote a lengthy extract from this play, I assume that Shakespeare himself wrote it and could not resist inserting a personal reprimand to those who were unable to appreciate his best work. (The digressions about the War of the Theatres, and about overacting and the 'pitiful ambition' of clowns who ruin a play [*Hamlet*, II.2.323ff., III.2.1ff.] strike me as similar self-indulgences). Hamlet's remarks about the failure of a lost 'Troy-play' are a sign – there are many more in the Sonnets – that gentle William Shakespeare sometimes reacted to the stupidity of others with irritation, as if he were rattled.

Although we cannot prove that a lost 'Troy-play' existed, the following hypothesis would explain several curious facts that appear to be related.

1 *Hamlet* refers to a 'Troy-play' in 1600–1 (the date usually assigned to *Hamlet*).
2 When Shakespeare wrote *Troilus and Cressida*, in 1601, he thought that this could give a new lease of life to the dead 'Troy-play', serving as the first of two plays dramatising the Trojan War. (It is widely assumed that Part 1 of *Henry VI* was written later than Parts 2 and 3, and generally agreed that *Henry V* followed many years after the *Henry VI* plays. In other words: the play that comes first, historically speaking, need not be written first).
3 While writing Acts IV and V of *Troilus and Cressida*, Shakespeare realised that it would help to bind the two Troy-plays together if Troilus, as well as other Greeks and Trojans, were kept alive.
4 The 'Troy-play' 'pleased not the million; 'twas caviary to the general', and *Troilus and Cressida*, 'never clapper-clawed with the palms of the vulgar', was not 'sullied with the smoky breath of the multitude'.

Whatever the reason, the two Troy-plays suffered the same fate. As regards the lost play, Hamlet gives us a clue when he adds, 'I remember one said there were no sallets in the lines to make the matter savoury, nor no matter in the phrase that might indict the author of affectation. . . .' This sounds like a reply to criticism: those who condemned the play alleged that it contained 'sallets' (spicy or bawdy lines) to make it more appetising, and that its style was affected; and Shakespeare could not refrain from repeating what had been said in his defence. The same two charges, by a strange coincidence, are sometimes made against *Troilus and Cressida*; and of course the 'Pyrrhus speech' recited in *Hamlet* (II.2.444ff.) particularly resembles the prologue of *Troilus and Cressida* in its stylistic inflation, and may likewise have been intended as a prologue, or as part of an epic chorus-sequence (as in *Henry V*). Enough 'coincidences' link the two Troy-plays, little as we know about the lost one, to make necessary some such hypothesis as I have outlined.

The stylistic link, suggested above, points to another possible explanation for the non-performance of *Troilus and Cressida*. If the lost 'Troy-play' failed to please partly because of its style, and if *Troilus and Cressida* was written in a similar style, would that style not have been the effective death-warrant of *Troilus and Cressida*? Here several special factors must be taken into account.

First, Shakespeare had grown aware of criticism of his 'bombast', or heightened style, by the time he wrote *Hamlet*, and reacted positively. As I have argued elsewhere,

> In *Hamlet* Shakespeare does not defend heightened speech and improbable action; he merely intimates, again and again, that he *knows* that what he writes sounds like wild and whirling words, or croaking, prating, mouthing, ranting, roaring, thunder, passionate speech, horrid speech, antic or distempered language, tearing a passion to tatters. Doing this he partly disarms criticism; he takes the 'bombast' out of its sails.[27]

Since someone apparently criticised the style of the lost 'Troy-play', Shakespeare could have protected himself in *Troilus and Cressida* by not writing so many 'inflated' speeches, and by other adjustments.

Secondly, the lost 'Troy-play', if we read between the lines, was thought to be heavy going – unappetising, therefore in need of 'sallets', and affected in its style. While Shakespeare did not abandon the stylistic mannerisms of the 'Troy-play' altogether when he wrote *Troilus and Cressida*, probably he tilted this other

Troy-play much more towards comedy, to make it more attractive. The epistle published with *Troilus and Cressida* in 1609 repeatedly describes this play as a comedy, which is not strictly accurate, and stresses its wit: 'So much and such savoured salt of wit is in his comedies that they seem . . . to be born in that sea that brought forth Venus. Amongst all there is none more witty than this . . . .' Again, Shakespeare reacted positively to criticism.

Thirdly, it is hard to believe that Shakespeare would make the same serious mistake twice over, writing two Troy-plays that failed to please for the same reason. The theory that Shakespeare and his colleagues suppressed *Troilus and Cressida*, because of its unintended 'Essex allusion', explains the play's fate more satisfactorily. (a) Total failure was most unusual for Shakespeare. (b) The writer of the epistle of 1609 did not see the play as a failure; rather, as one of Shakespeare's best. (c) Modern theatre-goers and critics also regard it highly. (d) The 'Essex allusion' fits *Troilus and Cressida* into a larger picture, as one of many texts that suffered a similar fate. The virtual disappearance of the play, from 1601 to 1609, becomes understandable; otherwise, without some such explanation, the play's stage history is an inexplicable anomaly in the Shakespeare canon.

To pursue the 'suppression' theory for a moment, let us turn from the play's stage-history to its printing-history. On three separate occasions the publication of *Troilus and Cressida* was obstructed – another oddity that has not received the attention that it deserves. When James Roberts entered the play in the Stationers' Register (7 February 1603) it was with the proviso that he should not print it for the time being. 'Master Roberts. Entered for his copy in full court holden this day to print when he hath gotten sufficient authority for it, the book of *Troilus and Cressida* as it is acted by my Lord Chamberlain's Men. 6d.' A. W. Pollard called this a 'blocking entry', and compared it with two others.

1 22 July 1598: 'James Roberts. Entered for his copy under the hands of both the Wardens, a book of *The Merchant of Venice* . . . provided that it be not printed by the said James Roberts, or any other whatsoever without license first had from the Right Honourable the Lord Chamberlain.'

2 4 August 1600: *As You Like It, Henry V, Every Man In His Humour* and *Much Ado About Nothing* were entered to Roberts 'to be stayed'.

Since Roberts enjoyed the exclusive right of printing play-bills, it was thought that he acted as the players' confidential agent, and made 'blocking entries' to prevent other publishers from issuing play-texts that the players did not wish to have printed. This view of Roberts has been challenged;[28] nevertheless, we may say that someone tried to 'block' the publication of *Troilus and Cressida*, and that the matter was taken even more seriously than in 1598 and 1600, having to be dealt with 'in full court holden this day'.

The second obstruction occurred in 1609, when someone insisted on the removal of the Quarto title-page, apparently because it stated that the play 'was acted by the King's Majesty's servants at the Globe'. The epistle makes it clear that 'the grand possessors' (the King's Men) were opposed to publication, but this could not have been for the reason usually given – namely, that a play would no longer draw big audiences once it was published. As *Troilus and Cressida* was not performed in public, and probably was not performed at all, there must have been a special reason for objecting to its publication. Four copies have survived of the Quarto in its first state, with the original title-page, and many more in the second state, with the revised title-page and epistle to the reader.[29] I deduce that the King's Men protested as soon as they heard of the Quarto's existence, and would have preferred to have the edition suppressed. Failing that, they insisted on having their name removed from the title-page. Why was this so important, when Shakespeare – whose name remained on the title-page, the publishers needing it there to sell the book – was known to be one of the King's Men? Shakespeare's colleagues, it seems, did their utmost to distance themselves from a play that was still felt to be dangerous.

A more extraordinary obstruction followed in 1623: until the very last moment it seemed that *Troilus and Cressida* could not be included in the First Folio. The printers in fact did set up three pages of *Troilus and Cressida* after *Romeo and Juliet*; the three pages had to be removed (they survived accidentally in some copies of the Folio), and the Folio publishers resigned themselves to issuing their precious volume, after many delays, without *Troilus and Cressida*. The 'Catalogue', or contents page, which listed all the other comedies, histories and tragedies in the Folio, omitted *Troilus and Cressida*; only when the Folio was about to be bound and issued did the syndicate receive, at last, permission to print, and it seems to have taken them by surprise. The usual explanation, or conjecture, is that the 'copyright'-owners of the Quarto of *Troilus and Cressida* would not agree to its inclusion. That remains a possibility, but again makes an anomaly of the play, as other Quarto owners came to an arrangement with the Folio syndicate before the 'Catalogue' was printed. We should therefore consider an alternative explanation: that *Troilus and Cressida* was a banned play, one that was known to have a very special history and that the stationers did not dare to print. How many other instances are there of plays that had to have their Quarto title-page replaced *or* had to have pages removed from the Folio? Once we see the Folio 'obstruction' as one of a series of events that all point in one direction (the non-performance of the play, its Stationers' Register entry in 1603, the cancelled title-page of the Quarto) we are driven to conclude that influential forces had sought to suppress the play's performance *and publication*, and were still operative in 1623. Fortunately Heminge and Condell secured permission to dedicate the Folio to the Earls of Pembroke and Montgomery; it may be that these admirers of Shakespeare intervened and helped to reverse a previous decision ('great command o'ersways the order') that *Troilus and Cressida* should not be reprinted.

We are now ready to consider the play's genre. Unlike any other play by Shakespeare it was described as a *history* (on the Quarto title-page), a *comedy* (in the Quarto epistle), and a *tragedy* (in the Folio); and modern critics still cannot agree what to call it. I have argued that there is textual and other evidence that it was to have ended with Troilus's death, a plan abandoned when the play was almost completed; and so drastic a change would inevitably have affected the 'genre' of the finished product. A tragedy ends with the death of the hero; if the hero fails to die, the play fails as a tragedy. Let us pause, however, and ask whether *Troilus and Cressida* could have passed as a tragedy supposing that Troilus had after all died in Act V. What a strange tragedy, it may be said, with so many scenes of unhurried comic chatter. Where is the tragic intensity, the tragic insight? Compare the play with *King Lear* or *Macbeth*, and the notion that it could have been intended as a tragedy seems unconvincing; compare it, on the other hand, with *Antony and Cleopatra* and there are striking similarities. Both plays give a considerable emphasis to comedy, especially in the opening acts; both divide equally into a political and a love story; both make the love-story the relationship of an artful female 'boggler' and an infatuated, put-upon male. In both plays, also, there is a perceptible shift of tone towards tragic urgency in Acts IV and V. The plays are so similar that, if *Antony and Cleopatra*, a 'Roman play', can be accepted as a version of tragedy, so can *Troilus and Cressida* rounded off, as it were, by the death of Troilus.

Would a dramatist willingly change direction so near the end of his play? Not every dramatist, perhaps – but 'myriad-minded Shakespeare', as I argue in other essays in this book, characteristically kept his options open, revised his plans as he went along, and broke genre-expectations, nowhere more so than in the problem plays. We need not look upon the late decision not to kill off Troilus as artistically irresponsible, a merely opportunistic swerve that would pay dividends by enabling Shakespeare to revive the failed 'Troy-play'. No: when the idea came to him that Troilus might be kept alive, Shakespeare would see that an inconclusive ending actually suited the play he had written. Influenced by the latest theatrical fashion, reacting against the doctrine of 'purity of genre', he had almost written the play described by Polonius – 'tragical-comical-historical-pastoral' (see p. 159) – and keeping Troilus alive at the end he made it even clearer that he had not set out to write a traditional play of recognisable genre.

If I am right about the play's date and suppression, we may sum up as follows. *Troilus and Cressida* was written in 1601 and given a 'try-out' performance, perhaps at Cambridge. The play's unintended echoing of the Essex story being noted, it was not performed at the Globe, even though Shakespeare changed his plans as he wrote Acts IV and V and hoped to make *Troilus and Cressida* the first of two linked Troy-plays. By 1601, however, a new play by Shakespeare would be an eagerly awaited event; one of his influential admirers heard of it, and wanted to read it. Either Shakespeare gave him the foul papers, if the Quarto derives from foul papers, or (as I think) he wrote out a fair copy, which was subsequently used by the Quarto printers. Exactly how the Quarto manuscript reached the printers eight years later remains a mystery: it may be significant, though, that in the very year that saw the publication of *Troilus and Cressida*, another Shakespearian manuscript reached print, presumably also from a private collection and also against the wishes of the author. The Sonnets (1609) carried a dedication as enigmatic as the epistle added to the second issue of the Quarto of *Troilus and Cressida*. In both cases there is a glancing acknowledgement that someone half-identified had rights in the text – Mr W. H., the only begetter of the Sonnets, and the 'grand possessors' of the play. It could even be that the two texts, besides being printed by the same printer, G. Eld, were previously presented to the same patron. As far as we know, Shakespeare did not make a habit of giving away his manuscripts; on the other hand, we are aware that he was willing to oblige the Friend of the Sonnets. And was this Friend not one of very few contemporaries who, prior to the publication of the Sonnets, would be able to savour a special piquancy in the play – namely, that the cynical portrait of Cressida was partly inspired by the Dark Lady?

As I said at the outset, all the 'problems' of *Troilus and Cressida* are connected. We cannot discuss the play's date, stage-history, textual transmission, genre, ending and general interpretation as separate issues: they are all connected, and should be taken together. We must look in all directions at once. After almost four hundred years we cannot hope to solve every problem, and must sometimes fall back on conjecture. The reader may think that I resort too readily to conjecture. Perhaps so; but I would reply, in self-defence, that many of the 'connections' proposed in this chapter have not been made before, and they deserve some attention.[30]

8

All's Well That Ends Well: a 'feminist' play?

Shakespeare is sometimes blamed because he expected woman to be beautiful and biddable in a male-dominated world. How unreasonable of him! His heroines, we are told, perpetuate the male myth of woman, as sanctified by the Bible and the marriage-vows of the Church of England; in so far as his feminine ideal was imprinted upon the consciousness of Europe, and later of the world, he was at least as guilty of the enslavement of woman as St Paul, who wrote that 'the husband is the head of the wife, even as Christ is the head of the church' (Ephesians 5:23).

Poor, mindless Shakespeare! At one time he was seen as a 'child of Nature' who, according to John Ward, a vicar of Stratford in the 1660s, 'was a natural wit, without any art at all'.[1] In our century E. M. W. Tillyard rehabilitated him as a man of ideas – second-hand ideas about authority and obedience, previously preached by spokesmen of the Tudor government, popularised by the dramatist. No sooner have we learned that Shakespeare was not necessarily uncritical of 'the Elizabethan world picture', even if he found it convenient to make use of such political platitudes in his plays, than we make the same mistake in the domestic sphere: Shakespeare popularised sexist platitudes about male authority and female obedience, once more repeating mindlessly. So we say to Shakespeare, as Hal said to Poins, 'thou art a blessed fellow to think as every man thinks' (*2 Henry IV*, II.2.52).

What is the truth? In his comedies Shakespeare taught women how to sparkle: he encouraged them to see themselves as intellectually equal to men, frequently more perceptive, more quick-witted in repartee. Far from restricting woman to a single man-pleasing stereotype, he delighted in those who shatter male expectations (Kate the Shrew, Beatrice in *Much Ado*) and, more than any other writer, he understood every kind of woman, from Juliet to Cleopatra. More than any single politician he helped to liberate woman, by portraying the infinite variety of femaleness.

As he grew older he also brought out more clearly that women are often morally stronger than their men-folk. That is already implied in *Romeo and Juliet* but not demonstrated in any clash between hero and heroine, whereas focal moments make the point quite explicit in later plays: 'Kill Claudio' (*Much Ado*, IV.1.287ff.), Portia's wound, which quells her husband's resistance (*Julius Caesar*, II.1.296ff.), Desdemona's attempt to shield Othello (V.2.127). It may be no more than a temporary ascendancy; in the plays that followed, however, it became more centrally important and psychologically meaningful. Cordelia, forced into the role of mother to her father; Lady Macbeth, Cleopatra and Volumnia, who dominate their men and decisively alter the course of events – in all of these cases the woman's moral victory is not fudged by an immediate flip-over into traditional sexual thinking. On the contrary: the woman's strength, and its effect on her father, lover or son, engaged Shakespeare's imagination seriously, at the highest level.

All's Well That Ends Well has been called 'the unfortunate comedy'. Its greatest misfortune, I think, is that it is always discussed together with *Measure for Measure*, largely because the two plays are influenced by folk-tale and there is a 'bed-trick' in both. One might just as well compare *All's Well* and *King Lear* – again, two plays influenced by folk-tale, with a rejected wife in both. Instead of attaching significance to superficial resemblances, I want to place *All's Well* where it more properly belongs, with a series of major plays that all explore the consequences of female dominance. Let us coin a phrase and call it Shakespeare's Thatcher phenomenon.

Helena's moral strength only reveals itself gradually, and can only be fully appreciated in retrospect. When the Countess charges her to confess her love –

> You love my son; invention is asham'd,
> Against the proclamation of thy passion,
> To say thou dost not. *Therefore tell me true*
> (I.3.164)

– she is caught in a trap, exactly as Bertram is later. We know the facts, as in Bertram's case, and yet, although we observe her wriggling in discomfort, she wins our protective sympathy, then our respect.

> I charge thee,
> As heaven shall work in me for thine avail,
> *To tell me truly.*
> HELENA.   Good madam, pardon me.
> COUNTESS. Do you love my son?
> HELENA.   Your pardon, noble mistress.
> COUNTESS. Love you my son?
> HELENA.   Do not you love him, madam?
> COUNTESS. Go not about; my love hath in't a bond
> Whereof the world takes note. Come, come, disclose
> The state of your affection; for your passions
> Have to the full appeach'd.
> HELENA.   Then I confess,
> Here on my knee, before high heaven and you,
> That before you, and next unto high heaven,
> I love your son.

> (174)

In this brilliant exchange, almost prose in its simplicity, we sense the strain of confession, not unlike the soul-crushing strain experienced by Bertram when he entangles himself in lies (V.3.80ff.). Helena has the moral strength to meet the Countess's challenge, and discovers that strength begets strength –

> COUNTESS. Had you not lately an intent – *speak truly* –
> To go to Paris?
> HELENA.   Madam, I had.
> COUNTESS.   Wherefore? *Tell true.*
> HELENA. *I will tell truth; by grace itself I swear.*

> (I.3.209)

As we appreciate more completely later, being able to 'speak truly' in a difficult situation is in itself a moral victory.

Helena's strength is also disclosed in decisions forced upon her by unexpected events. When Bertram rejects her, after the king's cure ('I cannot love her, nor will strive to do it' – II.3.143), she quietly makes a momentous offer.

> That you are well restor'd, my lord, I'm glad.
> Let the rest go.

> (II.3.145)

And when Bertram is about to leave her, she quietly demands recognition as his wife.

> HELENA. Pray, sir, you pardon.
> BERTRAM.   Well, what would you say?
>   . . . what would you have?
> HELENA. Something; and scarce so much; nothing, indeed.
>   I would not tell you what I would, my lord.
>   Faith, yes:
>   Strangers and foes do sunder and not kiss.
>
> (II.5.77)

She demands a kiss, and brings her relationship with him to a crisis. Each of the three passages (Helena's interview with the Countess, her offer to surrender Bertram, her asking for a kiss) was added to the story by Shakespeare; in each case Helena, under pressure, in so far as she is threatened with displeasure, skilfully redefines her rights, forcing the other party to support or reject her. Though seemingly at a disadvantage, she always makes a calculated counter-move – a gamble, which could wreck all her hopes, quietly resolved upon, forewarning us of a remarkable inner strength.

Before any of these episodes Shakespeare placed her encounter with Parolles, another addition to his source-story, the first of her many dialogue duels.

> PAROLLES. Are you meditating on virginity?
> HELENA. Ay. You have some stain of soldier in you: let me ask
>   you a question. Man is enemy to virginity; how may we
>   barricado it against him?   (I.1.104)

At one time this 'indelicate' passage was cut in production – a disastrous amputation for the unfortunate comedy, since the dramatist here shapes our response to all that follows. Parolles springs his question on her (compare Lucio to Isabella, 'Hail virgin, if you be' – *Measure for Measure*, I.4.16); she decides almost instantaneously that she can handle this kind of impertinence: it chimes in with her mood. By means of this dialogue, the first real testing of Helena's intellectual and moral fibre, Shakespeare possesses us of several essentials all at once. Helena, who has just soliloquised about her hopeless passion for Bertram, is not a

romantic fool: sex, and what we today would call sexual psychology
and know-how, holds no mysteries for her. She is able to switch
from romantic day-dreaming to earthy masculine humour, which
traditionally makes a woman a sex-object and virginity a joke.
And, even more important, she swiftly takes control of a
conversation that began as an attack upon her, willingly allowing
the masculine joke to drag on ('How might one do, sir, to lose it
to her own liking?' – I.1.141), finally making use of Parolles to
send signals to Bertram.

> Not my virginity yet.
> There shall your master have a thousand loves,
> A mother, and a mistress, and a friend . . . .
>   (153)

Although she seems to be on the defensive in her later exchanges
with the Countess, the King and Bertram, and speaks quietly, we
are meant to remember her skilful fencing with Parolles and
consequently to be aware of hidden strengths – whilst, locally, her
interlocutors are more impressed by her modesty and deference
('Your pardon, noble mistress'; 'Pray, sir, your pardon', to Bertram).
They accept her more or less as she presents herself ('I am a simple
maid' – II.3.64); we, the theatre-audience, begin to suspect that
she is also a formidable opponent, something of a Britomart.

Just before the virginity-dialogue Shakespeare placed Helena's
first soliloquy, in which an attendant lady, who had previously
spoken only once, suddenly drops the mask of maiden modesty
and unpacks her heart.

> O, were that all! I think not on my father;
> And these great tears grace his remembrance more
> Than those I shed for him. What was he like?
> I have forgot him; my imagination
> Carries no favour in't but Bertram's.
> I am undone; there is no living, none,
> If Bertram be away.
>   (I.1.73)

Her ability to cut loose from conventional thinking ('I have forgot
him'), and to sort out her priorities, prepares for her breath-taking
directness in the virginity-dialogue, and the soliloquy and dialogue

together give us glimpses of the less 'maidenly' parts of her character, which she is careful to screen from her social superiors.

The bed-trick in *All's Well*, sometimes described as a mere plot-mechanism taken over from the source and regrettably out of key with the play's realism, may be seen as Helena's very personal choice, reflecting the complicated character that Shakespeare created for her. For *All's Well* also resembles *Measure for Measure* (and of course several other plays) in dealing with overmastering sexual impulses; Helena's predicament is not unlike Angelo's, and, even if she cannot be accused of judicial rape, it is not unfair to describe her as sexually rapacious. Shakespeare does not wish to antagonise the audience, therefore sets to work discreetly, preparing for the bed-trick step by step, as a dynamiter assembles his time-bomb. Helena thinks of herself as 'The hind that *would be mated by* the lion' (I.1.85; note the force of that 'by'); in imagination she has languished for his physical charms ('His arched brows, his hawking eye, his curls' – 88); later, when he has gone to the wars, she worries about 'those tender limbs of thine' (III.2.103). She allows the virginity-dialogue to continue a little longer than is seemly, at last closes the door on it ('Not my virginity yet'), then rapturously flings it open again – '*There* shall your master have a thousand loves'. (Where, exactly?) Hers is very much a physical passion. The fact that the Steward overheard her confess it, 'in the most bitter touch of sorrow that e'er I heard virgin exclaim in' (I.3.109), that the Countess is also aware of it, and that she herself drops hints to Parolles, confirms that her impulses are violent; they drive her to Paris, to Florence, to the bedding of Bertram. Like the clown she is 'driven on by the flesh', and she 'must needs go that the devil drives' (28).

Shakespeare would never have considered a bed-trick as appropriate for Rosalind or Beatrice. Other tricks are used in their plays, expressive of their characters; Helena's bed-trick expresses hers, and we should notice in how many ways it differs from its counterpart in *Measure for Measure* (where, as I have argued [p. 163], Shakespeare also took some trouble to relate it to character, particularly the Duke's and Mariana's). She stage-manages the whole affair, persuades the Widow, instructs Diana – even, we must suppose, anticipating Bertram's reluctance to part with his ring and devising a verbal trick to overcome it ('Mine honour's such a ring:/My chastity's the jewel of our house' – IV.2.45). All her managerial and adversarial skills are brought into play.

Shakespeare, quite exceptionally, intimates that the physical consummation was a success, a point not to be taken for granted when the woman is a virgin and the man may 'Remain there but an hour' (58).

> But, O strange men!
> That can such sweet use make of what they hate . . . .
> (IV.4.21)

The credit for this success must probably go to Helena, whose afterglow once more reminds us of her highly sexed nature. Despite all her phrases of maidenly modesty, therefore, Shakespeare portrayed her from the beginning as an unconventional woman, the only woman in all of his plays who is right for this particular bed-trick – because she is so single-minded in her pursuit of Bertram. As she ringingly proclaims in the last lines of the first scene,

> my project may deceive me,
> But my intents are fix'd, and will not leave me!

Why did Shakespeare choose to make a play out of the short story translated by Painter from Boccaccio? The bed-trick is its focal event, and must have appealed to him – if only as a trial of his ingenuity, having to metamorphose the two-dimensional characters that are acceptable in a short story into more credible human beings. Helena becomes what she is because of the bed-trick – but Shakespeare chose the story, I believe, because he saw that she might speak for the New Woman of his age, who challenges Man in his time-honoured prerogatives. Had England not been ruled for forty-five years by Queen Elizabeth? And France, more briefly, by Catherine de Medici? Although the universities and inns of court did not admit women, many titled ladies were social and intellectual leaders – Sir Philip Sidney's sister, Lord Burghley's wife, George Herbert's mother – and others, high and low, shook off traditional female roles and sought equality with men. Mary Fitton, one of the Queen's maids of honour, used to dress as a page, so it was said, to slip away from the court and meet her lover. Moll Cutpurse dressed as a man, swaggered as a man, intimidated her sexual admirers, and had a play written about her by Middleton and Dekker (published 1611, written earlier). Foreigners who visited England marvelled at the emancipation of its women: 'they have more liberty than in other lands, and know how to make good use of it', going constantly abroad while 'the men must put up with such ways, and may not punish them for it'.[2] Perhaps Anne Hathaway, who married a boy eight years her junior when she was twenty-six, was an 'emancipated' woman; the Dark Lady of the sonnets must certainly have been one.

Long before *All's Well That Ends Well* Shakespeare had already flirted with the New Woman. In his first signed publication the heroine, Venus, is sexually aggressive, but the interest centres on situation-comedy, not psychology. Rosalind and Beatrice dare to challenge men in their thinking, even to outwit them in verbal duels, and they may claim to be the most 'liberated' women in English drama at the turn of the century. Thereafter the New Woman took two different roads: one the primrose path trodden by Cressida, Cleopatra and other 'white devils'; the second the way of self-confident virtue chosen by Helena and the Duchess of Malfi.

Helena is a special case, for, apart from her other talents, she has some professional skill. She may not be a qualified doctor but she was educated by her father (I.1.34), a famous doctor, who left her his prescriptions –

> Of rare and prov'd effects, such as his reading
> And manifest experience had collected . . . .
>
> (I.3.213)

She understands their application, and *knows* that one of them will cure the king.

COUNTESS.   Dost thou believe it?
HELENA. Ay, madam, knowingly.
                    (240)

The modern reader may misinterpret these hints, modern medicine being a closed shop. In the Elizabethan period one could count on a great variety of semi-trained and untrained practitioners (for example, Simon Forman, who set horoscopes and offered his female patients sexual services, as well as more traditional aids[3]) – and they included many women. 'Carry his water to th' wise woman!' cries Fabian, when Malvolio appears to be demented

(*Twelfth Night*, III.4.97). The wise woman of Brainford (*Merry Wives*, IV.5.10ff.), the wise woman of Hogsdon, and midwives generally, were credited with more than a little medical know-how, not to mention witchcraft and other forbidden arts.

In Shakespeare's age women competed with men in the medical world, as does Helena when all the most renowned doctors despair of curing the French king. A contemporary audience would understand that her success, although spoken of as if miraculous (II.3.1ff.), need not be a miracle – except in so far as 'miracle cures' have always had their place in the history of medicine. It suited Shakespeare to let bystanders talk of miracles, since he wanted Helena to impress us as, figuratively, a 'miracle-worker', triumphing over one impossible task after another; nevertheless, two-day cures (II.1.160) are by no means unheard of, and her success with the French king should be taken as possibly resulting from natural causes – and from a woman's professional brilliance, defeating the most learned doctors in their own masculine territory.

Helena also challenges a masculine prerogative when she demands, as her reward, the right to choose her own spouse. The idea comes from the source-story, significantly changed.

> 'Because thou are a maiden and unmarried [said the French King], if thou heal me according to thy promise, I will bestow thee upon some gentleman, that shall be of right good worship and estimation. . . . ' [She replied,] 'I beseech your grace, let me have such a husband as I myself shall demand.'[4]

In the play she herself broaches the subject, unprompted.

> HELENA. But, if I help, what do you promise me?
> KING. Make thy demand. . . .
> HELENA. Then shalt thou give me with thy kingly hand
>   What husband in thy power I will command.
>
> (II.1.189)

Shakespeare made her more direct, more masterful. Notice the ambiguity of 'in thy power': she will demand a husband who is in the king's power, and she will do this by *commanding* it 'in thy power'. She will assume his authority. Her switch to 'thou' and 'thy' at this point is noteworthy.

It was Shakespeare's idea to have a beauty-parade of young

lords. In the source Helena simply named her choice ('I have then, my lord, quoth she, deserved the Countie Beltramo of Rossiglione'); the parade again reverses sexual prerogatives, for it is usually the ladies who are on show, the men who select. We today are familiar with the Miss World meat-market and similar rituals, where the livestock has to show off its paces before a smirking male; the original audience might think of plays such as *Godly Queen Hester* or Peele's *Judgement of Paris* – or of dances or may-games, where it is also the man's prerogative to choose. The uncomfortableness of the lords should not be overlooked. Lafeu wonders, 'Do all they deny her?'; they respond politely, not enthusiastically, partly because the parade offends the dignity of the male.

Helena later pursues her chosen mate to his bed, in Florence. This, again, is thought to be a male prerogative ('Man is the hunter, woman is his game'), as exemplified by Bertram, 'a whale to virginity' (IV.3.203), who forces his way dishonestly into 'Diana's' bed. In the final scene Helena comes to her husband's rescue, the strong helping the weak. The ending was radically altered by Shakespeare, partly to make this point – Helena appearing at the very last moment, a *dea ex machina*, radiant, triumphant, just when Bertram's fortunes are at the lowest. In the source she returns to Bertram's palace,

> to the place where the count sat, falling down prostrate at his feet, weeping, saying unto him, 'My lord, I am thy poor infortunate wife. . . . Therefore I now beseech thee, for the honour of God, that thou wilt observe the conditions which [you] did command me . . . .

She presents him with twin sons and his ring, and he embraces her – 'and from that time forth, he loved and honoured her as his dear spouse and wife'. Shakespeare swept away the wifely submissiveness, and Bertram's spontaneous change of heart. Instead, Diana and the Widow are brought to France and Bertram reveals the full odiousness of his character –

> She's impudent, my lord,
> And was a common gamester to the camp
> (V.3.185)

– sinking to his lowest, it should be observed, after he has broken with Parolles, who is sometimes blamed for misleading him. Shakespeare also reintroduced the King, Lafeu and the Countess, authority-figures in whose absence Bertram might have rid himself of Diana less unpleasantly. Everything possible has been done, in short, to drag down Bertram, placing him in a position of weakness, reversing the normal relationship of husband (protector) and wife (the protected). He has to ask her pardon; she comforts him, if that is the right word, with a smiling allusion to his performance in bed:

> O, my good lord, when I was like this maid
> I found you wondrous kind.
>
> (303)

– the type of remark that men more often make to women. (Compare Iago: 'You rise to play, and go to bed to work' – *Othello*, II.1.115.) If Bertram actually kneels when he asks for pardon, as would be natural – overwhelmed as he is by the certainty that all of his deceptions must now be exposed – then the husband kneels to the wife, another reversal of sexual prerogatives. Wives knelt to their husbands (*Taming of the Shrew*, V.2.136ff., *Julius Caesar*, II.1.278, *Othello*, IV.2.31); Bertram's kneeling to Helena, when sexual roles were so stereotyped, would seem as extraordinary as Lear's to his daughters (*King Lear*, II.4.152; IV.7.59).

From the first stage-direction Shakespeare signals to the audience that *All's Well* is to be an unconventional comedy: the characters enter '*all in black*', and black was the colour of tragedy ('Hung be the heavens with black' – *1 Henry VI*, I.1.1). The Countess's husband has recently died, Helena mourns for her dead father, the French king 'hath abandoned his physicians' and is not expected to live. A strange beginning for a comedy! The sex-reversals that I have described were an equally deliberate break with comic convention, I believe, supported by other adjustments to the story: Shakespeare invented the Countess, 'the most beautiful old woman's part ever written', according to Bernard Shaw,[5] and made more of Diana's mother, a 'gentlewoman' in the source who also becomes a widow in the play. (All of the play's secondary characters lack a sexual partner, except for a clown, driven by the flesh, and Diana, solicited by Bertram: what would be considered normal domestic and romantic love is excluded, and predatory sexuality accentuated.) The Countess, Widow and Diana, being remarkably business-like, help to suggest that Helena's efficiency is not necessarily unfeminine, and the four ladies together, opposing the irresponsible Bertram and Parolles, tip the whole play firmly towards a feminine point of view. The King and Lafeu ensure that the men are not completely disgraced, but cannot restore the balance: already in the husband-choosing scene we sense that Helena is in control, and even more so in the final scene, where the King is reduced to the rank of a baffled spectator. His parting words to Diana, 'Choose thou thy husband, and I'll pay thy dower', may be meant to indicate that women have proved their worth, but also suggest that men will go on making the same mistakes, being more status-conscious than sensitive to the mutuality of love.

The Countess and Widow have other important functions. Conventional morality did not allow a girl to love, let alone love passionately, until the man had declared himself. (Helena, said the source, 'fervently fell in love with Beltramo, more than was meet for a maiden of her age'; she 'burned' in love.) By not condemning Helena's love the Countess establishes that it is not unfeminine ('Even so it was with me when I was young' – I.3.119); by actually encouraging her to go to Paris, that a poor physician's daughter might be socially acceptable as a count's wife. Shakespeare added the Countess's moral support and removed the King's disapproval (in the source, the King 'was very loth to grant [Bertram] to [Helena]'). Similarly, the Widow's support guarantees that the bed-trick will not strike us as scandalous; here Shakespeare closely followed his source, adding 'Violenta and Mariana', two friends of the Widow. Mariana's advice that 'the honour of a maid is her name', and warning against the 'engines of lust' (III.5.11ff.), defines the Widow's circle as morally conventional. Attaching Helena to a group of four women (27), Shakespeare created a feminine power-centre, corresponding to the Countess in Rousillon; and the five women together, observing the army as it passes (71), underline the sexist division of the play. I would repeat this visual point when Helena, the Widow and Diana arrive in France by making their 'two attendants' women, and, again, by arranging the women as a closed group at the end, when Helena and the Countess embrace (V.2.313). Perhaps the women should be dressed 'all in black', as at the beginning, surrounded by colourfully costumed creatures, male peacocks.

The Parolles sub-plot, added by Shakespeare, appears to

contribute little to the play's 'sexist' concern, apart from an insistently physical view of male – female relations. Parolles initiates the virginity dialogue, and loses no opportunity to degrade sex –

> He wears his honour in a box unseen
> That hugs his kicky-wicky here at home,
> Spending his manly marrow in her arms,
> Which should sustain the bound and high curvet
> Of Mars's fiery steed.
>
> (II.3.272)

'Kicky-wicky' is not recorded elsewhere, says the Arden editor ('keecky', though, is a term of endearment for a wife in Mrs Centlivre's *The Basset-table*, 1706). Unlike Cleopatra, who jokingly compares herself to a happy horse ('O happy horse, to bear the weight of Antony!' – *Antony and Cleopatra*, I.5.21), Parolles imagines sexual activity as equivalent to masterful horsemanship (hence '*kicky*-wicky'?). After encouraging Bertram in his follies, a Vice-figure counterpoising Helena's Virtue, Parolles becomes more important in himself in the 'drum' episodes, which some critics consider tedious. One sees, of course, that they have a structural function: blindfolded, he betrays his friends, abjectly hoping to save his skin, and this conditions our response to Bertram when he goes through similar motions in Act V, also 'blindfolded', equally dishonourable and cowardly as he tangles himself in lies. Later, Bertram's contempt for Parolles will rebound upon himself. The sexist function of the drum episodes is not quite so obvious, and may be illustrated from *The Alchemist* (III.3.38ff.): Face brutally tells Doll to get ready for a lustful Spaniard, who is to be thrown in a down-bed –

> Where thou shalt keep him waking with thy drum;
> Thy drum, my Doll; thy drum; till he be tame.

Either 'drum' was slang for hymen and vagina, or Shakespeare, ever inventive in his sexual imagery, gave Parolles the 'impossible task' of retrieving a drum as a suggestive analogy. At any rate it cannot be an accident that Parolles pretends to seek for the drum in the very night when Helena loses her virginity – indeed, that the lords persuade him to 'undertake *this business*' (III.6.79) just before Helena persuades the Widow, who is 'Nothing acquainted with *these businesses*' (III.7.5). Shakespeare had already looked forward to the drum's usefulness as a resonating symbol in Bertram's farewell to Helena –

> Go thou toward home, where I will never come
> Whilst I can shake my sword or hear the drum.
> (II.3.88)

A modern dramatist might have called the play *The Sword and the Drum*, but Shakespeare trusted his spectators to catch the cross-references. The ladies elaborately plan their bed-trick while the men plan a different trick, also a night ambush. The ladies are serious, the men amuse themselves; in both plots a drum is valued high and low: 'My chastity's the jewel of our house' (IV.2.46); 'A pox on't; let it go; 'tis but a drum' (III.6.40).

The Parolles sub-plot, added by Shakespeare, reinforces the play's feminist emphasis. Returning now to this larger theme, the play's patterned contrast of male and female, I have to acknowledge a problem. If Helena is as sensible as has been suggested, and Bertram as worthless, how can she love him? Does that not discredit her? Not initially, since the stage-response shields her: everyone admires or loves Bertram (the Countess, Lafeu, the King, as well as Helena). He is the image of his 'good father' (I.2.19ff.), just as Helena appears to repeat hers, and, the King's afterthought notwithstanding ('Thy father's moral parts/Mayst thou inherit too!'), there is no reason to think ill of Bertram. His overvaluation of Parolles only becomes worrying in Paris, and his other errors of judgement follow *after* she asks for him as her husband: until he rejects her everyone considers him, as she does, 'a bright particular star' (I.1.80). His faults thenceforth are carefully graded. He disdains her as his wife – unpleasant. He sulks and defies the king ('I cannot love her, nor will strive to do it') – unwise, yet no more so than Romeo and Juliet, and other lovers who wish to choose for themselves. He decides 'I will not bed her', writes to the king 'that which I durst not speak', promises Helena to join her in two days, and rides to Florence. Here, in his first batch of faults, the audience observes his lies and moral cowardice, but Helena remains ignorant of the worst. In Florence, his 'wanton siege' of Diana is more reprehensible; Helena knows about it, and still loves him. Back in France the inner logic of his character emerges fully as he tries to protect himself against Diana (and here Shakespeare departs from his source); all of his most selfish tendencies converge – disdain, cowardice, untruthfulness, treachery. Even if Helena is not a witness, she clearly stage-manages the humbling of Bertram; can she – *should* she – still love him?

It may not be sensible, but she does. Or, at least, she *offers* her love ('Will you be mine now you are doubly won?' – V.3.308) and, in a 'feminist' play, love may be allowed to triumph over sense as the highest good. Yet Dr Johnson was right: we cannot reconcile our hearts to Bertram – the sharp contrast of male and female continues to the end. In response to Helena's appeal he turns *away* from her, addressing the King, for he still feels threatened –

> If she, my liege, can make me know this clearly,
> I'll love her dearly, ever, ever dearly.
>
> (V.3.309)

He means: if she can convince me that the child is mine – and not before. He must be the only person who remains doubtful. To his credit, though, he does not pretend a love that he does not feel. We are left wondering whether the most impossible task of all, the winning of a husband's love after so public a disgrace, is not beyond Helena, and beyond human nature. The title *All's Well That Ends Well* could be just as ambiguous as *Measure for Measure*.

Should Helena reappear with a child 'in her arms', as in the source, or heavily padded and visibly pregnant? Bertram's letter required her to 'show me a child begotten of thy body that I am father to' (III.1.56). The second time round we hear

> And looke you, heeres your letter: this it sayes,
> When from my finger you can get this Ring,
> And is by me with childe, &c. This is done,
> Will you be mine now you are doubly wonne?
>
> (V.3.305, F)

Shakespeare knew that audiences would not remember the exact wording of a letter, so felt free to introduce minor changes. Yet the difference between 'show me a child' and 'is by me with child' could involve a significant change in staging, perhaps second thoughts by the dramatist.[6] But not necessarily: the second reading may refer to Helena's tasks, not to her return. She could therefore show a child, as Shakespeare certainly intended while writing Act III, or a bundle containing a child. I prefer this to a pregnant Helena, for nothing high-lights the division of the sexes better than the handling of a baby. She gives the bundle to Bertram, her female triumph, or holds it out to him, and, caught in this final trap, what can he say? what should he do? He will have to wait a couple of centuries for advice – from August Strindberg.

I have not paid much attention, so far, to the folk-tale elements in the play. Some readers may complain that my approach is too psychological and 'realistic' – to which I reply that the play's language must take the blame. One half of the dialogue consists of prose, and much of the verse is 'prosaic', in the sense that it serves for interrogations, information-giving, chat, and avoids the poetical. The language has the qualities that Dryden admired in Beaumont and Fletcher: 'they understood and imitated the conversation of gentlemen much better [than Shakespeare]. . . . I am apt to believe the English language in them arrived to its highest perfection.'[7] More than in most of his Jacobean plays Shakespeare aimed at naturalness in the language of *All's Well*, an easy 'modern' style uncluttered by mixed metaphors and syntactic snarls. No wonder that Caroline Spurgeon found so little to say about the play's imagery! This is a sign not of linguistic inadequacy but of deliberate choice, as – *mutatis mutandis* – with the language of *Julius Caesar* (cf. p. 29 above): 'natural' speech begat life-like men and women, which begat a life-like play.

No one will think, I hope, that natural speech must be artless. The Countess's examination of Helena merely repeats one word to prize open her defences, and by this means, though both women dissimulate, Shakespeare reveals their characters. 'I am a mother to you. – Mine honourable mistress. – Nay, a mother. / Why not a mother? . . . I say I am your mother' (I.3.130). An extraordinary tension builds up and explodes in 'Yes, Helen, you might be my daughter-in-law!' Three possible relationships interact in their minds. The fact that the Countess actually feels a motherly affection, and that Helena dare not confess her feeling, makes this little scene a double-bluff rather like Lear's interrogation of Cordelia, and yet the true characters of the participants show through the chinks quite differently.

In addition to its natural language *All's Well* contains an unusual number of rhyming speeches, the effect of which is the very opposite. At one time these were thought to belong to an earlier version of the play, fossil-deposits in an archaic style – a view that no longer prevails. G. K. Hunter has shown that Shakespeare oscillates between a 'remote, impersonal, and hieratic presentation of his subject, and a more immediate and human treatment of it', as in some of his other plays. But Hunter erred, I think, in concluding that 'there is a general failure in *All's Well* to establish a medium in verse which will convey effectively the whole tone of the play':[8] the tone of the play depends on this oscillation. Switching from rhymed verse, or from occasional passages of knotted syntax, to what I have called natural language, Shakespeare invests these lines of plain, direct speech with even more power.

> HELENA. I am a simple maid, and therein wealthiest
>   That I protest I simply am a maid.
>   *Please it your Majesty, I have done already.* . . . .
>   Blessing upon your vows; and in your bed
>   Find fairer fortune, if you ever wed!
> LAFEU. *These boys are boys of ice; they'll none have her. Sure, they are*
>   *bastards to the English* . . . .
> HELENA [*to Bertram*]. I dare not say I take you; but I give
>   Me and my service, ever whilst I live,
>   Into your guiding power. *This is the man.*
> KING. *Why, then, young Bertram, take her; she's thy wife.*
>
> (II.3.64)

Such effects are particularly important in *All's Well*, thanks to the sheer quantity of prose and rhymed verse, and, in key-scenes, the rapid alternation of natural and heightened language. The proximity of 'folk-tale' elements and more 'natural' action has a similar impact: one that is meant to be noticed, even though they are intermingled carefully, as is the language. And the division of male and female, which I think persists to the very end, must be part of the same design. If *All's Well* followed after the romantic comedies and preceded *Measure for Measure*, as is generally thought, this play should be venerated as one of the most consciously innovative in Shakespeare's long career.

9

Shakespeare's mingled yarn and *Measure for Measure*

This will not be a lecture for purists. I propose to examine a trend that troubled Sir Philip Sidney when he lamented the fashion for 'mongrel tragi-comedy' – a shift in literary taste that owed much to the genius of William Shakespeare. It started, perhaps, with the mixing of comic and more serious matter in medieval drama; Kyd and Marlowe gave it a new impetus; and it had certainly arrived by the time of *Measure for Measure*, Shakespeare's darkest comedy. But I have in mind something more far-reaching than the hybridisation of kinds, or the doctrine of purity of genre. As Elizabethan drama moved towards realism, and simultaneously lurched in several other directions as well, many kinds of 'mixing' were developed – prose and verse; natural and stylised language, and stage behaviour, and acting; Elizabethan and 'historical' costume, as in the Peacham sketch of *Titus Andronicus*; plot and sub-plot – to name just a few 'mixings' that must have been in general use by the 1580s. Then Shakespeare appeared on the scene, pressed a button, and the mixer-speed accelerated remarkably, much to the disgust of purists (such as Ben Jonson). Shakespeare delighted in mixed metaphor; Jonson reputedly said of some of the grandest speeches in *Macbeth*, which 'are not to be understood', that 'it was horror'. Shakespeare specialised in crazily complicated plots, cross-wooing comedies, plays with time-jumps, plays that zig-zag between different countries – disgraceful 'mixings' that Jonson castigated publicly. More modern critics discover the same tendency wherever they look: Shakespeare's expert interweaving of different views of the same person, of past, present, and future, of slow time and fast time, of conflicting motives, or the interplay of many emotions in a single phrase – 'Pray you, undo this button'; 'Kill Claudio'. If, as I shall argue, Shakespeare's mixing-skills were of the essence, as indispensable to his success as his inventiveness in metaphor, it may be no accident that he so often peaks as a poet in scenes of intense emotion or madness (Hamlet's, King

Lear's), where a 'mixer' mechanism in the play triggers off his own special talent. I believe that these mixing-skills are conscious artistry, not inspired fumbling, if only because the dramatist so often draws attention to them:

> You have seen
> Sunshine and rain at once: her smiles and tears
> Were like, a better way.
>
> (*King Lear*, IV.3.17)

We need not doubt that a writer who said that 'the web of our life is of a mingled yarn' would know, even without Ben Jonson's unnecessary help, that he himself was a purveyor of intricately mingled yarns.

The 'mixing'principle in Shakespeare is my subject today. Ben Jonson was merely the first of many good critics who could not come to terms with it, and one or two other examples will illustrate the range of problems. Dr Johnson, though he defended tragi-comedy, thought that 'the poet's matter failed him' in the fifth act of *Henry V*, 'and he was glad to fill it up with whatever he could get'; in Johnson's view, Act V did not mix with the rest. Coleridge repudiated the 'low' Porter-speech in *Macbeth*, which reminds us that bawdy, once removed by editors as intrusive dirt, is now praised as an integral part of the Shakespearian 'mix' in both comedy and tragedy. T. S. Eliot faulted Shakespeare's 'mixing' even more ingeniously, arguing that it is 'strictly an error, although an error which is condoned by the success of each passage in itself, that Shakespeare should have introduced into the same play ghosts belonging to such different categories as the three sisters and the ghost of Banquo'.[1] These are all 'mixing'-problems, and they warn us that Shakespeare's imagination scrambled the ingredients of a play in so many new ways that even the very best critics 'hoppe alwey bihinde'.

Examples of supposedly bad 'mixing' are alleged, and have to be endured, in almost every book on Shakespeare. Yet the mixing-principle itself has not had the attention it deserves. This may be because criticism finds it convenient to deal with detachable units – imagery, character, genre, scene-by-scene analysis – rather than with the intermeshing of such units, which I consider the heart of the mystery. After four centuries criticism is still largely defeated by a procedural problem, how to grapple with the play as a whole:

I suggest that we may solve this problem by focusing on the mixing-principle, searching for its unique functioning in each text. Not only Shakespeare criticism could benefit: we do not have to look far to discover similar needs elsewhere. Let me illustrate, tactfully, from *Juno and the Paycock*, where, it has been said, the tragic element 'occupies at the most some twenty minutes . . . for the remaining two hours and a half this piece is given up to gorgeous and incredible fooling'.[2] Who has not heard that *The Winter's Tale* consists of three acts of tragedy followed by two of comedy? Or that some scenes in *Measure for Measure* are 'tragic', others 'comic'? It is the interpenetration of comedy and tragedy that now needs our attention – or, more exactly, the interaction of everything with everything else, in these unfathomably rich plays.

O'Casey once remarked 'I never make a scenario, depending on the natural growth of a play rather than on any method of joinery.'[3] Shakespeare criticism, when it attempts to explain the mixing-principle, still tends to think too much in terms of joinery – as in a brilliant paper on *The Winter's Tale* in which Nevill Coghill showed that the bear, the famous bear, 'was calculated to create a unique and particular effect, at that point demanded by the narrative mood and line of the play. It is at the moment when the tale, hitherto wholly and deeply tragic, turns suddenly and triumphantly to comedy.'[4] Much that Coghill said about the bear seems to me perceptive, yet his is largely an explanation of joinery. Looking at the play as an organic growth, I am struck by the fact that each of its two movements ends with an addition to the story by Shakespeare – the bear, and the statue. In each case the bystanders, astounded, react aesthetically, as if the bear and statue are merely a thrilling spectacle, then struggle comically to adjust their bewildered feelings – and thus lift the scene, emotionally, in a very similar way. If the bear and statue are connected, as I think, then the mixing-principle works not only in local joinery but also, more elusively, in shaping dramatic units that are far apart.

I am going to assume, in what follows, that in 'organic' drama everything joins on to everything else; that bears and statues can shake hands, as over a vast, and embrace as it were from the ends of opposed winds. The logic of our bread-and-butter world need not apply; the linear structure of events, and of cause and effect, is not the only structure that concerns us. Although we are sometimes told that a literary work grows in the reader's mind as does a musical composition, being a process experienced in time, and should not be compared to a painting, which is frozen in time, a play that lasts two to three hours differs from longer literary works, such as an epic or a novel, in so far as its process can be held in the mind as a single experience, somewhat like a painting. Aided by memorable dialogue and good acting a poetic drama will not pass away from us while we surrender to its magic, as do the trivia of day-to-day existence: such a play grows in the beholder's mind in a present continuous, partly insulated from time, a single shared experience framed by the stage, one that remains present, like a painting, even as it unfolds, challenging us to connect the ends of opposed winds, a bear and a statue, Claudio's guilt and Angelo's, Angelo's ignorance of the world and Isabella's and the Duke's. 'Only connect' is the dramatist's command, and the more unexpectedly he mixes the play's ingredients the bigger the challenge.

I should like to illustrate the 'present continuous' of drama from a soliloquy that some of you may remember - 'To be or not to be, that is the question'. I find it surprising that, according to some competent editors, Hamlet here talks not of his own suicide but only of the general problem of life after death. Dr Johnson paraphrased the opening line succinctly, as follows: 'Before I can form any rational scheme of action under this pressure of distress, it is necessary to decide whether, after our present state, we are to be or not to be. That is the question. . . .' Another editor soon offered a different interpretation, 'To live or to put an end to my life', which, he thought, was confirmed by the following words. Johnson had his supporters, and I find this surprising not because of the following words but because of preceding speeches that prepare us for 'To be or not to be'. Hadn't Hamlet wished that 'this too too solid flesh would melt'? (Knowing what we know about the frauds and stealths of injurious imposters, I had better say firmly that 'solid flesh' is the reading of the only authorised text – of this lecture.) 'You cannot, sir, take from me anything that I will more willingly part withal – except my life, except my life, except my life.' These and other passages determine our immediate impression that in 'To be or not to be' Hamlet meditates upon his own suicide; the soliloquy is not a detachable unit, it throbs with implications planted in our minds in earlier scenes.

If my example seems fanciful, let us take two that are more straightforward. Let us take the one sentence that occurs in both *Othello* and *Macbeth*. Lady Macbeth waits for Macbeth; he appears, the daggers in his hands, blood on the daggers; the deed is done, and wrings from her a terrible, gloating cry – 'My husband!' Othello explains to Emilia that the murder of Desdemona proceeded upon just grounds ('Thy husband knew it all'), and she reacts in shocked surprise – 'My husband!' The same words, but the effect is totally different, because the words mingle with previous impressions, there is an inflow of power from very different sources. Lady Macbeth had taunted her husband that he was not man enough to commit the murder; when he has proved himself she cries, in effect, 'My true husband, at last!' Emilia had suspected that Desdemona had been slandered by 'some cogging, cozening slave, to get some office'; as soon as Othello names Iago she realises what has happened, and she feels that she has come to a crossroad in her life. Her exclamation marks the end of a marriage, Lady Macbeth's a new beginning (as she thinks) of hers. The words that are spoken out loud are only a small part of the complex communication that goes on at the same time; whether we are conscious of it or not, these words mix with other impressions – are, indeed, completely dwarfed by momentous implications that immediately rush in upon us.

So far I have concentrated on the play's organic growth, indicating how important lines or episodes grow out of others, mixing with what we may have heard or seen much earlier in the play's 'present continuous'. The mixing principle can also be illustrated from 'joinery', as O'Casey called it – an unkind word that refers, presumably, to the way one episode is cobbled on to the next. Such local joinery, in the hands of a Shakespeare, can serve to illustrate the highest skills, where the craftsman's conscious mixing and the play's organic growth are indistinguishable. We can observe how felicitously each episode joins on to its neighbour and fits the needs of its individual play by comparing three with very similar functions – the grave-digger episode in *Hamlet*, the Porter-scene in *Macbeth*, and Cleopatra's interview with the clown who brings the asp. In each case a clown's 'low' humour precedes and follows scenes of high tension, or of tragic seriousness, yet each of the three has unique features determined by its play. In *Hamlet*, where there had been much talk of suicide and the hereafter, the two clowns pick up these themes and fool around with them as naturally as grave-diggers pick up bones. Hamlet's interest in the question 'How long will a man lie i'th'earth ere he rot?' is related to an earlier topic, how long will a man's memory outlive his life (two hours? twice two months?) – two kinds of survival after death. The play being filled with mock-interviews, in which the prince pretends to misunderstand a questioner (Rosencrantz and Guildenstern; Claudius; Osric), first grave-digger turns the tables on him, answering knavishly – so the shape of their exchanges is another thread that hooks into a larger design. 'Alas, poor Yorick' mysteriously echoes 'Alas, poor ghost'; and so on. The grave-digger episode, in short, mixes with the rest of the play in its larger themes, in specific questions, in verbal echoes, and in using a special dialogue-device, the mock-interview; and no doubt in other ways too.

A word will suffice for *Macbeth*. The dramatic irony in the Porter's soliloquy is familiar: it is Macbeth who is an equivocator, who has 'hang'd himself on th' expectation of plenty'. True. I am equally struck by the Porter's exchanges with Macduff – for the Porter, in the delightful afterglow of his carousing, also resembles Macbeth in the previous scene in being present and not present; his tipsiness has the same effect as Macbeth's imagination – he only gives half his mind to the matter in hand. And in each case there is a cool observer and questioner, Lady Macbeth and Macduff, whose presence measures the distance of Macbeth and the Porter from normality. Just as the knocking in the Porter-scene spills over from the previous scene, the Porter's tipiness grew out of Macbeth's intoxicated imagination, and his slowness in answering the call of the here and now and his psychic distance from Macduff were also influenced by the previous scene. It should be noted in passing that alcohol plays a part in the grave-digger *and* Porter scenes, yet its effect is adapted to the needs of the play no less than is each clown's distinctive way of speaking and relating to others.

Next, Cleopatra's clown. Plutarch mentions a 'countryman', who brings the asp in a basket of figs, but not a word about his interview with Cleopatra, which is pure Shakespeare – perhaps his most daring 'mingle' in the tragedies, because here comedy modulates immediately into the tragic climax. Appropriately, it is comedy shot through with sexual innuendo, and even the chastest ears cannot miss it.

> You must not think I am so simple but I know the devil himself will not eat a woman. I know that a woman is a dish for the gods, if the devil dress her not.   (*Antony and Cleopatra*, V.2.270)

The richest insinuation and 'mingle' in the Clown-scene, however, grows out of one keyword, repeated eight times — 'Hast thou the pretty worm of Nilus there?', 'I wish you all joy of the worm'. It's a word not used by Plutarch at this point, and conjures up a very different image from Plutarch's one specific description of the asp: Cleopatra pricked the creature with a spindle, so that, 'being angered withal,' said Plutarch, 'it leapt out with great fury, and bit her in the arm' – not really what one expects from a *bona fide* worm. In Elizabethan English, of course, 'worm' could mean reptile, or serpent, or other things – and, since no one in the play's first audience is likely ever to have seen an Egyptian asp, the uncertain meaning of 'worm' was particularly useful. We are made to wonder exactly what this hidden worm may be. 'The worm will do his kind', the Clown explains, helpfully. 'The worm's an odd worm.'

I have dwelt on the spectator's inability to imagine exactly what to expect because there must have been a reason for the dramatist's teasing vagueness. I am reminded of another teasing device in the play – its concealed penis-imagery, a joke repeated several times, in different ways, by different characters. Since learned editors do not feel obliged to explain what cannot be seen, I had better give some examples. First, the soothsayer tells Cleopatra's ladies that their future fortunes are alike. 'Well,' says Charmian to Iras, 'if you were but an inch of fortune better than I, where would you choose it?' Reply? – 'Not in my husband's nose' (I.2.51ff.). Secondly, Cleopatra, bored, asks Charmian to play billiards; Charmian suggests Mardian the eunuch instead, and Cleopatra quips 'As well a woman with an eunuch play'd / As with a woman' (II.5.5). A third concealed image is given to Agrippa:

> Royal wench!
> She made great Caesar lay his sword to bed.
> He plough'd her, and she cropp'd.
>   (II.2.230)

The wicked word is not mentioned — indeed, was not known yet, though the English language was rich in alternatives. Here, then, are three examples of concealed penis imagery – a distinctive series in the play that puts us in a state of readiness for the Clown's 'worm'. We have to remember at this point the infinite variety of Shakespeare's sexual imagery, and that he had used the same image before, when Lucrece exclaims against rape – 'Why should the worm intrude the maiden bud?' (a traditional image long before Blake's 'The Sick Rose'). Recalling also how tirelessly the Elizabethans punned on the sexual sense of 'lie' and 'die', we observe that the general context also nudges us towards concealed imagery. 'I would not desire you to touch him', the Clown tells Cleopatra,

> for his biting is immortal; those that do *die* of it do seldom or never recover.
> CLEOPATRA. Remember'st thou any that have *died* on't?
> CLOWN. Very many, men and women too. I heard of one of them no longer than yesterday: a very honest woman, but something given to *lie*, as a woman should not do but in the way of honesty; how she *died* of the biting of it, what pain she felt – truly, she makes a very good report o' th' worm.   (V.2.245)

The extraordinary power and flavour of this clown-scene partly depends on concealed imagery, imagery reactivated by the puns on 'lie' and 'die', by 'a woman is a dish for the gods, if the devil dress her not', by the Clown's winking knowingness and by Shakespeare's teasing vagueness as to what the worm might be. At one and the same time the 'worm' refers to the asp (a word carefully excluded until the Clown has gone), to the worm in the grave, and to the sex-worm whose 'biting' is also immortal – hence the pungent rightness of the Clown's parting shot to sex-obsessed Cleopatra, 'I wish you joy o' th' worm!' Here, marvelling at a treble pun that has its tentacular roots in other local puns, and in concealed imagery that acts upon us subliminally, one is tempted to cry, with Cleopatra, 'O heavenly mingle!' – for what more is possible? Yet the mingling continues:

> Give me my robe, put on my crown; I have
> Immortal longings in me.
>
> (278)

'Longings for immortality', thought the New Arden editor. Perhaps; but, after 'I wish you joy o' th' worm' she also means 'immortal longings' as opposed to 'mortal longings' – a higher form of sexuality, a kiss from the curled Antony 'which is my heaven to have'. The sublime 'Give me my robe', a speech structured round the idea of 'immortal longings', grew out of the largely latent sexuality and low comedy of the Clown-scene.

The three clown-scenes, possibly written for the same actor, have been thought to have a similar function in three of the greatest tragedies. Yet they are not merely 'comic relief', since each one builds upon ideas, images, mental states, or relationships from previous scenes – that is, flashes back to more serious concerns, mingling seriousness with laughter. (Meredith's phrase 'thoughtful laughter' is peculiarly apt: an awareness that the clown-scene somehow mingles with what has gone before pulls us back from surrendering wholly to laughter, even though we cannot stop the play to trace all the connections.) More important for my purposes: not only are the clown-scenes sewn into the fabric of the play in so many ways – each one is sewn in in its own distinctive way. There may be superficial resemblances, but we fail to appreciate the dramatist's skill unless we see that seemingly similar devices always 'mingle' quite uniquely with their dramatic surroundings.

That brings me to the notorious 'bed-trick' in *Measure for Measure*. It was Shakespeare's error, we have been told often enough, that he chose to solve the problems of a realistic plot by resorting to pure folk-tale. After the 'realism' of the early scenes, of Angelo's passion for Isabella and of his demand that she buy her brother's life by yielding her virginity, comes the bed-trick – Angelo's betrothed, Mariana, takes Isabella's place in his bed – a hangover from folk-tale or romance, it is said, quite out of keeping with what has gone before. This account of the play assumes that Shakespeare had got into trouble with his plotting, and that the bed-trick was an attempt to slither round a difficulty. Shakespeare had departed from his sources in making Isabella a novice in an order of nuns, and in giving her a passionately virginal nature; unlike her prototype in the sources, therefore, she could not comply with Angelo's demand – so we have the bed-trick instead, a desperate expedient.

Before I argue that, on the contrary, the bed-trick is beautifully right where it is placed, no less than the bear in *The Winter's Tale*, a multiple 'mingle' in a self-consciously mingled yarn, let us examine our terminology – 'realism' and 'folk-tale'. So-called realistic scenes in the play do employ non-realistic devices: the low-life characters meticulously finish their sentences; Angelo soliloquises – in verse. Realism is adjustable; so, too, folk-tale episodes can be presented more or less plausibly. Much can be done to bring realism and folk-tale together, to make them tone in with one another; before we denounce the bed-trick as a desperate expedient it is our duty to ask how it mingles with its surroundings.

First, though, I must correct a common misrepresentation of the bed-trick in literature. Bed-tricks, though familiar in folk-tale and romance, were not restricted to one or two *kinds* of literature: we have all read Genesis 19:33, and *The Escapes of Jupiter*, and *The Magus*. Next: a bed-trick story can be told in the spirit of *The Reeve's Tale* or of *The Knight's Tale* or – somewhere in between. The use of significant detail will sharply differentiate one bed-trick story from another.

We can learn what Shakespeare might have done, had he thought a bed-trick too 'unrealistic' after his play's earlier scenes, by glancing at some other literary versions. Even Malory, not the most realistic of writers, felt that a drugged drink was needed to trick Lancelot into sleeping with the fair Elaine – 'as soon as he had drunk that wine he was so assotted that he wened that maiden Elaine had been queen Guinever' (xi.2); later Elaine's lady-in-waiting 'took him by the finger' (there's realistic detail!) 'and led him unto her lady'. Deloney's *Jack of Newberry*, a rip-roaring narrative, provides a more representative example of bed-trick realism. An English girl, Joan, had an importunate Italian lover, who became a nuisance until Joan's kinsman taught him a lesson. The kinsman gave a 'sleepy drench' to a young sow, put the sleeping sow in Joan's bed, 'drawing the curtains round about', and told the lover that his opportunity had arrived. But, he warned, 'you must not . . . have a candle when you go into the chamber, for . . . dark places fits best lovers' desires'. The Italian knelt down by the bedside, saluted the invisible sow with a love-speech, slipped into bed, ardently embraced her, and only discovered his mistake from her non-human grunting.[5] I hesitate to call this realism, but we may say that Deloney made room for more 'realistic' touches than Malory. In Marston's *The Insatiate Countess*, which is close to *Measure for Measure* in genre and date, two ladies plot to sleep with their own husbands (the husbands each having importuned the other's wife), 'and the better to avoid suspicion', one wife explains, 'thus we must insist: they must come up darkling'. 'But,' says the second wife, 'is my husband content to come darkling?' This problem solved, she thinks of another difficulty. 'I am afraid my voice will discover me.' 'Why, then you're best say nothing . . . .' 'Ay, but you know a woman cannot choose but speak in these cases.'[6] The dramatist positively delights in applying a 'realistic' imagination to the bed-trick, without damaging his play.

It appears, then, that you can choose between comedy and seriousness, between more and less realism. In bed-trick scenes you can adopt almost any position, as it were. This is hard for us to grasp today, because we have been taught to think of the bed trick as a purely literary device, one that belongs to literature at its furthest possible remove from life. Before the invention of electricity, however, the night-life of Europe must have been much more tricky than now, and there is plenty of evidence that strange things happened in the dark.

> Now 'tis full sea a-bed over the world,
> There's juggling of all sides . . . .
> This woman, in immodest thin apparel
> Lets in her friend by water. Here a dame
> Cunning, nails leather hinges to a door
> To avoid proclamation.
> Now cuckolds are a-coining, apace, apace, apace, apace!
> (*The Revenger's Tragedy*, II.2)

I have laboured the point that Shakespeare did not have to fall back on a 'ready-made' bed-trick, the figmentary bed-trick of folk-tale and romance, simply to suggest that he was free to devise his own. The stark contrast that so many critics have disliked in *Measure for Measure* as 'realism' is succeeded by the bed-trick, I conclude, was entirely of his own choosing. The play was written when he was at the height of his powers, when he had fully mastered the art of mingling one episode with another, yet this bed-trick jars all expectation. Why did Shakespeare choose it, in this form, when there were other options open to him?

As I mentioned at the outset, drama in the later sixteenth century introduced many new kinds of 'mingling'. Some of the dramatists no doubt did so unconsciously. By the turn of the century, however, the mingled yarn of literature was a matter of public debate. Italian critics defended tragi-comedy; Sidney moved with the times in defending pastoral, where some 'have mingled prose and verse. . . . Some have mingled matters heroical and pastoral', though he was not happy about 'mingling kings and clowns'.[7] In *The Faerie Queene* Spenser aimed at variety, copying the artful confusion of Italian epic so that, as he put it, many things are 'intermedled' with one another – again, the mingling principle, artful combination. Metaphysical poetry, said Dr Johnson, experimented with the 'combination of dissimilar images . . . the most heterogeneous ideas are yoked by violence together'.[8]

Similar experiments took place at the same time in the visual arts, and they also have a bearing on *Measure for Measure*. Mannerist painters of the later sixteenth century sought out new combinations, mingling realistic detail in a recognisably non-realistic ensemble, as in Arcimboldo's *Librarian*, a deplorably bookish gentleman, or his *Autumn*, a jolly old Bacchus made out of fruit and veg whose features are recognisably those of the Emperor Rudolph II. Sometimes the Mannerists even mingled different levels of realism: Pontormo's *Joseph in Egypt* in the National Gallery playfully distorts scale and perspective, and includes clothed figures standing on pedestals like statues, wholly fanciful architecture with stairways leading nowhere – an imagined world, consciously deviating from nature, in no sense intended as a copy of nature.

Whether such Mannerist experiments of the late sixteenth century were influential in England is difficult to determine. We do know, however, that illustrations in sixteenth-century English books often depicted mingled scenes: a single crude woodcut may combine the creation of Eve, the Temptation, and the Expulsion from Paradise. This is a tradition that goes back to medieval art; inevitably, it appealed to later book illustrators, and English readers would know it from Harington's *Orlando Furioso* of 1591, where the engravings are copied from an Italian edition. One unusual painting of the late Elizabethan age also belongs to this tradition – *The Life and Death of Sir Henry Unton* (it hangs in the National Portrait Gallery), an attempt to bring together many scenes from the life of one of Queen Elizabeth's ambassadors: his arrival at Oriel College, Oxford; his wedding-masque; his diplomatic missions; his funeral procession and burial. Although not strictly a Mannerist painting, it mingles different scales and different degrees of realism, and each scene mingles differently with its neighbours. The artist or artists may not have been of the highest quality (some of the detail is most delicately finished), but there can be no doubt that the 'mingling principle' is consciously employed. Remember, please, how the half-length figure of Sir Henry Unton holds the whole composition together. For there is a similar centre-piece in one of the greatest Mannerist compositions, El Greco's *View and Plan of Toledo*, which belongs to the same decade as *Measure for Measure* and deserves our closer attention. According to one admirer, El Greco here did his utmost

> to prevent the actual view of Toledo from dominating the picture. He put the figure of the river god of the Tagus in the left foreground. He also removed the monastery, which lay outside the town and for which he presumably painted the view of the town, from reality by transferring it from *terra firma* to a bright airy cloud. Above it he painted the vision of Mary borne high over the town by angels. . . . The painter further distorted the view of Toledo . . . by the addition of the half-length figure of a boy holding out the plan of Toledo to the spectator.[9]

Unlike the allegories of the High Renaissance, such as Botticelli's *Primavera*, El Greco's composition reassembles matter in jarringly new ways; his centre-piece, the monastery in the clouds, asserts the artist's right to make the most unexpected combinations, where heterogeneous ideas and images are yoked by violence together.

I have digressed in order to suggest that discussions of 'mingling' problems in tragi-comedy and pastoral, of 'intermeddling' in Italian epic and its derivatives, the self-conscious mingling of heterogeneous ideas and images in metaphysical poetry, and the radical rethinking of compositional norms by the Mannerists, all reflect the spirit of the age, no less than Guarini's *Compendio* of 1602, which Shakespeare could scarcely have seen, and all point forward to *Measure for Measure*. While we cannot demonstrate Shakespeare's knowledge of Italian and Spanish Mannerists, there are signs of similar experiments in England, and we can claim that he was aware of the new trends in literature. Polonius announces the actors in Elsinore – the best actors in the world for 'tragedy, comedy, history, pastoral, pastoral-comical, historical-pastoral, tragical-historical, tragical-comical-historical-pastoral, scene individable, or poem unlimited' (*Hamlet*, II.2.392). If even Polonius grasps that the dramatic poem no longer conforms to the traditional limits of genre, we may take it that Shakespeare and his public must have been interested in such technical developments as well.

In *Measure for Measure* Shakespeare went one step beyond any he had previously taken, not merely mingling the play's ingredients surprisingly, as often before, but making an issue of it, challenging the audience to put the pieces together and to think critically about a 'poem unlimited'. The notorious bed-trick comes at the point of no return, when a spectator *must* ask himself, even if he has previously failed to do so, 'What kind of play is this?' Terms such as 'problem play' and 'dark comedy' had not yet been invented; 'tragi-comedy' was sometimes discussed, but there was no agreed definition – in England there had been no serious attempt at definition. Up to Act III it would be reasonable to see *Measure for Measure* as a tragedy that includes a good deal of low comedy (like *Romeo and Juliet*), or as a new-formula play such as the 'tragical-comical-historical-pastoral' of Polonius, or as tragi-comedy. Whichever one favours, the important thing is that one cannot be certain – and, consequently, that one keeps returning to the question, 'What kind of play is it?' Even the modern spectator cannot avoid this question, since he still has to fit all the bits and pieces together. 'Is Angelo's self-accusing honesty, or Isabella's torment, too life-like, placed beside a disguised duke and a comic constable, in *this kind of play*?' The question has already nagged us for a while when suddenly Shakespeare introduces the bed-trick, a twist so unexpected that now we can no longer escape our dilemma – 'What kind of play?' Observe that the bed-trick, Shakespeare's addition to the story, whatever it may achieve in simplifying Isabella's problems, notably complicates the play's genre problems and the spectator's genre expectations.

The bed-trick resembles the bear in *The Winter's Tale*, and the 'Cinna the poet' scene in *Julius Caesar*, and the Porter-scene in *Macbeth*, in coming at the point where the play modulates from one mood into another. It is done differently in each one, of course, but nowhere more self-advertisingly than in *Measure for Measure*. For, just at this point, the play's style joltingly changes gear several times. The Duke soliloquises in rhyming tetrameters, a new voice for him –

> He who the sword of heaven will bear
> Should be as holy as severe;
> Pattern in himself to know
> Grace to stand, and virtue go;
> More nor less to others paying
> Than by self-offences weighing. . . .
>   (III.2.243)

Then follows (IV.1) the play's only song, and shortly thereafter the Duke switches in mid-speech from verse to prose – all warning-signals that the play is about to change direction. Then follows the play's most arresting modulation, Isabella's speech about the proposed midnight meeting with Angelo, a speech that the dramatist could easily have left to the audience's imagination. Shakespeare chose to give Isabella this speech, I think, because it allows him to suggest, in passing, a unique mingling of realism and romance, and the unique nature of his play: the speech combines a romantic sense of mystery, as in Mariana's song, with an insistent factualness.

> He hath a garden circummur'd with brick,
> Whose western side is with a vineyard back'd;
> And to that vineyard is a planched gate
> That makes his opening with this bigger key;
> This other doth command a little door
> Which from the vineyard to the garden leads.
> There have I made my promise
> Upon the heavy middle of the night
> To call upon him.
>   (IV.1.26)

Despite its factualness (the garden, brick wall, vineyard on the western side, the gate, the smaller door, the two keys), this speech cannot be called 'realism'; a garden *circummured* with brick and a vineyard with a *planched* gate also carry overtones from another world, the world of Mariana of the *moated grange*, the world of *The Romance of the Rose*. The mingle, and the sense of a special creative pressure, is supported by out-of-the-way words ('circummured' and 'planched', like 'moated', occur nowhere else in Shakespeare; 'circummured' was his coinage); and it is all bonded together by a concealed image – the Freudian slip when Isabella's imagination dimly anticipates sexual contact ('Upon the heavy middle of the night', an unusual turn of phrase that stamps her personal feeling upon this special bed-trick).

In this speech, neither realism nor romance, we are asked to give a willing suspension of disbelief to an experience as strange as the coming-to-life of the statue at the end of *The Winter's Tale* – a bed-trick as peculiar to this play as Hermione's statue is different from all the other statues that return to life in romances before Shakespeare. It is a far cry from Deloney's passionate Italian and his drugged sow, and from all other bed-tricks in literature, because

Shakespeare (like El Greco in *The View and Plan of Toledo*) has reassembled and mingled his material in new ways. Instead of the 'clever wench' or 'clever wife' who wishes to reclaim her husband (as represented by Helena in *All's Well*) he gives us Mariana, a mere pawn in someone else's clever game; and he changed the man, a mere sex-object for the traditional 'clever wife', into the brooding, vulnerable Angelo. The bed of the 'bed-trick' disappears from view, and Shakespeare eliminates the snigger found in other plays (including *All's Well* and *The Changeling*) when one of the principals goes to or returns from copulation: instead we are asked to apply our imagination to a garden, a vineyard, a planched gate. The actors, the moral implications of the action, the feelings involved, our sense of place, our awareness of a containing society – all are changed for the specific needs of *Measure for Measure*.

Shakespeare's immense care in fitting the bed-trick into his story is also evident in his handling of Mariana. It may seem, to those who believe that the dramatist snatched the bed-trick out of the air to solve an unforeseen plot-problem, that Mariana accepts it too readily. That is to presuppose that her character is reflected in the hauntingly romantic song sung for her when she first appears at the moated grange – 'Take, O, take those lips away'. Producers usually cast her thus, as a dreamy romantic, for which we must partly blame Tennyson's poem 'Mariana'.

> She only said, 'My life is dreary,
>   He cometh not,' she said;
> She said 'I am aweary, aweary,
>   I would that I were dead!'

Yet Shakespeare's pure and romantic maiden jumps without hesitation at the offer of a place in Angelo's bed; the whole complicated story is explained to her by Isabella while the Duke speaks a short soliloquy, and Mariana is ready. Out of character? No: Tennyson misrepresented her. Shakespeare had previously stressed that, when Angelo rejected Mariana's love, this, 'like an impediment in the current, made it more violent and unruly' (III.1.234). She suffers from an overmastering passion – easily conveyed to us if she has a picture or keepsake of her lover, kissing it passionately as the boy sings, 'But my kisses bring again, bring again'. Mariana's willingness to undertake the bed-trick is prepared for by what we are told about her 'violent and unruly' affection, and probably by her 'body-language' as she listens to the song; instead of being just a romantic dummy in the plot, she has character – sufficient character – to tone in with the near-realism of adjacent scenes. And she also tones in with all the other characters in the play who suffer from irresistible sexual impulses – Claudio and Juliet, Lucio, Mrs Overdone, Angelo.

To argue that Shakespeare by no means lost sight of the demands of realism, or near-realism, when he decided to introduce the bed-trick, may seem unwise. I should like to pursue this possibility for a moment, since the entire second half of the play appears to pull away from realism and indeed to pull away from the first half, and this requires some explanation. The sense that the play modulates into a new mood, or changes direction, comes in Act III scene 1, where the bed-trick is announced. Just before we hear of the bed-trick, it is important to notice, Shakespeare jolts our trust in the Duke, who proposes the bed-trick. How can the Duke say so confidently to Claudio, 'Son, I have overheard what hath pass'd between you and your sister. Angelo had never the purpose to corrupt her; only he hath made an assay of her virtue . . .' (160)? We *know* this to be false, since we overheard Angelo's soliloquies, whereas the Duke didn't. He continues, 'I am confessor to Angelo, and I know this to be true . . . .' Some critics have wondered whether the disguised Duke could be, or could ever have been, confessor to Angelo, and one has even expressed indignation that the secrets of the confessional should be revealed, contrary to the rules of the Church. The ordinary theatre-goer, however, is unlikely to encumber himself with such idle fancies: aware that the Duke's assertion, 'I know this to be true', is a fabrication, he is cued to regard 'I am confessor to Angelo' as another fabrication. Whatever his motives, the Duke appears to snatch arguments out of the air, and Shakespeare invites us to note his dexterity, and inventiveness. Then, within a few lines, the conjurer–duke produces from his hat the bed-trick – snatches it out of nothing, another brilliant improvisation, again one that he has scarcely had time to think through, any more than his right to say 'I am confessor to Angelo'.

Just as Angelo tangles himself in one deception after another, and Lucio, the comic foil, in one lie after another, the disguised Duke finds himself obliged to improvise more and more desperately – inventing the future, as it were, and becoming more and more unable to control it. We already feel uneasy about his reading of the future, I think, when he explains to Friar Thomas

that he needs a disguise because he wants Angelo to clean up
Vienna, and immediately adds that he half-mistrusts Angelo –

> Hence shall we see,
> If power change purpose, what our seemers be.
>
> (I.3.53)

At this stage the Duke sees his own future role as that of an
observer:

> And to behold his sway
> I will, as 'twere a brother of your order,
> Visit both prince and people.
>
> (43)

When he reappears, however, the observer feels impelled to throw
himself fully into his new role as a friar, interrogates Juliet ('Repent
you, fair one, of the sin you carry?' – II.3.19), and then improvises
impressively as he lectures Claudio on death. Has an observer the
right to impose thus on another human being, merely by virtue of
his disguise? The moral authority of his speech 'Be absolute for
death' (III.1.5ff.) is undercut by our awareness that he is playing a
part – a growing uncertainty about him, corresponding to our
uncertainty about the nature of the play. More unmistakably
disturbing is the Duke's sudden expedient that Barnardine's head
should be substituted for Claudio's; the Provost's amazement, and
reluctance to comply, inform the audience, if ordinary human
instincts fail to do so, that to play with life in this way is
presumptuous. What, we ask ourselves, is he up to?

Everything said and done by the Duke, from his initial decision
to appoint Angelo as his deputy and to look on as a 'friar', can be
read as improvisation, usually as hurried improvisation. We are
therefore prompted to think of the bed-trick not as an 'archaic
device' placed in uncomfortable proximity to psychological realism
by a fatigued dramatist, but as the Duke's device, just as much an
expression of his character as his disguise-trick, and his other
surprising and whimsical expedients. As the second half of the
play pulls away from realism, and the question 'what *kind* of play?'
grows more urgent, we look to the Duke to solve our problems,
while at the same time we half suspect that the dithering Duke
merely improvises irresponsibly. His awareness of Angelo's

intentions, and of all that happens, serves as a hint to the audience that a tragic outcome may be prevented; yet the Duke's sheer inefficiency, highlighted by his failure to control Lucio, by no means guarantees a happy ending. Our uncertainty about the nature of this mingled yarn therefore continues – augmented, I think, by our uncertainty about the Duke's double image (as duke and friar), and about his motives and his control.

In the second half of *Measure for Measure*, as we wonder whether the Duke and the dramatist know where they are going, we are teased with several possibilities. The shape of the play begins to resemble a familiar Elizabethan stereotype – the story of the clever man who overreaches himself, who initiates a dangerous action, and has to improvise more and more frantically to hold off disaster (Marlowe's Barabas, Shakespeare's Richard III and Iago). But, if we sense this kinship, Shakespeare refuses to conform to his model, for in this version of 'the sorcerer's apprentice' the fumbling friar reassumes control at the end, as the Duke, and the stereotype is shattered.

Another possibility is that the ending will be like that of *The Malcontent*, where a disguised duke resumes his ducal authority, forgives his enemies, and only one, the wicked Mendoza, is punished by being ceremonially kicked out of court. Yet Shakespeare also includes intimations of a tragic outcome – a possibility that remains open, even though neither of Angelo's intended crimes (the rape of Isabella, and the judicial murder of her brother) has been committed. The deputy's abuse of power deserves to be punished with death, as he himself recognises:

> When I, that censure him, do so offend
> Let mine own judgment pattern out my death . . . .
> (II.1.29)

And later:

> let my trial be mine own confession;
> Immediate sentence then, and sequent death,
> Is all the grace I beg.
> (V.2.370)

Angelo's death, or tragic humiliation, must be what Isabella intends when she denounces the 'pernicious caitiff deputy' and clamours to the Duke for 'justice, justice, justice, justice' (V.1.25). This echo of *The Spanish Tragedy*, of Hieronimo's cry to his king –

Justice, O justice, justice, gentle king! . . .
Justice, O justice!
(III.12.63, 65)

– brings to *Measure for Measure* a similar tragic intensity. There are even moments when we are reminded of a play performed by the King's Men shortly before *Measure for Measure*, another play in which a ruler withdraws from his responsibilities, leaving, in effect, a deputy, whom he has raised but distrusts, a man whose abuses are closely watched by the ruler's spies, who is at last trapped and exposed as theatrically as Angelo. And in the case of *Sejanus* the outcome is tragedy.

It appears to have been Shakespeare's strategy to leave open his play's outcome and genre to the very end. We recognise several possible models, including *The Malcontent* and *Sejanus*, but not one that really answers our question, 'What kind of play is it?' Until the very last minutes the execution of Angelo remains a possibility – all the more so since some spectators would know that in some versions of this widely dispersed story Angelo did lose his head. Then, just as we think we know where we are, Shakespeare springs two more surprises. The play seems to turn into a comedy of forgiveness – until the Duke remembers Lucio, and hacks at him with unforgiving vindictiveness. In addition, we have the Duke's proposal to Isabella, which invariably comes as a surprise, despite all the efforts of producers to prepare us for it – and surely was meant to be one, the 'happy ending' of another kind of comedy grafted on here with the same careful tissue-matching as we found in the bed-trick. Is a disturbing proposal not appropriate at the end of a deeply disturbing play?

It is particularly in the second half of the play that its genre is brought into question – and here Shakespeare protects himself, and teases the audience, by making it more emphatically the Duke's play. The Duke, of course, was given the role of inventor of the plot, and stage-manager, from the beginning. In the second half of the play he has to interfere more and more decisively, to resume the active responsibility that he had found so irksome, and becomes more completely the play's dramatist. After the bed-trick – *his* bed-trick, as I have said – there follows a little scene of comic misunderstanding, modelled on *The Spanish Tragedy*, that demonstrates exactly how far he may be trusted as a dramatist. Angelo's messenger arrives with a strict order that Claudio is to be executed punctually, and the Duke, all at sea, declares, preposterously, 'here comes Claudio's pardon', and again,

> This is his pardon, purchas'd by such sin
> For which the pardoner himself is in . . . .
>   (IV.2.103)

He's wrong, and Shakespeare wants us to notice it. The dramatist–Duke has lost control of his play – and, as he hurriedly attempts to reorganise his plot, he, almost as much as Shakespeare, becomes responsible for its genre, and for our genre-expectations. Knowing him as we do, we cannot expect artistic tidiness. He, the Duke of dark corners, is the inventor of almost all the improbable, 'non-realistic' twists of the story that make *Measure for Measure* Shakespeare's most challengingly mingled yarn before *The Winter's Tale* – his disguise as a friar; the bed-trick; the substitution of another head for Claudio's; the concealment of Claudio's escape from Isabella; the unexpected proposal of marriage. All these improbabilities, dreamed up by one man, are therefore rooted in psychological realism, being all expressions of the Duke's imagination, which is as individual as Hamlet's or Prospero's. Duke Vincentio's imagination, like that of a Mannerist painter, delighting in unexpected combinations, makes his bed-trick as necessary a centre-piece to the play's design as El Greco's monastery, which sits so solidly and improbably in a cloud of cotton-wool. The Duke, in short, with his love of mystification and ingenious twists and turns, forever revising his options, was the ideal dramatist to put into this mingled yarn – the distinctive feature of which is that it mystifies and keeps changing direction, both at the level of story and of seriousness, insisting on our revising our expectations to the very last.

And what have the Duke and the bed-trick to do with all my other examples – the bear and the statue in *The Winter's Tale*; 'To be or not to be'; the cry 'My husband!' in *Othello* and *Macbeth*; the grave-diggers in *Hamlet*, the Porter in *Macbeth*, and Cleopatra's clown? Only this: they demonstrate, together, how variously the 'mingling principle' works. Each example connects with its immediate context and with the present continuous of its play, but no two are the same. Isolated examples illustrate Shakespeare's habitual 'mingling' under the microscope, as it were, but of course each play consists of an infinite number of examples – reaching out in all directions, interpenetrating one another, enriching one another. *Measure for Measure* affords a different kind of example, in so far as Shakespeare also asks us to observe a violently 'mingling' dramatist, in the person of the Duke, and also a more efficient dramatist who tidies up, so to say, behind the Duke and ensures that all of the play's bits and pieces combine plausibly together.

My argument draws to its conclusion, and a scandalous conclusion it is. I have argued that in *Measure for Measure*, one of his most puzzling plays, Shakespeare wants the audience to take an interest not merely in the story but also in the nature of the play – an idea that we have all encountered before, in studies of other plays and of the novel. Having bowed politely to Mannerism and Structuralism and all things fashionable, the besotted lecturer drags in Metadrama as well. Is it really necessary? If I am told that a packed Bankside audience of prentices and prostitutes would be less alert to such questions than their distinguished descendants, whose haunt is Piccadilly,[10] I need only remind you that *The Old Wives' Tale* and *A Midsummer Night's Dream* also required the audience to ponder the nature of the play, and that the same challenge is built into the early plays of Marston and Jonson. In *Measure for Measure* Shakespeare addressed an audience already trained to query genre-boundaries, and to expect the forms of things unknown.

> And as imagination bodies forth
> The forms of things unknown, the poet's pen
> Turns them to shapes, and gives to airy nothing
> A local habitation and a name.
> Such tricks hath strong imagination . . . .
> (*Midsummer Night's Dream*, V.1.14)

The time has come for me to sum up, and I can do it in a single line from Shakespeare, slightly improved:

> Such *bed-tricks* hath strong imagination.

10

On not trusting Shakespeare's stage-directions

How authoritative are the stage-directions printed in modern editions of Shakespeare? That they are important will be readily granted, for a very large number goes beyond basic information, as contained in entries and exits, and reflects on character. 'Alas, poor Yorick!' says Hamlet, 'I knew him, Horatio: a fellow of infinite jest, of most excellent fancy; he hath borne me on his back a thousand times.' A moment later Hamlet *'Throws down the skull'* – or so we are sometimes told in editions of the play. How insensitive of him! Are skulls not brittle things, easily smashed? In this instance, however, it is the editors who are insensitive: Capell, in the eighteenth century, inserted the direction that Hamlet throws down the skull, and later editors simply copied from their predecessors, a time-honoured procedure. Apart from such 'editorial' stage-directions, printed in square backets in some modern editions to indicate that they have been interpolated, which have no more authority than the editor's say-so, there are others that first appeared in the original Quarto (Q) or Folio (F) texts – surely all of these can be accepted as authoritative? Unfortunately, not so. As is well known, some of Shakespeare's earliest printed texts contain few directions; he himself took little interest in them, his copyists and printers could be careless and / or high-handed, so we need to be on our guard. Both the placing and the significance of Q and F stage-directions has been misinterpreted, with serious consequences for modern readers and actors, who now find themselves hedged in by imperatives that ought to be questioned. One of the purposes of this chapter is to show that, in hundreds of instances, we have much more freedom of choice than the tyranny of the modern printed page appears to allow. I include speech-prefixes with other stage-directions, since they too give directions to the actors and they too have been interpreted in debatable ways; and occasionally I glance sideways, at the texts of Shakespeare's contemporaries, where we encounter similar problems.

I MISPLACED STAGE-DIRECTIONS

(a) Every editor of Shakespeare knows that scores of stage directions have been moved in the *textus receptus* from their position in Q and F texts, where they were inserted a line or more too early or too late. Such rearrangement elicits little comment, the usual assumption being that juggling with the text is established practice and needs no defence. What requires comment is that, in addition, many more stage-directions are still printed too early or too late; editors have merely tinkered with the problem, their *ad hoc* decisions have observed no overall policy, and much textual tidying remains to be done. Compare the following.

1 *Enter Oliuer. / Adam.* Yonder comes my Master (*As You Like It*, Q3ᵃ).
2 Heere comes Monsieur the *Beu. / Enter le Beau* (Q4ᵃ)
3 Yonder sure they are comming. Let vs now stay / and see it. / *Flourish. Enter Duke . . .* (Q4ᵃ)
4 *Enter Duke with Lords. / 2 lines / Looke*, here comes the Duke . . . (Q5ᵃ)
5 *Enter Corin and Siluius. / Ros.* I, be so good *Touchstone*: Look you, who comes / here . . . (Q6ᵃ)
6 *Enter Iaques. / 1. Lord.* He saues my labor by his owne approach (R1ᵃ)
7 But who comes here? / *Enter Orlando* (R1ᵃ)
8 Heere comes yong Mr *Ganimed . . . / Enter Rosalind* (R2ᵃ)
9 *Enter Celia with a writing. / Ros.* Peace, here comes my sister reading (R2ᵃ)[1]

In the Folio text of *As You Like It* alone there are twenty such entries, preceded by 'see where they come' or its equivalent eight times, and followed by similar words twelve times. How important are these differences? Editors usually stick to the Folio's placing of the stage-directions, which could suggest that Rosalind is seen by the stage characters before the audience sees her whereas Celia is seen first by the audience (8, 9, above). If no such suggestion is intended it would surely be better to standardise the placing of the stage-directions, either just before of just after 'see where they come': so many other stage-directions are moved up or down because Shakespeare and his copyists are thought to have been careless about such matters that we must reckon with the possibility that 'see where they come' entries are further examples of carelessness.

As it happens, there are some signs that a Folio editor or collator was interested in such trivialities. When the Folio copy for *Othello* was prepared, many entries were moved to a later point in the text, compared with their placing in the Quarto.

1 But looke, what Lights come yond?/*Enter Cassio, with Torches*. (*Othello*, F, 2s4ᵇ)
2 Here comes another Troope to seeke for you. / *Enter Brabantio* . . . (ibid.)
3 *1. Senator*. Here comes *Brabantio*, and the Valiant Moore. / *Enter Brabantio* . . . (2s5ᵃ)
4 *Enter Desdemona, Iago, Rodorigo, and Æmilia*. / Oh behold, / The Riches of the Ship is come on shore (2s6ᵇ)
5 Loe, where he comes. / *Enter Othello* . . . (2t1ᵃ)
6 *Enter Othello*. / Looke where he comes . . . (2t5ᵃ)
7 *Enter Iago, and Cassio*. / Looke you, Cassio and my Husband. (2t6ᵃ)

Yet, though sufficiently interested to improve on his Quarto copy[2] in the placing of all these entries and many more, the Folio collator of *Othello* seems to have cared very little whether he put the stage entry first or 'see where they come'. From this I deduce that other 'Elizabethans' concerned with the transmission of texts will have cared even less, and that modern editors are free to standardise.

If we wish to standardise, however, let us note that there will be special cases. An entry accompanied not by a statement but by a question ('But who comes here . . . ?') may be meant to suggest a greater distance between the speaker and those he fails to recognise immediately: either the full width of the stage lies between them, or the speaker sees others before they appear on the stage. In some such instances there might well be a gap of several lines between the question and entry, or the entry may have to come second even though it is normally placed first.

(b) Editors have been so haphazard in dealing with a very common 'entry' formula that one wonders what else they have neglected. I find it strange that they are sometimes so uninterested in the precise placing of directions, especially those that should be inserted in the middle of a verse-line.

1 By this I challenge him to single fight. / *Throwes downe his*
   Gauntlet   (*3 Henry VI*, q2ª)
2 Downe, downe to hell, and say I sent thee thither. / *Stabs him*
   againe   (*3 Henry VI*, q4ª)
3 Take that, and that, if all this will not do, *Stabs him*.   (*Richard*
   III, r3ª)
4 Die, die, *Lauinia*, and thy shame with thee, / And with thy
   shame, thy Fathers sorrow die. / *He kils her*. (*Titus Andronicus*,
   2e2ª)

Where a single, sudden action is concerned it would be useful to
indicate the precise moment for it (namely, following 'this',
'downe', 'that', 'die'). Most of the editors leave the stage-direction
where they find it in the Folio or Quarto – which I mention
not because it leads to serious misunderstanding but because it
illustrates my general case against editorial inertia. Although they
know that Elizabethan dramatists and copyists were careless about
the precise placing of stage-directions, although they themselves
move *some* directions, when they feel they have to, editors usually
prefer to leave well alone, if they think they can get away with it.
Yet by moving a stage-direction a line or two we can quite often
improve the sense or stage-effect, and so we must ask ourselves
whether there is any real need to follow the first Quarto or Folio.

5 I am husht vntill our City be afire, & then Ile speak a litle
       Holds her by the hand silent.
   Corio. O Mother, Mother!
       What have you done? Behold, the Heauens do ope,
                                        (*Coriolanus*, 2c2ᵇ)

When Coriolanus yields in Act V scene 3, after listening to his
mother's long speech, the actor has the very difficult task of
conveying an overwhelming emotion without the help of words.
Is that really what Shakespeare intended? The actor's task would
be easier if he could at least begin to express his emotion – an
alternative that involves moving the stage direction one or two
lines down ('*Corio*. O mother! mother! What have you done? *Holds*
her by the hand, silent'). Here as elsewhere we may assume that the
direction was written in the margin and not properly aligned with
the text – a common fault in surviving MS texts of the period.
And in this instance the form of the stage-direction supports

rearrangement. In *Coriolanus*, and normally in other texts, a direction lacking a subject refers to the previous speaker, not the next one: '*Kneeles*' (2a5ᵃ), '*Pushes him away from him*', '*Beats him away*' (2b5ᵇ), '*Kneeles*' (2c5ᵃ), but compare '*Corio. drawes his Sword*' (2b2ᵇ) where Brutus is the previous speaker. So '*Holds her by the hand silent*' ought to be inserted after Coriolanus has begun his speech. The fact that Shakespeare closely followed Plutarch at this point convinces me that the placing of this stage-direction in the Folio, and in many modern editions, is again unacceptable. Volumnia and the rest, said Plutarch, fell down on their knees. 'Martius, seeing that, could refrain no longer, but went straight and lift her up, crying out: "Oh, mother, what have you done to me?" And holding her hard by the right hand, "Oh mother," said he, "you have won a happy victory for your country, but mortal and unhappy for your son. For I see myself vanquished by you alone." '

> 6 *Duk.* Oh *Hippolito?* call treason.
>   *Hip.* Yes my good Lord, treason, treason,
>   treason.   *stamping on him.*
>   *Duk.* Then I'me betrayde.
>   (*The Revenger's Tragedy*, 1606, F2ᵇ)

'Then I'm betrayed' from someone who has been stamped on sounds out-of-place. The stage-direction should be moved down, perhaps as much as ten lines (to go with '*Vind.* T'is I, 'tis Vindici, tis I').

> 7   You shall get no more children till my brothers
>   Consent to be your Ghossips: haue you lost your
>   tongue? 'tis welcome:
>   For know whether I am doomb'd to liue, or die,
>   I can doe both like a Prince.   *Ferdinand giues*
> *Ferd.* Die then, quickle: *her a ponyard.*
>   (*The Duchess of Malfi*, 1623, F4ᵃ)

To print the stage-direction at the end of the Duchess' speech is to associate it with Ferdinand's command, 'Die then', but leaves ' 'tis welcome' a puzzle. Editors insert another direction after 'lost your tongue', namely '*she turns and sees Ferdinand*', which helps to give some sense to ' 'tis welcome', though the words still sound odd.

The difficulty disappears, however, if we move the direction two lines up: and if Ferdinand *'gives her a poniard'* silently, before he tells her what to do with it, his enigmatic gesture prefigures the later offer of the dead man's hand (IV.1). The direction, of course, was added to the text while it was being printed (in the corrected sheets of Q), when there was no room for it where I think it should have gone (before ' 'tis welcome'): all the more reason for distrusting its placing in Q.

II DEATHS

Next, a problem already touched upon – the timing and performance of death. It is a curious fact that the familiar stage-direction *dies* (or *he* or *she dies*) appears in not one of the good quartos, even though deaths are plentiful there, particularly in *Titus Andronicus, Romeo and Juliet* and *Hamlet*. Supremely careful as he was in writing his dialogue, Shakespeare never bothered to record the precise moment of death in the 'good Quarto' texts, no doubt because he trusted his actors and, if necessary, could give guidance at rehearsals. In the good Quartos the stage-direction – in the rare cases when there is one – usually describes a death-blow, which may but need not imply instantaneous death. We find *'Here Exton strikes him downe'* in *Richard II, 'They Fight'.* Tibalt *falles'* in *Romeo and Juliet.* In the good Quarto of *Hamlet* the deaths of Polonius, Claudius, Gertrude, Laertes and Hamlet are not marked by any stage-direction – nor is Hector's death in *Troilus and Cressida.* The deaths of Paris, Romeo and Juliet are also unmarked. In *Titus Andronicus* we read, *'He kils her', 'He cuts their throats', 'He stabs the Empresse',* yet even *'He kills her'* need not mean instant death, for in *1 Henry IV* the stage-direction *'The Prince killeth Percy'* is followed by ten lines of verse from Hotspur, who has already received his death-blow ('O Harry, thou hast robb'd me of my youth . . . '). Similarly, in the Folio *King Lear* Cornwall's servant cries, 'O, I am slain' *after* the stage-direction *'Killes him.'* It would seem, then, that all or almost all of the stage-directions of the genus *he dies*, which occur here and there in Folio texts, were added by a playhouse scribe or prompter, or by a Folio editor, and have little authority. Later editors have enjoyed themselves adding even more such stage-directions, since the Folio failed to mark numerous deaths – and have done so on the assumption that every death-blow kills immediately, despite the fact that many deaths apart from Hotspur's prove the contrary. Othello speaks two more lines after stabbing himself, Emilia in the same play speaks twice after receiving her death-wound, Julius Caesar speaks after being stabbed many times – why, then, is it taken for granted that the theatrical opportunities afforded by a slow death were normally disregarded by Shakespeare?

The death of King Lear, according to the Folio, comes as he finishes his last speech.

> Do you see this? Looke on her? Looke her lips.
> Looke there, looke there.   *He di[e]s.*

Not all of the bystanders, however, are persuaded that he dies. Edgar says, 'He faints, my Lord, my Lord', and again 'Looke vp my Lord.' Although Lear may indeed die at the point indicated, the crucial fact is that we are left in uncertainty for a while, in the theatre: the moment of death is not obvious. As John Donne said in 'A Valediction: forbidding mourning', some men

> pass mildly away
> And whisper to their souls, to go,
> Whilst some of their sad friends do say
> The breath goes now, and some say no.

Long before *King Lear*, Shakespeare had presented the death of King John in the same way – Faulconbridge reports the latest news to the dying king, and then is told, 'You breathe these dead news in as dead an ear.' In these circumstances, to mark the arrival of death at a particular moment in time is to be oblivious to the wishes of the dramatist.

The death of Enobarbus in *Antony and Cleopatra*, usually marked by an editorial *'Dies'* at IV.9.23, raises more complex issues. Different characters in this tragedy commit suicide in significantly different ways: Eros more decisively than Antony, Cleopatra more painlessly. How then should Enobarbus die? And when? The soldiers who observe his curious behaviour are by no means clear as to what has happened. One says 'he sleeps', addresses him ('Awake, sir, awake; speak to us'), another adds 'Hear you, sir?'; the centurion thinks Enobarbus dead ('The hand of death hath raught him'); but the first soldier has the last word, 'He may recover yet' – an exit-line, and exit-lines carry special weight. Should editors impose certainty upon this confusion, or could Shakespeare have wanted uncertainty? The problem is aggravated by our not knowing exactly how Enobarbus dies, if indeed he does. He speaks of 'the poisonous damp of night', and may drink poison; also, of his heart, dried with grief, so perhaps he dies of a broken heart, if that is possible; or he could use his sword. Does it matter? Yes, because the manner in which the living approach 'the secret house of death' (IV.15.81) affects our response to later deaths. Also, because uncertainty can be functional in a play, and seems to be so here (Antony's will to survive, Cleopatra's professions of love, and so on). Accordingly, I think it all the more obligatory to respect the implied wishes of the text and to leave Enobarbus' fate in doubt. He fumbles, and collapses (back-stage; the soldiers observe him front-stage); he is carried off, probably dead, but we do not know. It makes good sense in a tragedy to leave the fate of some secondary characters unspecified, as Shakespeare was aware: compare the case of Lear's Fool, and Kent's puzzling last line ('My master calls me; I must not say no' – *King Lear*, V.3.322).

III ASIDES

Modern editions of Shakespeare contain many more asides than are found in the Folio and quartos, as often as not a legacy from eighteenth-century editors who maimed and deformed where they undertook to cure. Some of these asides merely raise questions about editorial consistency, while others involve interesting points of interpretation.

1 When Romeo eavesdrops on Juliet in the balcony-scene (II.2), why should his second speech be called an aside ('Shall I hear more, or shall I speak at this?') but not the first? The first is much longer, and perhaps editors think that asides ought to be short; yet as neither Q nor F indicates an aside, and Romeo's two speeches are equally inaudible to Juliet, why treat them differently?

2 POINS. Ay, four, in buckram suits.
   FALSTAFF. Seven, by these hilts, or I am a villain else.

PRINCE. [*Aside to Poins*] Prithee, let him alone; we shall have more anon.   (*1 Henry IV*, II.4.198)

3 TIMON. . . . I prithee let's be provided to show them entertainment.
FLAVIUS. [*Aside*] I scarce know how.   (*Timon*, I.2.175)

When an editor adds '*Aside*' he often implies that the speaker would not have dared to utter the same words openly; in short, he passes judgement on the relationship of two or more dramatic characters. Clearly, if the situation includes an impudent speaker or an inattentive listener the case for an aside is weakened. Hal, in fact, speaks bitingly to and of Falstaff in his presence, and to give him an aside (2, above) is to make him more considerate than is necessary; while Flavius tells Timon a little later that his previous warnings went unheeded ('You would not hear me' – II.2.128), so there is no reason why he should not protest openly (3, above).

4 KING. . . . But now my cousin Hamlet, and my son –
HAMLET. [*Aside*] A little more than kin, and less than kind.
KING. How is it that the clouds still hang on you?
HAMLET. Not so, my lord; I am too much in the sun.

(I.2.64)

Traditionally printed as an aside (since Theobald), Hamlet's first speech expresses the riddling impudence that is characteristic of all of his exchanges with Claudius before Act V. Are we to assume that he would not have dared to speak out loud, and that the only alternative is an aside? There is surely evidence enough in the play that Hamlet's angry contemptuousness could not be muzzled. Nevertheless, a third possibility should be considered: that Hamlet, the arch-soliloquiser, not infrequently mutters to himself and cares not a rap whether or not others catch his words. Shakespeare had earlier broken the convention of 'inaudible soliloquy' when it suited him (as in the balcony-scene in *Romeo and Juliet*); now he modifies the aside, which becomes audible or semi-audible as he chooses, so that many of Hamlet's speeches resemble an aside in being partly addressed to himself ('These tedious old fools!'; 'Marry, this is miching mallecho . . . '). The 'semi-aside', or aside half overheard, has an important function in *Hamlet*, and in some other plays.

> 5 HAMLET. [*Aside to Horatio*] Dost know this waterfly?
> HORATIO. [*Aside to Hamlet*] No, my good lord.
> HAMLET. [*Aside to Horatio*] Thy state is the more gracious; for 'tis a vice to know him. He hath much land, and fertile. Let a beast be lord of beasts, and his crib shall stand at the king's mess. 'Tis a chough; but, as I say, spacious in the possession of dirt.   (V.2.83)

To label these exchanges 'asides' is to deprive them of much of their nervy edge. Hamlet enjoys insulting those he despises to their face (Claudius, Polonius, Rosencrantz and Guildenstern), and we have no grounds for supposing that he must treat Osric differently. Hamlet may half turn away, and slightly lower his voice, still allowing Osric to 'listen in' if he wishes, and in the course of this 'semi-aside' Hamlet may suddenly raise his voice for Osric's benefit on certain phrases: ' 'tis a vice to know him . . . spacious in the possession of dirt'. Such opportunities are lost if the editor prints '*Aside*'; I think it best, therefore, to return to the Quarto and Folio texts and to omit the stage-directions in this passage and in others that are similar.

IV 'ALL' SPEECHES

Many texts contain speeches assigned to 'All', or to an indefinite number of speakers (Lords, Plebeians, etc.), which ought to be looked at as a group. When two or more dramatic characters miraculously utter the very same words in scenes that are psychologically 'realistic' I believe that this is often a result of editorial misunderstanding.

The tradition of simultaneous speech goes back to choric passages in pre-Shakespearian drama. No one can quarrel with simultaneous speech in more 'realistic' drama where it has an obvious choric or ritual function – the incantations of the ghosts in *Richard III*, or of the Weird Sisters, or appropriate salutations or responses such as '*All*. God saue the King, God saue the King' (*2 Henry VI*, O1[b]), '*All*. Amen' (*Richard III*, S2[b]). And short and appropriate exclamations need no defence either: '*All*. The Troians Trumpet' (*Troilus and*

Cressida, ¶ ¶ 3ᵇ), '*All*. Longer, longer' (*Hamlet*, 2n6ᵃ). But when '*All*' hit upon words that cannot be thus explained, what should be done? '*All*. Against him first: He's a very dog to the Commonalty', '*All*. Nay, but speak not maliciously' (*Coriolanus*, 2a1ᵃ): here, and in many other places, we have '*All*' speeches that are individualised, not ritualistic, and they always sound wrong in the theatre if uttered by more than a single voice.

To get the problem into focus let us turn to the three pages in *Sir Thomas More* now generally ascribed to Shakespeare, where, it seems, the dramatist wrote at such speed that he did not trouble to indicate all the minor speakers' names in a crowd-scene. Shakespeare's 147 lines include four speeches assigned not to a named person but to 'other' (i.e. another), a speech prefix that shrinks to 'oth' and even 'o';³ and, in addition, no less than ten 'All' speeches. A scribe concerned with the play was dissatisfied with so many vaguely assigned speeches, deleted the four 'other' prefixes and substituted more specific ones, 'GEO BETT' and 'WILLIAN'; and, significantly, he also ·deleted one 'All' prefix and substituted 'LINCO' (= Lincoln).

Let us remember, too, that there are 'All' speeches that cannot be taken to imply simultaneous speech of the kind mentioned above. '*Fairies*. Readie: and I, and I, and I. Where shall we goe?' (*Midsummer Night's Dream*, Q, D3ᵇ); '*All People*. Teare him to peeces, do it presently:/He kill'd my Sonne, my daughter, he kill'd my Cosine/*Marcus*, he kill'd my Father' (*Coriolanus*, 2c3ᵇ). The dramatist clearly wanted each fairy to answer individually, and so the Quarto's single speech is usually chopped up to read '*PEASEBLOSSOM*. Ready. *COBWEB*. And I. *MOTH*. And I', etc. In *Coriolanus* it is equally certain that different individuals cry out about the death of a son, daughter, cousin and father (though editors do not identify them as individuals, as I think they should, most of them printing '. . . He kill'd my son. My daughter. He kill'd my cousin Marcus', etc.). Compare also Petruchio's calling for three servants when he returns home (*Taming of the Shrew*, T3ᵃ): 'Where is *Nathaniel*, *Gregory*, *Phillip*. / *All ser*. Heere, heere sir, heere sir. / *Pet*. Heere sir, heere sir, heere sir, heere sir.'

From these examples we learn that Shakespeare sometimes used the '*All*' speech-prefix loosely, no doubt because he wrote in haste and thought that he could explain the details later – just as he might fall back on 'other', or on an actor's name, when he was too impatient to pause. We learn that an 'All' prefix could be reassigned to a single speaker (*Sir Thomas More*), or could indicate that different consecutive speakers are required (*Midsummer Night's Dream*). In *Coriolanus* and *Shrew* we encounter a third possibility, simultaneous 'confused' speech, for which *Antony and Cleopatra* gives an unambiguous direction (y4ª):

2. How now Maisters? *Speak together.*
Omnes. How now? how now? do you heare this?
1. I, is't not strange?
3. Do you heare Masters? Do you heare?

It would be quite wrong, of course, to urge that individualised or longer 'All' speeches must never be delivered as simultaneous 'choric' speech. Two unusual directions in *Titus Andronicus* (Q, B4ᵇ, C1ª) put this beyond doubt:

Titus two sonnes speakes.
And shall or him wee will accompanie.

they all kneele and say,
No man shed teares for Noble *Mutius*,
He liues in fame, that died in vertues cause.

On the other hand, editors have not made as much as they could or should of the fact that 'All' speech-prefixes were used more loosely than single-name prefixes and may therefore be variously interpreted.

1 Very often an 'All' speech in a crowd-scene may mean no more than that one person speaks while the rest howl or clamour or contribute what was known as 'confused noise':

All. That would hang vs, euery mothers sonne
(*Midsummer Night's Dream*, Q, B2ᵇ)

All. Most true, the Will, let's stay and heare the Wil.
(*Julius Caesar*, 2l ᵇ)

All. We will so: almost all repent in their election.
(*Coriolanus*, 2b1ᵇ)

2 Many 'All' speeches could be divided between two or more consecutive or simultaneous speakers. '*All*. A Clifford, a Clifford,//Wee'l follow the King, and Clifford' (*2 Henry VI*, O1ᵇ), and '*All*. It shall be so, it shall be so://let him away://Hee's banish'd, and it shall be so' (*Coriolanus*, 2b4ᵃ) could thus be assigned to two or three (new speakers indicated by //).

3 Some short 'All' exclamations may have been repeated more than once. '*A long flourish. They all cry, Martius, Martius, cast vp their Caps and Launces : Cominius and Lartius stand bare*' (*Coriolanus*, 2a4ᵃ): if caps and lances are flung up and retrieved this would take longer than the shouting of 'Marcius, Marcius'. I assume that an 'All' speech involving the repetition of a word or phrase indicates repetition but may leave it to the actors to decide how often to repeat. '*Warwicke and the rest cry all, Warwicke, Warwicke, and set vpon the Guard, who flye, crying, Arme, Arme*' (*3 Henry VI*, p6ᵇ). Indeed, even when an 'All' exclamation is printed only once, repetition may have been intended in 'ritual' situations where one would normally expect it: '*Cry, S. George, A Talbot*' (*1 Henry VI*, K5ᵃ; compare K5ᵇ: '*Enter a Souldier, crying, a Talbot, A Talbot*'). *2 Henry VI* perhaps confirms when the bad Quarto indicates twice that the Folio's 'All' cry was repeated. (The bad Quarto, admittedly, is not a perfect witness.)

> *After the Beadle hath hit him once, he leapes ouer the Stoole and runnes away: and they follow, and cry, A Miracle.* (F, m₆ᵃ) . . . they run after him, crying, A miracle, a miracle. *Hump.* A miracle, a miracle, let him be taken againe . . . .   (*The Contention*, C3ᵃ)

And sometimes we find echoes in the dialogue immediately after an 'All' cry that suggest, again, that the cry was meant to be repeated:

> *Within crie arme.* / The word is giuen, arme, arme flies through the camp   (*Sir Thomas Wyatt*, 1607, E1ᵃ)

> *A great noise, follow.* / *Enter Wyat* . . . / *Within.* Follow, follow (Ibid., E4ᵇ)

V 'BOTH' SPEECHES

Most of my remarks about 'All' apply equally to 'Both' speeches. While the existence of some choric 'Both' speeches cannot be denied, we should always consider alternative possibilities.

1 In a 'realistic' context where non-ritualistic lines are concerned it may be that there ought to be only one speaker, who indicates by a gesture that he speaks for both: '*Both*. Why? how are we censur'd?' (*Coriolanus*, 2a4[b]).[4]

2 'Both' speeches may signify nothing more than the author's hasty composition. This must often be so, I think, in *Timon*, a text that includes so many other non-specific speech-prefixes (an exceptional number of 'All' speeches, as well as '*Some speake*' and '*Some other*' – 2h1[a]): '*Both*. Giue vs some Gold good *Timon*, hast $\frac{u}{y}$ more?' (2h2[a]); '*Both*. More counsell with more Money, bounteous *Timon*' (2h2[b]); '*Both*. What we can do, / Wee'l do to do you seruice' (2h4[b]); and so on.

3 When the text names two speakers, instead of using the speech prefix 'both', it is more likely that simultaneous 'choric' speech is required. In Shakespeare such speech-prefixes are usually reserved for short replies or exclamations that any two persons might well make independently, and 'choric' speech is then quite acceptable.

> *Cleo. Dio.* All this we sweare. (*Winter's Tale*, 2A6[a])
> *Macb. and Lenox.* What's the matter? (*Macbeth*, 2m3[a])
> *Hor. & Marc. within.* My Lord, my Lord. (*Hamlet*, 2O1[b])
> *Gui. Arui.* Stand, stand, and fight. (*Cymbeline*, 3b2[b])

Occasionally, however, this type of 'Both' speech sounds less natural (but, occurring at moments of social or legal ritual, it stops short of the unnatural): '*Ang. Esc.* Happy returne be to your royall grace' (*Measure for Measure*, G4[a]); '*Gray. Scro.* To which we all appeale' (*Henry V*, h3[b]).

VI CRYPTO-DIRECTIONS

If editors have erred in the treatment of stage-directions it could also be said that they have not helped readers as they should with Elizabethan 'crypto-directions'. I refer in particular to expletives, some of which appear to have served as short-hand directions for a great variety of noises. To take one example, the ubiquitous 'O! – o!' is sometimes described as an 'actor's vulgarisation' – as if no self-respecting dramatist would stoop to write such stuff. Yet the metre confirms that even the greatest dramatists could sometimes write 'O! – o!' etc., while the context makes it equally clear that at other times this expletive was nothing more nor less than a familiar signal, like Malory's 'ha, ha' (indicating anger) or Molière's 'Ah, ah, ah' (indicating laughter); a different kind of signal, however, since it directed the actor to make whatever noise was locally appropriate. It could tell him to sigh, groan, gasp, roar, weep.

1 all the perfumes of Arabia will not sweeten this little hand. Oh, oh, oh. / *Doct.* What a sigh is there?   (*Macbeth*, 2n2^b)

2 Oh! / *Lou.* Why do you sigh?   (*A New Way to Pay Old Debts*, 1633, F2^a)

3 Ooh. – *Within.* / *D'am.* What groane was that?   (*The Atheist's Tragedy*, 1611, K2^b)

4 *Cont.* Oh. / 1. *Sur.* Did he not groane?   (*The Devil's Law Case*, 1623, F1^b)

5 Ooh. / *D'am.* His gasping sighes are like the falling noise of some great building.   (*The Atheist's Tragedy*, K3^a)

6 Oh, oh! / *Ver.* What horrid sounds are these?   (*The Changeling*, V.3.140)^5

7 *Oth.* Oh, oh, oh. / *Emil.* Nay, lay thee downe, and roare   (*Othello*, 2v5^a)

8 Ooh. / *Ruf.* Hell grinnes to heare this roaring   (Dekker, *If It Be Not Good*, 1612, L3^b)

9 Oh- oh. / *Mel.* Doe not weepe, what ist?   (*The Maid's Tragedy*, 1622, F1^b)

Middleton even resorted to 'O! o! o!' to express gloating;^{6} and when the immediate context gives no further explanation, the wide range of possibilities elsewhere suggests that the actor could do as he liked. Editors, I think, should deal with such crypto-directions as they deal with other private signals in Elizabethan texts: they should replace them with the appropriate equivalent (as they remove actors' names and substitute character-names). Thus 1 and 7 (above) might be printed as

1 all the perfumes of Arabia will not sweeten this little hand. [*A long sigh.*] *Doct.* What a sigh is there!

7 *Othello cries out in pain.* / *Emil.* Nay, lay thee downe, and roare.

In short, I assume that quite often what the original audience heard was not 'O! – o!', and that it will only mislead a modern reader or audience to print the dramatist's signal in this form.

VII   SERIES

Almost all 'Elizabethan' stage-directions resemble others in form or phrasing. As will have become clear, we are only ready to interpret stage-directions when we have identified them as members of a group, or series: and awareness of a series may prompt us to question the received text in many other places, where editors have in the past looked too narrowly at a single play, or author.

> 1 *Ege.* Full of vexation, come I, with complaint
> Against my childe, my daughter *Hermia.*
> > *Stand forth Demetrius.*
> My noble Lord,
> This man hath my consent to marry her.
> > *Stand forth Lisander.*
> And my gratious Duke,
> This man hath bewitcht the bosome of my childe
> > (*Midsummer Night's Dream*, Q, A2ᵃ; so F)

Editors normally emend to read ' / Stand forth, Demetrius. My noble lord, / This man hath my consent to marry her. / Stand forth, Lysander. And, my gracious Duke, / '. Yet Q would scan if the italicised words are treated as stage-directions, which is what one would normally expect them to be. The fact that a similar formula is found in other stage-directions inclines me to believe that emendation is unjustified ('*Lucillius and Messala stand forth*' – *Julius Caesar*, 214ᵃ; '*Berowne steps forth*' – *Love's Labour's Lost*, Q, 12ᵇ).[7]

> 2 *Ob.* Silence a while. *Robin* take off his head:
> *Titania*, musick call, and strike more dead
> Then common sleepe; of all these, fine the sense.

> *Tita.* Musicke, ho musicke, such as charmeth sleepe.
> > *Musick still.*
> *Rob.* When thou wak'st, with thine own fooles eies peepe.
> *Ob.* Sound musick; come my Queen, take hands with me
> > (*Midsummer Night's Dream*, O1ª)

It is not easy to decide when the music starts and stops. Editors normally omit '*Musick still*' and add '*Music*' after 'take hands with me', or misinterpret '*Musick still*' as 'Still music' or 'Soft music', with Theobald, Dyce, and others. Compare, however, *King Lear*, 2r2ªff.: '*Storme still*' (repeated at the beginning of three scenes, and three times in mid-scene); *Julius Caesar*, 215ª: '*Alarum still*'; *Coriolanus*, 2C3ª: '*A shout within* [7 lines] *Sound still with the Shouts*'; *Old Fortunatus*, 1600, G2ᵇ: '*Musicke sounding still*'. '*Musick still*' must have meant something like 'the former music continues', whereas '*Music*' on its own implies something very different, 'music starts at this point'. I take it that the '*Rurall Musicke*' called for earlier in the same scene in *A Midsummer Night's Dream* (a stage-direction added in the Folio, as was '*Musick still*') continues at Titania's command, viz. music 'such as charmeth sleep'. Puck, thereafter, speaks his one line when the rural music stops, and Oberon then calls for another kind of music (dance music).

> 3 *Officer.* It is his Highnesse pleasure, that the Queene
> > Appeare in person, here in Court. *Silence.*
> *Leo.* Reade the Indictment.
> > (*Winter's Tale*, 2A5ᵇ)

Most editors print '. . . here in court. Silence!', changing what appears to be a stage-direction into a spoken command. In this instance it is helpful to cite another stage-direction where the staging, if not the phrasing, follows a similar formula – from the trial-scene in *Henry VIII* (V2ᵇ).

> *Crier. Katherine* Queene of England, &c.
> > *The Queene makes no answer, rises out of her Chaire, goes about the Court, comes to the King, and kneeles at his Feete. Then speakes.*

The *Henry VIII* stage-direction spells out what must have happened in *The Winter's Tale*. Hermione, like Katherine, is asked to appear in court, and evidently walks to her appointed place. '*Silence*' in the Folio looks like a stage-direction, and should not be altered since it makes good sense as one. It tells us that a very special silence is required. Not the short 'pause' of modern play-texts, but a protracted silence at the end of which Hermione stands face to face with Leontes – stands, perhaps, not only silent but motionless, like a statue. The unusual stage-direction, in short, may point forward to the statue-scene, where Leontes and Hermione once more face one another and Paulina comments, '*I like your silence*, it the more shewes off / Your wonder' (my italics).

VIII   FOLIO STAGE-DIRECTIONS

Readers of Shakespeare who have not looked carefully at his early texts may think that all Quarto and Folio stage-directions have the same unimpeachable authority. If only that were true! Every text, however, passed through different hands, and many Quarto and Folio texts are bound to include stage-directions not written by the dramatist. One elderly scrivener employed, as he said in 1621, by

> those civil, well-deserving men
> That grace the stage with honour and delight,
> Of whose true honesties I much could write

certainly took it upon himself to tidy and rewrite the stage directions in plays that he transcribed. Ralph Crane[8] did not see himself as dishonest or unprofessional – quite the contrary. As Crane's writing-habits were highly distinctive, we can trace his hand in manuscripts and also in printed plays, even in some of Shakespeare's Folio texts. Other scriveners will have tidied other Folio texts, though probably not on the same scale; several Folio texts, in addition, were based on prompt-books and printed stage directions supplied not by Shakespeare but by a prompter. At some point, again, an editor or editorial team prepared copy for the Folio printers, inserting act and scene division as well as a new stratum of stage-directions intended to help the reader. We can see how this was done by glancing at Folio texts that are, in effect, reprints of earlier Quartos slightly improved with a sprinkling of new stage-directions (e.g. *Much Ado, The Merchant of Venice, A Midsummer Night's Dream*). The editor(s) wrote in '*The Clownes all Exit*', '*Enter Piramus with the Asse head*', '*shifting places*', '*Lye down*', and so on, in *A Midsummer Night's Dream* (F,N4^b,N6^b), probably copying from a manuscript, but not necessarily in every case. These new directions fall into several classes: one, directions for music, which are likely to derive from playhouse manuscripts; another, attempts to tidy up entrances and exits, which sometimes introduce new errors and must therefore be regarded as less authoritative.

For many reasons, stage-directions printed only in the Folio have a smaller chance of being Shakespeare's than those in the good Quartos. The Folio, of course, is a priceless volume, but, as I have argued elsewhere,[9] editors have tended to overrate its reliability. If we need to re-examine the meaning and reliability of Shakespeare's stage-directions, we shall have to be particularly cautious in dealing with all those that are transmitted only by the Folio.

IX CONCLUSION

This discussion of stage-directions builds on assumptions which are not, I believe, controversial. First, Shakespeare was careless about stage-directions. He often omitted them, or left them incomplete, or inserted them in approximately but not precisely the correct place. Secondly, some stage-directions in the good Quartos, and many more in the Folio, were added or misplaced by scriveners, prompters, Folio editors or compositors. Thirdly, a very large number of the stage-directions printed in modern editions which were added by eighteenth-century editors or their successors have only the authority of good sense (or not, as the case may be). Accepting these assumptions, we cannot avoid giving a higher authority to the 'implied stage-directions' of the dialogue than to directions printed as such. Indeed, our general understanding of a character (Hamlet's asides), or of what can and cannot be done successfully in the theatre (fast and slow deaths, 'all' and 'both' speeches), must always override the printed stage-directions. By identifying every stage-direction as one of a group or series, as I have attempted to do in this chapter, we can now advance beyond the eclectic methods of the past. We have a great opportunity, and a great responsibility: to see the plays, not as editors direct, but as we would wish to direct them ourselves.

11

Shakespeare at work: preparing, writing, rewriting

How did William Shakespeare prepare for and actually write his plays? We know a good deal about the writing-habits of later authors, and sometimes they throw light on the finished literary product. The work sheets of Dickens reveal how he planned ahead, or left problems to sort themselves out later, or changed his mind; his manuscripts show that some passages gave him trouble, and that others came easily; his letters defend some of his literary decisions. His friends also recalled what they knew about his working-methods; Frederic Chapman, one of his publishers, said that Dickens started a novel by 'getting hold of a central idea', made this into a 'skeleton story', then 'set to work and gave it literary sinew, blood and life'; also, that 'up to the moment of the appearance of the book' Dickens went on correcting and altering it.[1] Could it be that *Persuasion* and *Dombey and Son* and *Measure for Measure* began life in the same way? Sometimes we know whether or not a literary work's title shaped its growth from the beginning, or was simply a happy afterthought; as far as Shakespeare is concerned, we do not know.

Four hundred years after the event, much of the evidence about Shakespeare's writing-habits has disappeared. Nevertheless, much remains, or can be inferred: there are oddities in the earliest Quarto and Folio texts – most of them smoothed away in modern editions – that give us glimpses of the dramatist at work; three pages of the play *Sir Thomas More* are generally thought to be by Shakespeare and afford us other insights, 147 lines of dramatic composition in his original manuscript (all else has survived only in printed versions). His friends remarked upon his fluency as a writer, and upon some other characteristics; he himself glanced at his own performance as a poet in the Sonnets. In addition, contemporary descriptions of poets and dramatists at work help us to place the references to Shakespeare in a wider context.

First, some of the things we do not know but can guess. When did he find time to write his plays? It is on record that some authors are afternoon-men, whereas others believe that they write most effectively before breakfast, or during the morning, or at one particular time of day. As long as he remained a full-time actor Shakespeare would not have been free to write in the afternoons, when plays were performed in public; the turnover of plays being what it was – considerably greater than in modern repertory companies[2] – he would have had to give several hours a day to rehearsals, as an actor. He probably rehearsed his colleagues in his own plays, read manuscripts submitted to his company by other dramatists,[3] and had to find the time for dealing with financial and professional problems, as a leading sharer and housekeeper. Greene's reference to him as 'an absolute *Johannes factotum*'[4] could not have been far off the mark: the man who seemed to be 'in his own conceit the only Shakescene in a country' was exceptionally busy, and efficient. Perhaps he stopped full-time acting once he had established himself as a writer – no other major dramatist of the period carried as many responsibilities as Shakespeare – yet until that happened one wonders how he found the leisure, or the energy, to write plays.

Considering his circumstances, it is not surprising that he acquired a reputation as an exceptionally fluent writer. 'His mind and hand went together', said his friends, Heminge and Condell, 'and what he thought he uttered with that easiness, that we have scarce received from him a blot in his papers'. Ben Jonson confirmed that 'he flowed with that facility that sometime it was necessary he should be stopped'.[5] Stories about Shakespeare's ready wit made a similar point, as did references to him as England's Ovid, for Ovid was renowned for his fluency. 'The sweet, witty soul of Ovid lives in mellifluous and honey-tongued Shakespeare', declared Francis Meres in 1598; Shakespeare himself implicitly claimed as much by choosing a motto from Ovid's *Amores* for *Venus and Adonis*, the first publication to which he set his name.[6] Yet even if other pressing duties and his natural talent made him a fluent writer, we must not take the 'unblotted papers' quite literally: as will appear, there is also some evidence to the contrary.

Not so long ago some biographers still thought of the greatest writer of his age as a reluctant reader. Seventeenth-century stories about his fluency seemed to support the myth of a 'child of nature' who needed no art or preparation to write his plays. 'I have heard that Mr Shakespeare was a natural wit, without any art at all',

John Ward (vicar of Stratford from 1662 to 1681) confided to his notebooks[7]. In the eighteenth century this form of bardolatry developed, and it came to be accepted that Shakespeare lacked 'learning', which meant book-learning. Edmund Malone, the most important Shakespeare scholar of the later eighteenth century, convinced the world that many of the dramatist's plays were revised versions of earlier plays, and therefore subsequent scholars, whenever they discovered signs of wide or careful reading in one of Shakespeare's works, postulated a 'lost source-play' that predigested this reading in a manageable form for the book-weary dramatist. I have discussed this damaging view of Shakespeare elsewhere[8] – it rests on shaky assumptions, and it contradicts common sense – and agree with E. K. Chambers: 'One may reasonably assume that at all times Shakespeare read whatever books, original or translated, came in his way.'[9] I would go further; he did not always wait for books to 'come in his way' – now and then he actively sought out the books he needed, and engaged in what can only be called research. While preparing to write some of the history plays he consulted several volumes of English chronicles. There are grounds for thinking that they lay beside him as he composed.

Where did he enjoy the peace to write? When in London, he lived in lodgings. Our only sighting of him as a lodger suggests that, like the poets and dramatists in *Satiromastix* and *Poetaster*, he could not count on much privacy. He lived for a while with Christopher Mountjoy, a French Huguenot tiremaker, in St Olave's parish; Mountjoy had an apprentice, Stephen Belott, who married Mountjoy's daughter Mary on 19 November 1604. It seems that Belott was not too eager to marry; Shakespeare later deposed under oath that Mary's mother 'did solicit and entreat' him (Shakespeare) to move and persuade Belott to marry, that he had heard Mr and Mrs Mountjoy 'diverse and sundry times say' that Belott was 'a very honest fellow', and 'they had amongst themselves many conferences about their marriage'. To withdraw from such household battles would not have been easy.

For the history plays Shakespeare needed to refer to volumes that were too heavy to carry around. Did he build up a library of his own? Half of his plays were largely based on only two source-books (Holinshed and Plutarch) – hardly a library – yet, as I have indicated, many of his plays reflect wide reading. There were no public libraries. He might have collected a private library in

Stratford, writing some of the plays in quick bursts when he went home, or he may have had access to the private library of one of his noble patrons. The fact that no books were mentioned in his will is neither here nor there. Some of his contemporaries bequeathed books in theirs, for special reasons; any household goods not otherwise disposed of would go automatically to the testator's heirs, and we may assume that Shakespeare's books, whether few or many, would take this normal route. The inventory of his goods prepared at the time of his death has disappeared.

The most productive writers have sometimes worked well under the greatest pressures. Some have had to work against the clock, and found it exhausting (Scott, Dickens, Balzac); Trollope wrote his forty pages a week, very often in railway-carriages, observed by 'four or five fellow-passengers', apparently without much sense of strain. The story that Shakespeare wrote *The Merry Wives of Windsor* in a fortnight suggests that his dialogue here came as fluently as Trollope's prose, yet we may wonder whether his best poetry gave him more trouble. What is certain is that for much of his working life the purely physical obstacles to composition were far from negligible: he had many other commitments, little privacy, and probably sometimes lacked the books that he needed to continue writing his plays.

Let us suppose that the time is propitious, and that he undertakes a new play. How did other dramatists make a start? We hear in the diary and papers of Philip Henslowe of 'plots' which were sometimes vetted by actors before a play was begun – 'Lent unto Benjamin Jonson the 3 of December 1597, upon a book which he was to write for us before Christmas next after the date hereof, which he showed the plot unto the company . . . xxs'; 'Lent unto Robert Shaw and Jewby the 23 of October 1598 to lend unto Mr Chapman on his playbook and two acts of a tragedy of Benjamin's plot, the sum of £3'; in 1613 Field wrote to Henslowe that 'Mr Daborne and I have spent a great deal of time in conference about this plot, which will make as beneficial a play as hath come these seven years . . . .'[10] Such plots (a) should be distinguished from (b), the plot or 'plat' prepared for the use of the prompter once a play had been completed and cast. The first would be a synopsis of the play's action, probably not very different from the 'argument' printed with some plays, and would be useful in persuading the actors to offer a cash advance, and in making it possible to assign the writing of parts of a play to different dramatists. The second

(b) gave a breakdown of all the *dramatis personae* in every scene, often substituting an actor's name for a character's, and also listed properties (furniture, books, etc.) that had to be available. When Francis Meres called Munday 'our best plotter',[11] and when Chapman followed 'Benjamin's plot', (a) must have been meant. This kind of plotting required a creative talent; the prompter's plot (b) could be prepared by a nameless hack.

Shakespeare, once established, did not need cash advances, and disdained the help of collaborators (so Leonard Digges informs us; now and then, however, he seems to have collaborated – for instance, in *Sir Thomas More* and *The Two Noble Kinsmen*). Two reasons for preparing a plot before starting to write a play would not apply to him, during the best years of his creative life. And, although a plot might still be useful to a dramatist working on his own, there are signs that Shakespeare sometimes managed without one. For instance, 'ghost' characters, who are named in stage-directions and given nothing to do. '*Enter Leonato gouernour of Messina, Innogen his wife, Hero his daughter, and Beatrice his neece, with a messenger*' (*Much Ado*, Q, I.1), '*Enter Tybalt, Petruchio, and others*' (*Romeo and Juliet*, Q2, III.1.36): one would expect that a dramatist who had prepared an 'author plot' would know whether or not a fairly important character such as 'Innogen his wife' had a part in his play. Again, several plays seem to change direction unexpectedly, as if the dramatist, having steered towards one conclusion, substituted another. This seems to have happened in *1 Henry IV*, as Harold Jenkins has shown. We may not have access to Shakespeare's secret intentions, said Jenkins, yet we know what he warns us to expect. The play elaborately contrasts Hotspur and Falstaff, and repeatedly prompts us to expect their catastrophes.

> The moment at the end of the third act when the Prince goes off to challenge Hotspur is also the moment when he leaves Falstaff's favourite tavern for what we well might think would be evermore. It is at the exit from the tavern that the road to Shrewsbury begins; and all the sign-posts I see indicate one-way traffic only. There should be no return.
>
> The various dooms of Hotspur and Falstaff are now in sight; and we reasonably expect both dooms to be arrived at in Act 5. What we are not at all prepared for is that one of the two will be deferred till five acts later than the other.[12]

I have argued that something similar occurred as Shakespeare approached the end of *Troilus and Cressida* (cf. p. 123 above). In both cases he wanted to stretch a five-act play to ten acts, substituting an inconclusive ending for the planned deaths of Henry IV and Troilus. This might have been done even if he had followed an author plot; for our purposes the important point is not to insist that he could or could not have prepared an author plot, but to note that he felt free to improvise when it suited him. Shakespeare revised his plotting as he wrote.

Dickens once observed that some characters developed as he composed in ways that he had not foreseen. 'As to the way in which these characters have opened out, that is to me one of the most surprising processes of the mind in this sort of invention. Given what one knows, what one does not know springs up. . . .'[13] Mrs Gamp and Pecksniff surprised their creator, and critics of Shakespeare have felt that he too allowed some of his characters to 'open out', upsetting the balance of their play: for instance, Mercutio, Shylock, Falstaff, Benedick and Beatrice. 'Shakespeare showed the best of his skill in his Mercutio, and he said himself that he was forced to kill him in the third act, to prevent being killed by him.'[14] Whether or not Dryden's anecdote is true, such things certainly happened, and many have independently explained the seemingly lopsided structure of different plays on some such ground.

Another indication that Shakespeare may have dispensed with an author plot comes from stage-directions that look like the author's notes for continuing his plays, rather than directions needed by readers or for performance. For example, in the Folio: '*Enter Lord Timon, addressing himselfe curteously to euery Sutor*' (*Timon*, I.1.97); '*Enter Lord Timon, the States, the Athenian Lords, Ventigius which Timon redeem'd from prison. Then comes dropping after all Apemantus discontentedly like himselfe*' (I.2.1); '*Flaminius waiting to speake with a Lord from his Master*' (III.1.1); '*Enter the King with diuers yong Lords, taking leaue for the Florentine warre*' (*All's Well*, II.1.1); '*She addresses her to a Lord*' (II.3.60); '*Parolles and Lafew stay behind, commenting of this wedding*' (II.3.181). Of the directions in *Timon*, W. W. Greg said that they 'are reminiscent of what may have been jottings in the author's original plot; where the drama has only half disengaged itself from the matrix of thought, it is natural that the directions should not have been fully adapted to the needs of the stage.' Of those in *All's Well*, Dover Wilson thought one 'may be Shakespeare's direction to a collaborator how to continue', yet 'it might equally well be a note for his own future guidance. But it has more the appearance of a phrase from an author's plot or scenario that has been accidentally preserved.'[15] Why, though, suppose that these curious directions derive from an author's plot, rather than that they replace such a plot? No firm evidence survives to prove that Shakespeare normally prepared an author plot, whereas many little and not-so-little signs suggest that plotting and writing sometimes went along together, rather than in two clearly distinct phases. Since Shakespeare almost always chose an existing story (history, biography, romance, etc.) as the source of his play, this source might serve as his author plot, and the rest he could carry in his head.

On one occasion, however, he did prepare a synopsis. Not for a play, but for *The Rape of Lucrece* – a very 'literary' poem, the second work signed by Shakespeare and definitely a bid for wider recognition. The dedication to the Earl of Southampton signalled to the reading public that Shakespeare has arrived – 'The love I dedicate to your Lordship is without end: wherof this Pamphlet without beginning is but a superfluous Moity. The warrant I have of your Honourable disposition, not the worth of my untutord Lines, makes it assured of acceptance. . . .' Then follows the 'argument', another signal that the poet, on his best behaviour, understands all the due formalities. Interestingly, the 'argument' diverges here and there from the poem. 'Lucrece, in this lamentable plight, hastily dispatcheth messengers [plural], one to Rome for her father, another to the camp for Collatine. They came, the one accompanied with Junius Brutus, the other with Publius Valerius . . . .' In the poem, Lucrece sends only one messenger, to her husband; while her father also arrives, Publius Valerius is not named at this point. Further, the 'argument' envisages a bigger part for Brutus:

> bearing the dead body to Rome, Brutus acquainted the people with the doer and manner of the vile deed, with a bitter invective against the tyranny of the King; wherewith the people were so moved, that with one consent and a general acclamation the Tarquins were all exiled . . . .

All this is huddled up in the last two stanzas, and we can guess why. A poet may think, like Christopher Sly, ''Tis a very excellent piece of work . . . . Would it were done!' So – away with the second messenger, and Publius Valerius, and the bitter invective. This argument for *The Rape of Lucrece* must have been written first, and when Shakespeare actually wrote the poem he decided to cut some corners. If he prepared an author plot for his plays he no doubt felt equally free to modify it as his writing progressed; *The Rape of Lucrece*, though, being a very special venture, could well have been more carefully and 'correctly' planned than the plays.

An author plot, like a 'skeleton story' by Dickens, might take many forms. I have suggested that it could resemble the 'arguments' prefixed to some poems and plays, and these again differed, depending on the author and the readers he had in mind. The one printed with *Gorboduc* seems too short (13 lines) to have been of much use to the authors during composition. Another, printed with Jonson's *The New Inn*, is so literary and long (126 lines in the Oxford *Ben Jonson*) that one suspects that it was added to impress the reader. Neither of these is likely to have been an author plot. Another, printed with the fragment of *Mortimer his Fall* after Jonson's death, seems about the right length (39 lines), and must have been written before the play, since this was left incomplete. (Someone added a note that 'He died, and left it unfinished.') It summarised the play's contents, perhaps more self-consciously than was necessary: 'The first act comprehends . . . . The second act shows . . . . The third act relates . . . . The fourth act expresseth . . . .' If Shakespeare prepared any author plots I imagine that they would have been less polished. His writing-habits, it seems, were totally different from Jonson's. (Jonson told Drummond 'that he wrote all his [verses] first in prose, for so his master Camden had learned him'; this may have applied to Jonson's dramatic verse as well.)

A younger contemporary who knew Shakespeare personally,[16] and who wrote two sets of verses in his honour filled with his own first-hand observations, marvelled that it gave the dramatist so little trouble 'to contrive a play'.

> First, that he was a poet none would doubt
> That heard th' applause of what he sees set out
> Imprinted; where thou hast, I will not say,
> Reader, his Works – for to contrive a play
> To him 'twas none – the pattern of all wit,
> Art without art, unparalleled as yet.

To 'contrive a play' (i.e. to devise or invent it) may also refer to writing and producing it, but must refer in the first instance to plotting. Leonard Digges here confirms our general impression of Shakespeare's seemingly effortless control of his material.

One other preparatory task must be mentioned – the *dramatis personae* list. A professional playwright knows how many actors are normally available; if attached to a company, as was Shakespeare, he would be aware of the special skills of every actor, and would have to make sure that all the 'sharers' – his employers – were satisfied with their parts. We may assume that, for these and other reasons, most professional playwrights started with a list of names, especially if they followed a source and wished to change some of the names. Shakespeare, being exceptionally sensitive to the sound of names, seems to have invented some (Shylock, Ophelia, Othello, Caliban), and to have rejected many that another playwright might have adopted quite happily. In *As You Like It* he kept the names Rosalind and Adam, and also the disguise-names Ganymede and Aliena, changing Celia, Oliver, Orlando, Sir Rowland de Boys and others (from Alinda, Saladyne, Rosader, Sir John of Bordeaux). The changes may be significant, or inexplicable whims; Orlando, Oliver and Rowland appear to allude to the *Chanson de Roland* story even if much else in *As You Like It* strikes us as 'Elizabethan'. (Several Huguenot immigrants in London in the 1590s had the name De Bois.) Whatever Shakespeare's reasons for renaming his characters, we should expect him to do so before he began to write the dialogue – although, as we shall see, there are some exceptions to this practice. Quite often he pinned down a new character with a name at his first entry, even though the name is never used in the dialogue (e.g. Claudius in *Hamlet*, Prince Eskales in *Romeo and Juliet*, Ferdinand in *Love's Labour's Lost*), and very minor parts, including some that never appear, are given names, we may think unnecessarily. In *King John* one man speaks a total of four words, yet Shakespeare invented a name for him: 'James Gurney, wilt thou give us leave awhile?' (I.1.230).

Names keenly interested Shakespeare. He took some trouble with them – nevertheless, we find two characters in *As You Like It* called Jaques. In this play, then, he may have dispensed with a *dramatis personae* list; or the melancholy Jaques could have been an afterthought. In *Hamlet* a minor character is referred to as Claudio (IV.7.40): perhaps Shakespeare forgot, as he neared the end of this long tragedy, that he had called the King Claudius (a name, as I have said, never used in the dialogue).

Seven *dramatis personae* lists were printed in the First Folio. Some were clearly inserted to fill blank spaces in the Folio – 'hence', it has been claimed, 'we must infer that they were drawn up in the printing house'.[17] Not necessarily, for some prologues and epilogues were also inserted in the Folio to fill blank spaces, yet no one would assign the prologue of *Troilus and Cressida*, or the epilogue of *2 Henry IV*, to any hand except the author's. A *dramatis personae* list might equally be authorial, and in that case could take us back to the preparatory phase of a play, before a word of dialogue was written. Particularly intriguing, I think, is the one that goes with *Measure for Measure*.

The Scene Vienna.	*Thomas.* ⎫
The names of all the Actors.	*Peter.* ⎬ 2. *Friers.*
Vincentio: the Duke.	*Elbow, a simple Constable.*
Angelo, the Deputie.	*Froth, a foolish Gentleman.*
Escalus, an ancient Lord.	*Clowne.*
Claudio, a young Gentleman.	*Abhorson, an Executioner.*
Lucio, a fantastique.	*Barnardine, a dissolute prisoner.*
2. Other like Gentlemen.	*Isabella, sister to Claudio.*
Prouost.	*Mariana, betrothed to Angelo.*
	Iuliet, beloued of Claudio.
	Francisca, a Nun.
	Mistris Ouer-don, a Bawd.

W. W. Greg commented as follows:

At the end F. adds one of its rare lists of personae. This gives 'Mistris Over-don, a Bawd', but only 'Clowne' for Pompey; it distinguishes Thomas and Peter as '2. Friers'; it omits the Justice and Varrius; but it gives the Duke's name as Vincentio, though it appears nowhere in the text. From this Wilson concludes that 'the F. list, whencesoever derived, relates to a form of the play different from that which has come down to us'. This is an attractive fancy, but for what purpose could such a list have been prepared?[18]

The purpose must have been to aid the author in his plotting. A list compiled in the printing-house for the benefit of readers would have been more accurate, and would not have given a name to the Duke that did not derive from the text. The fact that he is called Vincentio in the list, and nowhere else, has importance when we recall Shakespeare's ingrained habit of attaching names to his characters, often superfluously. (Compare also Francisca in *Measure for Measure*, another unnecessary name.) From the *Measure for Measure* list we learn that Shakespeare, as usual, devised names for almost all the principal actors at an early stage of planning, except the Provost (who remained nameless) and the clown (later Pompey); some minor parts were probably not thought of till later, and extras (V.1.1: 'Lords . . . Citizens') did not matter. If I am correct, Shakespeare had already worked out much of the detail in his plotting that departs from his sources: Mariana, far from being a last-minute substitute to save Isabella from Angelo's bed, must be seen as integral to Shakespeare's original conception of the play (cf. p. 162 above).

After studying his 'sources', and sometimes preparing an author plot and *dramatis personae* list, Shakespeare could begin to write his dialogue. How 'unblotted' were his papers? 'What he thought he uttered [expressed in words] with that easiness, that we have scarce received from him a blot [a correction or deletion] in his papers' – can we take this assurance literally? W. W. Greg commented,

> We may suspect that what we are told of the unblotted condition of Shakespeare's papers is exaggerated — 'scarcely' is an elastic term – and we may allow that they were probably not all of a kind; but unless a substantial proportion of those papers showed manifest signs of free composition, such as careful fair copies would not, to appeal to them as proving the author's ease of utterance would be absurd.[19]

Yet we now know that Heminge and Condell's praise of Shakespeare's fluent writing, like much else in their prefatory epistles in the First Folio, simply echoed the clichés of their time. A good writer was expected to be fluent. Jonson and Webster resented it when others accused them of crabbed, slow writing; Heywood was proud of having had a hand, 'or at least a main finger', in well over two hundred plays. The notion that fluency was somehow meritorious goes back to Ovid and other classical authors,[20] and won wide support in the Elizabethan period. 'Give me the man,' wrote Thomas Nashe, 'whose extemporal vein in any humour will excel our greatest art-masters' deliberate thoughts; whose inventions, quicker than his eye, will challenge the proudest rhetorician to the contention of like perfection with like expedition'. Nashe particularly admired Robert Greene: 'In a night and a day would he have yarked up [thrown together] a pamphlet as well as in seven year; and glad was that printer that might be so blest to pay him dear for the very dregs of his wit.'[21]

Four men who knew about Shakespeare's First Folio before it was published, and helped in various ways to bring it about, worked together on other literary ventures and prove that the literary world made as much capital as it could of an author's fluency at this time. Edward Blount, one of the principal publishers of the Folio, and Ben Jonson, who wrote two sets of verses for the Folio, and Leonard Digges and James Mabbe, both of whom also contributed verses, actively supported each other in their books – as in Mabbe's translation of Aleman's *The Rogue* (1622), which was published by Blount and decked out with complimentary verses by Jonson and Digges. Mabbe claimed that he translated this large volume in 'a few weeks', and he was praised as an author 'whose quill both writes and flies / With equal speed' (A4[a]); we are also told that Aleman's own fluency 'may almost be counted a miracle'.

> Putting his papers from hand to hand to the press, and wanting matter for that day's work, I knew for certain that, overnight, he composed so much stuff as did serve to keep the press going all the next day following: for he was troubled at that time with diverse other businesses, which did necessarily require his help and assistance. And in those short hours of the night he was seen to employ himself with a great deal of diligence, as well in the affairs of his other businesses as in the ordering and sorting of papers to send them to the printers, as also in the composing of more matter for the press.[22]

Heminge and Condell, who praised Shakespeare's unblotted papers a few months later, sound quite restrained in comparison.

It should be observed, too, that the remarks about Shakespeare's fluency are partly sales-talk. Before the publication of the Folio, Heminge and Condell inform 'the great variety of readers', you were 'abused with diverse stolen and surreptitious copies, maimed and deformed by the frauds and stealths of injurious impostors'. Those plays are now offered to your view cured, and perfect of their limbs; and all the rest, absolute in their numbers, as he conceived them. Who, as he was a happy imitator of Nature, was a most gentle expresser of it. His mind and hand went together: and what he thought he uttered, with that easiness that we have scarce received from him a blot in his papers.

Heminge and Condell are not attacking good Quartos, but 'stolen and surreptitious' texts, which could be distinguished by their unnatural language, as in this version of a famous soliloquy:

> To be, or not to be, I there's the point,
> To Die, to sleepe, is that all? I all:
> No, to sleepe, to dreame, I mary there it goes,
> For in that dreame of death, when wee awake,
> And borne before an euerlasting Iudge,
> From whence no passenger euer retur'nd,
> The vndiscouered country, at whose sight
> The happy smile, and the accursed damn'd . . . .

The bad Quarto of *Hamlet* may here be a little more 'maimed and deformed' in its language than the average stolen and surreptitious text, but helps to illustrate Heminge and Condell's point: bad Quartos give themselves away by their deformed language, whereas the authentic texts – *our* Folio texts – are 'absolute [*OED*, 4: free from all imperfection] in their numbers', the work of a most supple master of the art of expression (*OED*, gentle, 5; expresser, 1b). The 'easiness' of Shakespeare's writing helps to confirm his linguistic mastery, which in turn authenticates *our* versions as against *theirs* (the bad Quartos). In context, the 'unblotted papers' are part of a sales campaign; this does not invalidate what Heminge and Condell say, and yet must again make us wary of accepting their assurances too literally.

When we turn to the 'good' printed texts, those that appear to derive more or less directly from Shakespeare's own papers, the surviving evidence of 'false starts' and other deletions contradicts the myth of unblotted papers. A well-known example, which is longer than most and also illustrates Shakespeare's extraordinary attention to detail when rewriting, occurs in *Love's Labour's Lost*, IV.3.292ff.

And where that you haue vowd to studie (Lordes)
In that each of you haue forsworne his Booke
Can you still dreame and poare and thereon looke.
For when would you my Lord, or you, or you,
Haue found the ground of Studies excellence,
Without the beautie of a womans face?
From womens eyes this doctrine I deriue,
They are the Ground, the Bookes, the Achadems,
From whence doth spring the true *Promethean* fire. . . .

Shakespeare wrote twenty-two and a half lines in this vein, then decided that he could do better, and started again.

O we haue made a Vow to studie, Lordes,
And in that Vow we haue forsworne our Bookes:
For when would you (my Leedge) or you, or you?
In leaden contemplation haue found out
Such fierie Numbers as the prompting eyes,
Of beautis tutors haue inritcht you with: . . . .

The speech grows much longer than the cancelled 'false start', which was printed by mistake in the first Quarto, yet Shakespeare kept his eye on the scrapped passage and rescued – and improved – some of its lines.

From womens eyes this doctrine I deriue.
They sparcle still the right promethean fier,
They are the Bookes, the Artes, the Achademes,
That shew, containe, and nourish all the worlde.

It is thought that 'false starts' that found their way into print were inadequately deleted, and that the printers did not realise that the first version had been superseded. That sounds plausible; we should note, however, that Elizabethan printers were not wholly incompetent: if they overlooked some 'false starts', we may assume that they spotted others, and sensibly omitted them. There must have been more 'false starts' than those that were accidentally printed in the Quartos.

'The Shakespearian pages in *Sir Thomas More* and Heywood's *Captives* alike prove that an author's foul papers may be reasonably free from alteration', said W. W. Greg. And again – 'What

Shakespeare could produce as a draft we may, I believe, see in the famous three pages of *More*, and I imagine that it was something of this sort that he often handed to the company.'[23] Greg here made two assumptions that ought to be questioned. First, that Shakespeare's three pages in *Sir Thomas More* represent free composition, i.e. his 'foul papers' or first draft. For the three pages replace a scene missing from the original manuscript before folio 10, and therefore Shakespeare could have copied rather than composed some of the dialogue, supposing the lost scene was his or partly his. A recent discussion of *Sir Thomas More*, arguing that Shakespeare was one of the original authors of the play, not one of the much later revisers,[24] and the fact that a scene very like Shakespeare's must have existed before he rewrote it, both need to be taken into account before we accept the three pages as typical of Shakespeare's foul papers. And of course the three pages, though clean by most standards, do contain several deletions and could not be fairly described as 'unblotted'.

Greg's second assumption, one that seems to be widely shared by textual specialists, sounds like common sense – until one remembers the actual circumstances of authorship in the Elizabethan period. Greg assumed that a dramatist first wrote his play as 'foul papers', then made out a 'fair copy' or arranged to have this done by a professional scrivener. Yet, although we know that Shakespeare's contemporaries referred to foul papers and fair copies, we are not entitled to assume that an author's foul papers were all of a piece. Why not? Because plays were written on loose sheets of paper, which were later tied together — a small point that has several important consequences for students of 'Shakespeare at work'. Innumerable passages in Henslowe's *Diary* and in the *Henslowe Papers* prove what is equally clear from the surviving manuscripts of the period. 'Mr Henslowe, I have heard five sheets of a play of the conquest of the Indies, and I do not doubt but it will be a very good play, therefore I pray ye deliver them forty shillings in earnest of it and take the papers' (S. Rowley to Henslowe, 4 April 1601); 'Mr Henslowe, I pray ye let Mr Hathway have his papers again of the play of John of Gaunt' (Rowley to Henslowe, 1601); 'on Friday night I will deliver in the 3 acts fair written and then receive the other 40*s*., and if you please to have some papers now ye shall' (R. Daborne to Henslowe, 3 May 1613).[25] Heminge and Condell referred to Shakespeare's unblotted *papers*. We must take it that Shakespeare also wrote on loose sheets of paper, and could always make a fair copy of individual sheets where he had got into a tangle (as in *Sir Thomas More*), even though other sheets might be genuine first drafts. In short, Heminge and Condell may never have seen Shakespeare's more 'blotted' papers, which could be easily replaced, and might have inferred from some signs of authorial afterthoughts in a manuscript that the entire manuscript represented 'first draft' writing. We, too, must beware of rashly assuming that texts such as the first Quarto of *Love's Labour's Lost* or the second Quarto of *Romeo and Juliet*, despite all the clues of 'foul paper' provenance – revised passages, indecision about the names of the characters – must therefore represent foul papers from beginning to end.[26]

In the last hundred years no one has done more than W. W. Greg to advance the study of Elizabethan printed texts and manuscripts. I respect his memory, on this side idolatry, as much as any; nevertheless, Greg seems to me to have taken Heminge and Condell's assurances too literally when he declared that 'an experienced dramatist would doubtless be able to produce at once a sufficiently coherent text', and that 'Shakespeare doubtless composed fluently and seldom went back over what he had written.'[27] When Greg himself closely examined the printed versions of Shakespeare's plays, and described the textual characteristics of the foul papers from which they appeared to derive, this evidence sometimes pushed him to a different conclusion: 'a rather heavily corrected manuscript' (*Othello*), 'foul papers, with sundry alterations and corrections' (*Troilus and Cressida*), 'foul papers that had been left in a rather rough state' (*Measure for Measure*).[28] As I have already indicated, Heminge and Condell may well have exaggerated Shakespeare's fluency; their sweeping generalisation is not easy to reconcile with the evidence of some of the individual texts.

Shakespeare's fluency having been an article of faith for so long, it has been taken for granted that he wrote his plays from beginning to end, as we now read them. Many authors of major literary works preferred a different procedure (witness *Gulliver's Travels, The Prelude, In Memoriam, The Waste Land, Tender is the Night*); a dramatist writing on loose sheets of paper might work on a scene whenever a good idea came to him, out of its sequential order, or he could finish the main plot and attend to the sub-plot later, and his papers, pieced together, would not look any the more 'blotted' as a consequence. When two or more Elizabethan dramatists collaborated such piecemeal composition seems to have been quite normal, as is proved by Henslowe's *Diary* and generally accepted as the obvious explanation of plays such as *Eastward Ho* or *The Changeling*. Interestingly, Shakespeare's hypothesised collaborations are usually divided by editors into Shakespearian scenes and episodes interspersed amongst scenes by another, a *modus operandi* which suggests willingness to abandon sequential writing. Shakespeare has been credited with I.2.90ff., Act II, and Act IV scene 4 of *Edward III*, and with Act I scenes 1 and 2, Act II scenes 3 and 4, III.2.1–203, and Act V scene 1 of *Henry VIII*. Whether or not we accept all such divisions, no one disputes that they are theoretically possible. E. K. Chambers, assigning *Henry VIII* to Shakespeare and Fletcher, noted that 'Shakespeare starts most of the themes', and commented on *Timon of Athens* that 'Shakespeare seems to have worked chiefly on the beginning and end of the play, and to have left the middle acts in a very imperfect state'; he added, 'I do not suggest that *Timon* throws much light upon Shakespeare's normal methods of working.'[29] If Shakespeare worked 'irregularly' in *Henry VIII* and *Edward III* and *Timon*, this would throw several beams of light in one direction.

The frequent 'inconsistencies' in Shakespeare's plays also point in the same direction. Once explained as 'fossil' traces of earlier versions of a play, particularly in the New Shakespeare volumes edited by J. Dover Wilson, these inconsistencies should not be dismissed as merely typical of Shakespeare's carelessness: they could have resulted from the conditions in which he worked. His company made many provincial tours; if he left his books and papers behind, in Stratford or London, and continued writing a play – or several plays – as opportunities arose, it would be the most natural thing in the world that, unable to check what he had already written, he might sometimes contradict himself. In *The Winter's Tale* the chorus Time announces 'I slide / O'er sixteen years' (IV.1.6), yet Camillo says, 'It is fifteen years since I saw my country' (IV.2.4). In *Measure for Measure* Angelo enforces laws that had been neglected for 'nineteen zodiacs', or years (I.2.161), and almost immediately afterwards the Duke confesses that he had ignored the state's strict statutes for 'fourteen years' (I.3.21). Either Shakespeare did not write these consecutive scenes consecutively or he did not refer back to the previous scene because he did not have it at hand. Some such explanation seems at least as likely as the theory that he forgot what he had just written (there are many indications that he had a tenacious memory), or that he failed to look back at the previous scene when that lay in front of him. In *Love's Labour's Lost* Ferdinand, King of Navarre, is also referred to as a duke (I.1.179, I.2.36, 121, etc.) and the French princess as a queen (IV.2.124, 131). In *Much Ado*, Act IV scene 2, Dogberry and Verges are called by various other names, including 'Kemp' and 'Cowley', the names of two leading actors in the Lord Chamberlain's company, but not Dogberry and Verges, even though they had already appeared as Dogberry and Verges in Act III scenes 3 and 5. Did their creator not remember these unforgettable names? It seems more likely that he wrote Act IV scene 2 *before* Act III scenes 3 and 5, could not make up his mind about these names when he first thought of the characters, and fixed on Dogberry and Verges later, when he wrote Act III. Uncertainty about names in other plays, or different titles for the same character, may also betray 'irregular' writing.

Sometimes two or more inconsistencies at the same point in a play strengthen the case for 'irregular' writing. In *Measure for Measure* the reference to nineteen years in Act I scene 2, conflicting with the fourteen years of Act I scene 3, occurs in a scene exhibiting multiple confusion about Claudio's crime.

(1) The bawd informs others, including Lucio, that Claudio has been sentenced 'for getting Madam Julietta with child' (58–77);

(2) the bawd asks the clown why Claudio has been sentenced, and does not know what she herself has just announced ('What! is there a maid with child by him?') (78–109: Lucio is not present here);

(3) Lucio asks Claudio the reason for his restraint ('What's thy offence, Claudio?'), even though he had heard the reason in the course of (1).

I conclude that (2) and (3) belong together, and were composed separately from (1): this explains the muddle that both the bawd and Lucio first know and then do not know the facts. As (2) and (3) fail to connect with (1), which precedes, and also with the immediately following scene (in the matter of the fourteen and nineteen years), it looks as if (1) and Act I scene 3 were written out of sequence and not at the same time as (2) and (3).

We can go further. Since (2) and (3) cover the same ground as (1), Shakespeare must have cancelled (1), replacing it with (2) and

(3): here we have another deletion that was printed by mistake (cf. p. 201). And the reason for the change is not hard to find. The verbal quibbling of Lucio and the two gentlemen had gone on long enough; by scrapping (1) and substituting (2) and (3), Shakespeare prevents the quibbling from becoming wearisome, and introduces Pompey, whose coarser humour tightens what would otherwise have been a slack scene.

Once we have noted that alternative and cancelled passages could find their way into Shakespeare's printed texts, it is natural to ask whether we have identified all of them. Must the evidence always be equally clear-cut? Is it conceivable that we print, and perform in the theatre, episodes or scenes that Shakespeare thought of as superseded? Take

(1) the two reports of the death of Portia in *Julius Caesar* –
     (a) IV.3.141–56, 164;
     (b) IV.3.179–93

– a much-discussed problem. T. S. Dorsch, the New Arden editor, agreed with 'most recent editors' that (b) was written first, and 'was not clearly cancelled in the MS.' when Shakespeare substituted (a); he added that a minority thinks 'that Shakespeare intended both passages announcing Portia's death to stand'. Before we try to decide for ourselves, let us glance at two other connected passages in the same play.

(2) There is no terror, Cassius, in your threats;
     For I am arm'd so strong in honesty
     That they pass by me as the idle wind
     Which I respect not. I did send to you
     For certain sums of gold, which you denied me;   70
     For I can raise no money by vile means.
     By heaven, I had rather coin my heart,
     And drop my blood for drachmas, than to wring
     From the hard hands of peasants their vile trash
     By any indirection. I did send   75
     To you for gold to pay my legions,
     Which you denied me . . . .
                                                    (IV.3.66)

'I did send . . . indirection' (69–75) could be a cancelled passage
(a), superseded by (b), 'I did send . . .' (75ff.).

(3) Asked by Cassius what he will do if they lose the battle, Brutus
makes two seemingly inconsistent statements.

(a) Just as he blamed Cato for committing suicide, Brutus will arm
   himself with patience.

> I do find it cowardly and vile,
> For fear of what might fall, so to prevent
> The time of life . . . .
>
> (V.1.103)

(b) Cassius asks his question again, and now Brutus answers quite
   differently:

> You are contented to be led in triumph
> Thorough the streets of Rome?
> BRUTUS. No, Cassius, no. Think not, thou noble Roman,
> That ever Brutus will go bound to Rome;
> He bears too great a mind.
>
> (108)

Dorsch thought that there is 'only a partial inconsistency. The
views of Brutus the philosopher conflict with those of Brutus the
Roman soldier facing the possibility of capture and degradation.'
Dorsch knew, of course, that Plutarch distinguished between
Brutus' *former* opinion and his *present* one ('being now in the midst
of danger, I am of a contrary mind'[30]); Shakespeare's Brutus, quite
differently, appears to hold contrary views at the same time, and
that is more puzzling.

In all three instances, an editor who retains (a) and (b) makes
Brutus more short-sighted, or more muddled, than one who
chooses between (a) and (b). If (1b) is not cancelled, Brutus gives
a performance of stoicism that may impress Messala, but overlooks
the fact that Cassius must be aware of it (from 1a) as a performance.
If (2a) is retained, Brutus overlooks that, since Cassius raised
money by vile means, it is grotesque to ask him for money, and
proclaim 'I can raise no money by vile means'. And, if (3a) remains,

the determination not to commit suicide conflicts with the known facts of Brutus' end, which is about to be presented. In each of the three, Brutus appears to contradict himself, and to be unaware that Cassius must notice it, if the (a) and (b) passages are both allowed to stand. That may have been Shakespeare's intention, continuing Brutus' earlier errors of judgement; on the other hand, this very point had been forcefully made already, and it could be argued that a tragic hero might lose the audience's sympathy if he seems both too rigid and too muddled in his thinking in the final scenes. Two views of Brutus are at stake, and also two hypotheses about the manuscript from which the Folio text was printed. For if deletions in the manuscript were not clearly marked, as I suspect, every possible 'alternative passage' in a play-text increases the likelihood that others in the same text have been preserved accidentally.

To proceed from the likely to the even more likely, let us consider a puzzle at the end of *Timon of Athens*. Timon's epitaph does not make sense as it stands:

> 'Here lies a wretched corse, of wretched soul bereft;
> Seek not my name. A plague consume you wicked caitiffs left!
> Here lie I, Timon, who alive all living men did hate.
> Pass by, and curse thy fill; but pass, and stay not here thy
>   gait.'
>
> (V.4.70)

The New Arden editor explains that 'there seems little doubt that Shakespeare copied down from North's *Plutarch two* epitaphs, each in a couplet, meaning to omit one or the other . . . on revision. As it is, they contradict each other ("Seek not my name", "Here lie I, Timon").'

No one will deny that 'alternative passages' survive in Shakespeare's printed texts, although argument may continue about individual instances. The paired passages that I have quoted share certain common characteristics: both passages go over the same ground and yet contradict each other, or one omits a detail that conflicts with other parts of the play; or they begin with the same words, as if the author meant to cancel the intervening lines and start again. Why, though, assume that 'alternative passages' will always cover roughly the same ground? Is it not conceivable that a dramatist – even a Shakespeare – might feel dissatisfied with what he has written, and substitute something entirely different? Such passages will be more difficult to detect; scenes and speeches that are normally cut in the theatre may well belong to this category – cancelled passages that were printed by mistake.

General misgivings about the 'unblotted papers', and about the unproven but wide-spread assumption of Shakespeare's 'sequential writing', lead on to other, quite fundamental questions that have not been asked. For instance, if Shakespeare, like other dramatists, composed some scenes out of sequence, might he not find a use for earlier, independently written material in some of his plays? Chaucer seems to have reused earlier work in *The Canterbury Tales*, Wordsworth inserted existing poems (e.g. 'The Simplon Pass') in *The Prelude*, T. S. Eliot did so in *The Waste Land*. Perhaps no one has considered this possibility with regard to Shakespeare because of the myth of the 'unblotted papers'. Yet another supposedly fluent dramatist, Oscar Wilde, reused the same epigrams in different texts, and Shakespeare seems to have inserted previously known songs in his plays, so why not speeches, or bits of speeches, left-overs from unprinted or abandoned works? Ferdinand's sonnet in *Love's Labour's Lost* (IV.3.22ff.) could be any lover's complaint, and may be such a left-over. To take a more deliberately provocative example, is it not curious that Hamlet talks of 'The undiscover'd country, from whose bourn / No traveller returns' (III.1.79) in one of the very rare plays in which someone actually claims to have come from that undiscovered country?

> I am thy father's spirit,
> Doom'd for a certain term to walk the night,
> And for the day confin'd to fast in fires . . . .
> (I.5.9)

It could be dismissed as a typical oversight, were it not for other oddities. All of Hamlet's major soliloquies except 'To be or not to be' (where he speaks of 'The undiscover'd country . . .') refer directly to the events of the play: 'or ere those shoes were old / With which she follow'd my poor father's body'; 'O most pernicious woman'; 'This is most brave, / That I, the son of a dear father murder'd'; 'I will speak daggers to her, but use none'; 'A villain kills my father; and, for that, / I, his sole son . . .'; 'How stand I, then, / That have a father kill'd, a mother stain'd . . . .' Only 'To be or not to be' debates general questions, and fails to mention

Hamlet's parents and his immediate, personal situation (though that may be touched on in the concluding lines, 'Thus conscience does make cowards of us all . . .'), and this is the soliloquy that 'overlooks' that a ghost has recently returned from 'The undiscover'd country'. Moreover, until its closing lines, 'Nymph, in thy orisons . . .', this soliloquy ignores Christianity and its certainties and instead seems to consider 'outrageous fortune' as the presiding power. Remembering that an earlier, lost version of *Hamlet* was ridiculed as excessively Senecan, and may have been written by Shakespeare himself;[31] also, that Seneca, a pagan philosopher, blamed Fortune for many of man's calamities – one asks whether 'To be or not to be' could be a hang-over from the lost *Hamlet*, in general argument if not in expression, or could have originated elsewhere. I have suggested that the Player's speech (II.2.446ff.) looks like a transplant from another play (cf. p. 124) – might 'To be or not to be', so strangely incongruous, turn out to be another? We think of it as quintessential Hamlet, but could one not imagine almost anyone making this impersonal speech? Is that not, perhaps, one of the secrets of its popularity? I do not wish to press a point that cannot be proved, and raise it only to show that questioning the traditional notion of 'unblotted papers' may force us to think again about significant interpretative problems – the character of Brutus or Hamlet's most famous soliloquy.

Having already touched on 'alternative passages' in Shakespeare, we can now proceed to the larger issue of authorial revision. First, though, we must rid ourselves of an inherited prejudice, the assumption that every author finalises his own text. For if authors fall into two classes – those who, like Chaucer, curse a copyist who does not 'write true' and those who, like Wordsworth, tell a friend 'you would greatly oblige me by looking over the enclosed poems and correcting any thing you find amiss in the punctuation'[32] – then Shakespeare very definitely belongs with Wordsworth. Even if he cursed whoever might move his bones, he was altogether more easy-going concerning his plays – an attitude that the modern literary critic, and some editors, find hard to accept. They see Shakespeare as a classic; they think of his texts not as foul papers and prompt-books but as Holy Writ, delivered in tablets of stone. We know that many authors feel free to change words or phrases in copying out their own work, and there are many signs that quick-thinking Shakespeare introduced afterthoughts in his plays, and did not regard them as finalised for ever. High-quality variants provide one kind of evidence, as in these examples from *Troilus and Cressida*.

1   tis madde Idolatry
      To make the seruice greater then the God,
      And the will dotes that is *attributiue*;
      To what infectiously it selfe affects, ...
                    (II.2.56, Q; *inclineable* F)

Would a copyist or compositor invent one of these out-of-the-way words, both 'hard readings' yet both acceptable in the context? (The New Shakespeare gloss explains that 'Q. = prepared to pay tribute to, F. = prepared to bow down to'.)

2 Speake then *thou vnsalted* leauen, speake, I will beate thee
   into hansomnesse. (II.1.14–15, Q; *you whinid'st* F)

Neither reading looks like a misreading of the other, or a copyist's unconscious substitution. ('Whinid'st' = vinnied'st, i.e. mouldiest.)
   Apart from 'high-quality variants', Elizabethan dramatists probably introduced many 'indifferent variants' when they copied out their plays (that is, alternative readings that are neither markedly better nor worse: synonyms, singulars for plurals, tense changes, etc.). Two autograph texts of Middleton's *A Game at Chess* may illustrate.

1 (a) Hold *Monster-Impudence*, wouldst *heape* a murder, on thy
       first fowle *attempt*, tis time that thou *wert* taken; . . . .

  (b) hold, *bloudie Villayne*, wouldst *thou heape* a murder on thy
       first fowle *offence*, tis time that thou *art* taken; . . . .

2 (a) this of all others beares the *hiddest* Venom the *smoothest*
       poyson, – *I am* an Arch-Dissembler Sr, . . . the time is yet
       to come that ere I *spake* what my heart mean't!

  (b) this of all others beares the *hiddenst* Venom the *Secretst*
       poyson; *Im'e* an Archdissembler (Sir) . . . the time is yet
       to come that e're I *spoke* what my heart mean't![33]

Whenever there are signs that Shakespeare copied out his play –

for instance, the 'high-quality' variants in *Troilus and Cressida* – we may take it that many of the hundreds of indifferent variants in the same two texts betoken authorial afterthoughts as well. Not always self-evident improvements, but, if nothing more, guarantees that Shakespeare did not think of his plays as finished and unimprovable.

Shakespeare's willingness to tinker with his plays may even be confirmed by the 'bad quartos', which could easily transmit afterthoughts that found their way into the prompt-book.

> *Fal.* I will not lend thee a penny.
> *Pist. Why then the world's mine Oyster, which I, with sword will open.*   (*Merry Wives*, II.2.1, F)

> *Fal.* Ile not lend thee a peny.
> *Pis. I will retort the sum in equipage.*   (Q)

Does the Quarto give us a reporter's botching, or the true voice of Pistol? Compare also, in *Henry V*, I.2.146ff.

> For you shall reade, that my great Grandfather
> Neuer *went with his forces into France*
> But that the Scot, on his vnfurnisht Kingdome,
> Came pouring like the Tyde into a breach, ...
>   (F)

> For you shall read, neuer my great grandfather
> *Vnmaskt his power for France,* . . . .
>   (Q)

The bad Quarto has a short line which, however, contains a wonderfully suggestive image in a scene where Henry himself unmasks his power ('The strawberry grows underneath the nettle', I.1.60). Moreover, Shakespeare experimented with the 'un' prefix in many clever ways, and coined dozens of new words with it – 'unbosom', 'unbuild', 'unclew', 'unsex me here', 'Unshout the noise that banish'd Marcius' – so the new idea that a king unmasks *his army* for France seems Shakespearian in conception and expression.

Most of the examples of revision that I have given so far have been purely local, single words or lines or short passages being replaced by others, with few knock-on effects. The changed titles in *Love's Labour's Lost* (King–Duke, Queen–Princess), and the deletion of some of Brutus's high-toned passages in *Julius Caesar*, cannot be called merely local – so how far might Shakespearian revision go? Of late, the revision of *King Lear* has become a battle-ground, one view being that the Quarto and Folio represent two different versions of the play. 'The apparent motive for many of the major Folio changes from the Quarto text is to strengthen the structure of act IV. . . . The Folio has done this by cutting superfluities . . . and strengthening the narrative line, largely by accelerating and clarifying the movement toward war.' Several of the Folio's changes are related to one issue, who leads the army against Goneril and Regan. In the Quarto there are many references to a French invasion, whereas the Folio changes the emphasis, 'systematically removing verbal and visual reminders of the French presence, so that Cordelia seems to lead not an invasion but a rebellion'. Gary Taylor's article 'The war in *King Lear*', one of many like-minded books and articles published in 1978 and thereafter, contended that Shakespeare restructured a group of scenes in the Folio version.[34] Is there any supporting evidence for revision on this larger scale? The question is important because the arguments for Shakespeare's revision of *King Lear* are not all equally convincing, and should some turn out to be unsound it may be thought that the rest are tainted by association. That does not seem to me to follow; nevertheless, other examples of more than merely local revision would reinforce the case for a revised *King Lear*.

Even before 1978 a similar revision-theory had been proposed for *Othello*, instead of the traditional view that the Quarto and Folio texts derive from a single parent text. Nevill Coghill observed that many of the passages added to the Folio text of *Othello* have serial connections, precisely what was later claimed for the 'war' passages in *King Lear*. In one series

> it is the character of Emilia that receives the fullest benefit, though others profit as well. It is as if Shakespeare had set himself methodically to strengthen her part at the four key-points we have considered; his purpose seems to have been to *endear* her to the audience: it is as if he had sensed that Emilia's guilt in the matter of the handkerchief had been insufficiently wiped out in the eyes of her critics.[35]

Previously such *Othello* passages had been considered Quarto cuts, rather than authorial additions in the Folio; Coghill replied that all of these 'cuts' would have saved a mere eight minutes of playing-time, out of two and three-quarter hours. And not only would it have been ludicrous to snip out lines in threes and fours, the laborious procedure taken for granted by others; Coghill showed that the fashionable theory of 'cuts' in effect postulated someone who consistently misunderstood the needs of the play. 'Nothing', said Coghill, 'entitles us to assume stupid cutting, still less destructive cutting, except a blind reliance on the supposed axiom that Shakespeare never revised his work.'

Revision on this larger scale, not necessarily by the author, was certainly not unknown in the Elizabethan period, as in the case of *The Spanish Tragedy* and other plays performed or published with 'additions' (e.g. *Dr Faustus*). Moreover, all 'cutting' of a text involved revision, no less than 'additions', in so far as a different emphasis is given to a theme or motive, or to the whole play. Who can doubt that the cutting of most of Act IV scene 4 of *Hamlet* had a significant effect? The Folio omitted IV.4.9–66, including the whole of Hamlet's soliloquy 'How all occasions do inform against me, / And spur my dull revenge. . . .' Even if Hamlet's 'delay' remains visible elsewhere, the removal of 'How all occasions' makes his delay far less prominent.

Harold Jenkins, who is properly cautious about revision-theories that cannot be proved, accepted one lengthy passage as an addition to *Hamlet*:

> It is not hard to envisage as an interpolation the whole passage about the players and their misfortunes, from the query 'What players are they?' to the announcement of their arrival (II.2.324–64). Their arrival is what matters to the play and it needs no explanation. That a passage of topical interest should be inserted in a play and when no longer topical removed is not inherently unlikely.[36]

Philip Edwards found more wide-spread revision in the same play.[37] The removal or insertion of several long passages must affect the character of a play; and, though only some of the evidence has survived, it is clear that shortened versions of many plays existed, and involved some restructuring. The bad Quarto of *Henry V*, according to Greg, 'is certainly an abridgement, in which, for example, the whole of I.1 and many later passages are suppressed';

Chorus disappears, and Bourbon replaces the Dauphin in the Agincourt-scenes. The bad Quarto of *The Merry Wives of Windsor* 'is also a deliberately shortened text', even though 'whoever prepared it evidently knew the full text'. Only one version of *Macbeth* has survived, and 'it is almost certain,' said Greg, 'that the text as we have it has undergone at least some cutting. It has, for instance, many short lines. . . . There are also some inconsistencies in the action which suggest that we have not got the whole story.'[38]

Arguing for the interpolation of II.2.324–64 in *Hamlet*, Harold Jenkins noted that 'one might not have supposed that an addition to a play already in performance would attach itself to the author's foul papers from which we believe Q2 to have been printed'.[39] This point has far-reaching implications. It is often assumed that printed texts based on foul papers or a prompt-book transmit the 'finalised' foul papers or prompt-book – that is, the play as Shakespeare first wrote it, or a fair copy then prepared for the stage, nothing added, nothing taken away. We have seen, however, that the printed texts sometimes included cancelled passages as well as later insertions, and that at least two acting versions may have existed of some plays. It would be more useful to think of the printed texts as transmitting 'full' – rather than 'finalised' – foul papers or prompt books, in so far as they often printed *everything* in the relevant manuscript; and the 'full' text seems to have included passages that were never or only rarely performed.

Here we must keep in mind the fact that Elizabethan actors performed on many different stages, and had to improvise accordingly. Even before they acquired the Globe and Blackfriars theatres, quite unlike each other in size and structure, Shakespeare's colleagues performed in different London theatres, at court, in inn-yards, in private houses; when on tour, they might have to perform on several different stages in a week. On tour, again, fewer actors would be available, and this enforced some 'doubling' or the dropping or amalgamation of some small parts. Is it likely that,in such ever-changing circumstances, the literary text of a play remained inviolate? 'That any play should have been twice and differently cut for representation', said Greg, 'is hard to believe.'[40] Even harder to believe is the notion that very long plays – some were considerably longer than the average 2000 lines, *Hamlet* being around 4000 lines – would always be performed in the full 'prompt-book version'. The Folio text of *Hamlet*, said Harold Jenkins, 'while manifestly having undergone some preparation for the stage, itself contains more than can be supposed to have been regularly played at the Globe.'[41] Some so-called 'prompt-book' texts are more likely to have been either 'intermediate manuscripts' annotated for production, already marking some but not all cuts, or 'full' prompt-books, incorporating more text than would normally be performed. The reported text of the First Quarto of *Hamlet*, most interestingly, follows some of the Folio's 'prompt-book' cuts, yet these two shortened versions also shortened in different ways.

> Q1 evidently derives from the already shortened version represented in F, which it often concurs with in variant readings and for the most part follows in cuts (though of two of the passages cut from F it shows some recollection). But Q1 makes many more omissions of its own, notably including: the first part of the King's first speech (I.2.1–25) . . . over twenty lines from the Pyrrhus speech (II.2.470–93) . . . all but the first two and the last four lines of the long speech of the Player King (III.2.183–206); the King's dialogue with Rosencrantz and Guildenstern (III.3.1–26) . . . the King's tête-à-tête with Laertes (IV.7.1–35) . . . an account of the gentleman from Normandy (IV.7.75–99). . . . Some, perhaps most, of these, like the clean cut in the Player King's speech, must have been deliberate excisions. Stage abridgement may have been progressive . . . .[42]

Such cutting involved a 'restructuring' of the play, even if not one as radical as has been suggested for *King Lear*. In the case of *Hamlet*, the restructuring occurred in two or more stages, not to mention the probable interpolation of II.2.324–64.

Hamlet itself lends some support to the hypothesis of an 'unfinalised' prompt-book. 'You could, for a need, study a speech of some dozen or sixteen lines which I would set down and insert in't, could you not?' (II.2.534) What is the Player's reply? Not 'Heaven forbid! We never depart from our prompt-book!' No: he readily agrees. And when the clowns are told to 'speak no more than is set down for them' (III.2.37), this implies that clowns sometimes did otherwise. Elizabethan plays must have expanded and contracted much more in performance than their modern counterparts.

An epistle from the stationer to the readers in Beaumont and Fletcher's *Comedies and Tragedies* (1647) provides contemporary evidence for 'full' texts, and for different kinds of abridgement in performance; and this epistle, of course, refers to the practices of Shakespeare's own company, in his lifetime and shortly thereafter.

> When these comedies and tragedies were presented on the stage, the actors omitted some scenes and passages, with the authors' consent, as occasion led them; and when private friends desired a copy they then, and justly too, transcribed what they acted: but now you have both all that was acted, and all that was not; even the perfect full originals, without the least mutilation.

If, as the evidence suggests, Shakespeare's plays were sometimes revised, we need not suppose that he himself was always responsible. Would he have inserted 'the other three Witches' in *Macbeth* (IV.1), and some of the play's other incongruities? The mangling of *Macbeth* may date from a time when the author could not be contacted, but what of revisions made in earlier years, when he undoubtedly enjoyed a pre-eminent place in his own company? Why should anyone else be asked to undertake even the simplest form of revision – cutting – if the author was available? Would he not wish to cut his own work, or to be consulted (as Beaumont and Fletcher were), to ensure that 'some necessary question of the play' (*Hamlet*, III.2.40) did not suffer as a consequence? Even 'bad Quartos', if they transmit a shortened text written down or performed by actors in Shakespeare's own company, probably represent an 'official' shortened version, however corrupt their dialogue.

The simplest form of cutting would be to omit whole scenes. Shakespeare's plays were not normally shortened in this high-handed way but more thoughtfully, by the removal of blocks of twenty or so of the least indispensable lines (as in the first Quarto of *Hamlet*: see p. 216), or even quite painstakingly, removing a few lines or half lines, leaving the metre and sense more or less intact. Dover Wilson admired the skilful amputation of some lines from *Hamlet*; for example, in a passage perhaps written too quickly in Act III scene 4 (second Quarto; Folio cuts in italics).

Assume a vertue if you haue it not,   160
That monster custome, who all sence doth eate
Of habits deuill, is angell yet in this
That to the vse of actions faire and good,

> *He likewise giues a frock or Liuery*
> *That aptly is put on* refraine to night,   165
> And that shall lend a kind of easines
> To the next abstinence, *the next more easie:*
> *For vse almost can change the stamp of nature,*
> *And either the deuill, or throwe him out*
> With *wonderous potency*: once more good night, ...   170

Although 'refraine to night' hangs loose in the Folio, 'we cannot help being struck with the delicacy and skill of the operation', said Dover Wilson. 'It was no careless reader, or thoughtless hand, which went out of its way to spare those middle portions; it would have been so easy just to run a pen through the whole thing. . . . Shakespeare himself could hardly have pruned his own verse more tenderly.'[43]

Shakespeare himself might have pruned his own verse – and, for that matter, might have added to an existing speech when he rewrote or revised a play. I am reminded of Dover Wilson's explanation of *A Midsummer Night's Dream*, V.1.2ff., where the Quarto's mislineation reveals the author's afterthoughts, a grafting operation even more skilful than the excisions from *Hamlet*. W. W. Greg, usually so cautious about Dover Wilson's theories, found this one irresistible.

A brilliant contribution [said Greg] was his demonstration of revision at the beginning of Act V. Here in the first 84 lines there are eight passages of varying length in which the line-division is disturbed. Omit these passages and a perfectly consecutive text remains. There is no escaping the conclusion that in this we have the original writing, which was supplemented by fresh lines crowded into the margin so that their metrical structure was obscured.

> *The.* More straunge then true. I neuer may beleeue
>   These antique fables, nor these Fairy toyes.
>   Louers, and mad men haue such seething braines,
>   *Such shaping phantasies, that apprehend / more,*
>   *Then coole reason euer comprehends. / The lunatick,*
>   *The louer, and the Poet / are of imagination all compact.*
>   One sees more diuels, then vast hell can holde:
>   That is the mad man. The louer, all as frantick,

Sees Helens beauty in a brow of Ægypt,
The Poets eye, in a fine frenzy, rolling, / doth glance
From heauen to earth, from earth to heauen. / And as
Imagination bodies forth / the formes of things
Vnknowne: the Poets penne / turnes them to shapes,
And giues to ayery nothing, / a locall habitation,
And a name. / Such trickes hath strong imagination,
That if it would but apprehend some ioy, ...
    [*A Midsummer Night's Dream*, V.1.2.ff., Q; italicised
    passages are thought to be marginal insertions in text;
    sloping bars indicate correct line-endings][44]

Sometimes we marvel at the genius of the person responsible for such interpolations, very like the skill of the person responsible for obviously sensitive cuts: we get more or less seamless stitching either way. At other times editors ask us to believe, as Nevill Coghill has said of *Othello* (see p. 214), that an insensitive person was given the task of shortening one of Shakespeare's greatest plays, someone guilty of stupid or destructive cutting. And why? Because these editors distrust the hypothesis of skilful authorial interpolation. Let us explore these alternatives – the genius or another – by comparing two forms of a famous passage in *King Lear*. It is verse misprinted as prose in both the Quarto and Folio; I quote from a modernised text, which arranges it as verse, and italicise about five lines found only in the Folio. With or without these five lines the continuity is perfect.

Through tatter'd clothes small vices do appear;
Robes and furr'd gowns hide all. *Plate sin with gold,*
And the strong lance of justice hurtless breaks;
Arm it in rags, a pigmy's straw does pierce it.
None does offend, none – I say none; I'll able 'em.
Take that of me, my friend, who have the power
To seal th'accuser's lips. Get thee glass eyes,
And, like a scurvy politician, seem
To see the things thou dost not. Now, now, now, now!
                    (IV.6.164)

The shorter (Quarto) version makes good sense, and scans. Is it possible, then, that Shakespeare *added* 'Plate sin with gold . . . '? Added an interpolation in mid-speech? Why take the trouble to do something so complicated? On the other hand, supposing 'Plate sin with gold . . . ' stood in the original version, what would be gained by deleting these magnificent lines? An accidental omission is most unlikely in this case, because 'Plate sin with gold . . . ' begins and ends in mid-line, so we have to choose between the genius and someone indifferent to Shakespeare's best poetry. And why not the genius, if we accept that Shakespeare added lines in mid-speech to *A Midsummer Night's Dream*?

Twenty years ago such a question would have been dismissed as preposterous. The new work on Shakespeare as a reviser has changed the climate of opinion and obliges us to look more carefully at such alternative passages, more especially when they occur in texts with 'serially connected' changes. I think that this is a healthy development. We must not forget, however, that the very texts that seem to transmit the first, unrevised version of a play are sometimes undeniably disfigured by accidental omissions or substitutions which, restored or corrected in the second version, may there look like 'revisions'. How can we distinguish between error in the Quarto *King Lear* and revision in the Folio? To be honest, many variant passages leave us guessing, taken on their own; yet when there are signs of skilful grafting elsewhere in one text, or of 'serially connected' changes, we must assume that other variant passages in the same text, even if not self-evident improvements, come from one and the same hand.

The debate about Shakespeare's 'rewriting' has entered a new phase, and will continue in the foreseeable future. I conclude with two observations, which show how far we have travelled from the notion of 'unblotted papers'. First: all that we have learned about Shakespeare's fluidity of mind as a writer must affect our thinking about him as a reviser. From first conception and throughout the process of writing, a play went on growing in his mind; if he copied out a second text, or prepared a shortened version, or planned a new production, this no doubt refired his creative energies. The fluidity of his mind matched the fluidity of theatrical performance, ever adjustable, and of the play itself as he himself and his contemporaries must have seen it. Second: since most of Shakespeare's plays have reached us, in effect, in only one text – several Folio texts being mere reprints, without independent authority – is it not significant that so many of the remaining plays appear to have been revised or restructured? Each one of the four great tragedies – *Hamlet, Othello, King Lear, Macbeth* – shows signs of revision of one kind or another. It follows, I think, that some 'single-text' plays will have been revised as well, even though we cannot prove it because the evidence, so often provided by a second text, has disappeared.

To sum up, the 'unblotted papers' view of Shakespeare supposes, at one extreme, that he 'composed fluently and seldom went back over what he had written', and that when he delivered a play to his colleagues that was the end of it, as far as he was concerned – he left it behind, he moved on to other things. The alternative proposes a myriad-minded dramatist who remained creatively engaged with every one of his plays, apart from the few that were never revived, until he retired from the theatre.

12

Shakespeare on his deathbed: the last will and testament

> In the name of God amen I William Shakespeare of Stratford upon Avon in the county of Warwick gentleman in perfect health and memory God be praised do make and ordain this my last will and testament in manner and form following. That is to say first I commend my soul into the hands of God my creator, hoping and assuredly believing through the only merits of Jesus Christ my Saviour to be made partaker of life everlasting, and my body to the earth whereof it is made.

With these words Shakespeare began his will, shortly before his death in 1616, bequeathing to the world a statement of his assets and naming several of his closest friends. The will appears to adopt the impersonal jargon of lawyers and thus, despite the famous 'second-best bed,' to conceal rather than reveal the testator. I want to compare the will with others of the same period and to suggest that Shakespeare's failure to observe some testamentary conventions makes his a most unusual document, one that gives us unexpected insights into his personality and even into his relationship with his wife, Anne Hathaway.

Placing Shakespeare's will in the cultural traditions of its period, we must compare it not only with London and Stratford wills but, more specifically, with those made by testators belonging to the same social class. After the preamble of a gentleman's will there were often directions for the funeral. John Heminge said, 'And my body I commit to the earth to be buried in Christian manner in the parish church of Mary Aldermanbury in London,' and he requested 'that my funeral may be in decent and comely manner performed in the evening, without any vain pomp or cost.' Shakespeare commended his soul to God 'And my body to the earth whereof it is made.' In itself this abruptness might have little significance – yet it needs to be seen in a larger context. A gentleman at this time would often leave a sum for the repair of his parish church, another sum for a funeral sermon or an annual sermon, and now and then for a monument – not for all but for some of these 'social obligations'. Shakespeare's colleague Thomas Pope left directions in 1603 for his funeral in the parish church and 'towards the setting up of some monument on me in the said church and my funeral £20'. Another colleague, Augustine Phillips, asked in 1605 to be buried in the chancel of the parish church and gave 'to the preacher which shall preach at my funeral . . . twenty shillings'. Shakespeare left no such bequests and this may indicate a lack of interest, or even disaffection. The haste with which his will was prepared cannot be wholly blamed for such omissions since he found time to add other small bequests, which were interlined. Moreover, he did give a generous sum to the poor of Stratford: 'Item, I give and bequeath unto the poor of Stratford aforesaid ten pounds.' Some testators asked their churchwardens to distribute such alms. Shakespeare did not – is that significant? He remembered only one godchild in his will – is that significant? Taken singly these points attract no attention; taken together they are a puzzle. Compare John Combe of Old Stratford, gentleman, who directed in 1612, 'Item, I give and bequeath to every one of my godchildren before not named five shillings apiece.' Combe also asked to be buried in the parish church, left £60 for a tomb, and twenty shillings a year for ever 'to make a sermon twice a year – evidently a more committed son of the church than W. Shakespeare.[1]

Before I try to explain other curious omissions it will be helpful to remind you of the story of Judith Shakespeare's marriage and its effect on her father's will. E. K. Chambers, though he did not know all the facts, guessed correctly, and I follow his narrative. Shakespeare probably first gave instructions for a will in January 1616; a draft was prepared by his lawyer, Francis Collins, consisting of three sheets. On 25 March Shakespeare decided to change his will – 'The changes he desired in the opening provisions were so substantial that it was thought best to prepare a new sheet 1.' Sheets 2 and 3 'were allowed to stand, with some alterations; and in this form it was signed on each sheet by Shakespeare'. Sheet 1 is 'mainly occupied with bequests to Shakespeare's daughter Judith', so 'it is reasonable to suppose that it was her marriage on 10 February 1616 which determined the principal changes'.[2] A lack of confidence in Thomas Quiney, Judith's husband, could explain these changes, thought Chambers – and a later discovery proved him to be correct.

Others have shown that Shakespeare had cause to mistrust his new son-in-law,[3] for Thomas Quiney was forced to appear in open court in the parish church and confess to 'carnal copulation' with one Margaret Wheeler. That was to be on 26 March; one day earlier, on the twenty-fifth, Shakespeare sent for Collins and had his will redrafted to protect his daughter – in effect to ensure that Quiney received none of his money, except under stringent conditions.

Other wills survive in which a member of the family is sharply rapped on the knuckles, most often a son-in-law, as in Shakespeare's case. Elizabeth Condell, the widow of Shakespeare's colleague, said of one bequest 'yet so I do intend the same as that my said son-in-law Mr Herbert Finch shall never have possession of the same; and therefore my will is that my said executors shall keep those goods in their hands for the good of my . . . grandchildren . . . unless my said son-in-law . . . shall first give good security'. Jacob Meade, who had an interest in the Hope theatre, asked his executors to retain a sum for his daughter – 'the principal to remain unto and for the only use and behoof of my said daughter, so long as it shall please almighty God that she shall live with her husband Michael Pyttes, whom I will shall have nothing to do or meddle therewith'. Shakespeare's unloved son-in-law was put in his place even more humiliatingly. He was not mentioned by name, his very existence was not acknow-ledged, even though the most carefully hedged clauses of the will were clearly devised in response to his unwelcome arrival in the bosom of the family. The thought is not unlike that of Elizabeth Condell and Jacob Meade, but notice the curious phrasing. Daughter Judith was to have £150, and another £150 after three years 'if she or any issue of her body be living at the end of three years. . . . Provided that if such husband as she shall at the end of the said three years be married unto or attain after do sufficiently assure unto her . . . lands answerable to the portion by this my will given . . . then my will is that the said £150 shall be paid to such husband as shall make such assurance to his own use.' Such husband? Who could be responsible for this phrasing, just six weeks after Judith Shakespeare married her first husband, Thomas Quiney?

The treatment of Quiney resembles that of another member of the family by marriage – William Hart, the husband of Shakespeare's only surviving sibling, his sister, Joan Hart. I think that it is fair to say that Joan Hart's future prospects worried her brother, almost as much as Judith Quiney's. Her husband was an obscure hatter and, it seems, a poor relation, for Shakespeare left his sister a life-tenancy of his house in Henley Street 'wherein she dwelleth,' for the peppercorn rent of one shilling a year, and also twenty pounds, 'all my wearing apparel,' and five pounds to each of her three sons. William Hart died a few days before Shakespeare, in mid-April, a fact that could not have been known when Shakespeare revised his will three weeks earlier; therefore, the absence of any reference to Hart seems odd, the more so since his sons were too young to wear their uncle's apparel. But we must not overlook an indirect reference to Hart. A provisional bequest to Joan Hart of fifty pounds, should Judith Quiney not live for three years, was to remain in the hands of Shakespeare's executors, who were to pay interest to Joan, 'and after her decease the said £50 shall remain amongst the children of my said sister' – in other words, it was not to go to her husband. The various bequests to the four other members of Hart's immediate family imply that Shakespeare neither loved nor trusted his brother-in-law.

Elizabeth Condell and Jacob Meade named the sons-in-law who had displeased them. Shakespeare's will carefully avoids naming Thomas Quiney and William Hart, and names omitted, for one reason or another, seem to me a peculiarity of his will as a whole. Bequests to several friends were interlined, and therefore were afterthoughts: for instance, those to Hamlet Sadler, William Reynolds, and to 'my fellows John Heminge, Richard Burbage and Henry Condell.' More astonishingly, there was not a single reference to the testator's wife in the will as first completed. Had it occurred to Shakespeare before the draft was completed that he ought to remember his friends and his wife, he could have added more clauses at a later point in the will: instead they were inserted awkwardly, and none too legibly, between lines that were already written.

I shall return to Anne Hathaway in a moment, but first, some other 'omissions' from the will. Shakespeare, the owner of one of the largest houses in Stratford, must have kept servants. A gentleman usually remembered his servants in his will – individual bequests to some and very often a year's wages for all the rest. 'Item, I give . . . unto those my servants whose names are expressed and declared in the schedule to this my will . . . the several sums to their names written,' said William Combe of Warwick. Shakespeare left nothing to his servants. Leading actors left bequests to each other and also, in some cases, to the hired men of the company and to their apprentices; Shakespeare left bequests to just three 'fellows', as an afterthought, a smaller number than one might have expected, and nothing at all to hired men or former apprentices, after at least 22 years with, basically, the same company.

Another fairly common practice at this time was to forgive all debts in one's will, or at least small debts, or the debts of impecunious friends or relations. John Combe of Old Stratford, the 'noted usurer' who bequeathed five pounds 'to Master William Shakespeare,' had his own way of forgiving debts – fractionally forgiving them, perhaps inspired by professional instinct. 'Item, I give and bequeath to every one of my good and just debtors for every twenty pound that any man oweth me twenty shillings.' Shakespeare, who *may* have been a money-lender and certainly took others to law to recover debts, forgave no debts in his will.

Compared with other testators from the same social class it may appear that William Shakespeare was totally self-centred and shockingly tight-fisted. Before we jump to conclusions I want to mention another omission, for which I blame not the testator but his lawyer. A wise lawyer made sure that the will he helped to prepare would stand scrutiny in a court of law. If there were deletions in a will it was prudent to certify their authenticity, as on the verso of Samuel Rowley's will (1624): 'Memorandum that these words, "and said lease in Plough Alley" interlined between the 11th and 12th lines within written [i.e., in the will, not quoted here], were interlined before the ensealing and delivery hereof' – with the names of four witnesses. Any insertion or deletion in a will could cause trouble. No one took the precaution of authenticating all the changes in Shakespeare's will, a more heavily revised will than any I have seen. More extraordinary still, the date at the beginning was interlined above an almost illegible deletion, without being validated by witnesses, although a changed date could have become a vital issue had the will been contested.

I think that we are driven to two conclusions, one old and one new.[4] The old one is that the testator was a very sick man, thought to be on his deathbed, hence the messiness of the will, only one page of which was rewritten (a most unusual procedure); hence the fact that his seal could not be found. (The will ends, 'In witness whereof I have hereunto put my seal,' then 'seal' was crossed out and 'hand' substituted.) In short, the will was a draft from which a fair copy was to have been made, had there been time – and, just in case time might run out, the testator and five witnesses there and then added their signatures. We happen to know that Shakespeare lived another month: I assume that after 25 March he was in no condition to sign his name again, and that this was the reason why the draft had to serve as his 'original will,' the definitive document.

My second conclusion, in which I depart from Chambers and other authorities, is that I see all the unusual features of the will as evidence that the testator himself, and not his lawyer, was largely responsible for its wording and structure. One suspects that it was the shock of hearing the news about Thomas Quiney and his misdemeanors that triggered off the rewriting of the will, and, quite possibly, Shakespeare's final illness as well. The testator's first priority on 25 March was to sort out his financial relationship with his new son-in-law – nothing else mattered so much to him. He was not in a forgiving mood, and he may have been too ill for his advisers to wish to nudge him to do whatever else was customary – for the church, for his servants, for debtors, and for other unremembered friends.

Now, back to Anne Hathaway. 'Item, I give unto my wife my second-best bed with the furniture' – interlined, evidently an afterthought. Beds figure more prominently in wills of the period than any other kinds of furniture, so there is no need for raised eyebrows. Nor is it significant that she was not called 'my loving' or 'my beloved' wife, as wives normally were, rightly or wrongly. Unlike most other testators, Shakespeare did not use terms of endearment anywhere in his will. Yet neither did his lawyer, Francis Collins, who signed his own will just a year later, in 1617. Legally speaking it scarcely mattered what you called your wife, though, incidentally, it was most unusual not to refer to her by name. One would have expected 'Item, I give unto *my wife Anne* my second-best bed. . . .' The only similar case that I remember of a wife not named occurs in the will of the actor Alexander Cooke

(1614), which was also unusual in one other respect. It begins 'In the name of the Father, the Son, and the Holy Ghost, I, Alexander Cooke, sick of body but in perfect mind, do with mine own hand write my last will and testament. . . .' Wills written by the testator himself are rare, and, as in the case of Alexander Cooke, are likely to depart from some of the customary forms and phrases. Others have recently suggested that Shakespeare penned his own will: I do not agree, yet, as I have said, the thinking and some of the actual words of the will often seem to be the testator's own, not the time-honoured rigmaroles of scriveners and lawyers.

Did Shakespeare, perhaps aware that he was on his deathbed, intend a snub to his wife when he left her the second-best bed? Some have argued that it was a gesture of affection: it would be the marital bed, whereas the best bed would be kept in the best room, reserved for important visitors. Another probable reference to Anne Hathaway persuades me, however, that the wife who was given only a bed, and no jewels or other keepsakes, was not as great a comfort to her husband as he may have wished. On sheet 2 the will initially said, 'Item, I give, will, bequeath and devise unto my daughter Susanna Hall all that capital messuage or tenement with the appurtenances called the New Place wherein I now dwell. . . .' etc. At some stage this was changed to 'I give . . . unto my daughter Susanna Hall [and then, interlined] for better enabling of her to perform this my will and towards the performance thereof . . . ,' a puzzling insertion. What can it mean? New Place and the other properties were going to Susanna in any case. The words 'for better enabling of her to perform this my will and towards the performance thereof' seem to imply that the 'performance' might be hindered. How, by whom, for what reason? I can think of one person who might have had different thoughts about the disposal of Shakespeare's 'plate, jewels and household stuff,' as they are lumped together and collectively bequeathed in the will – a person who would continue to reside at New Place and who might indeed have hindered the 'performance'. If I am right, this oblique allusion to Mistress Shakespeare, who is not named, resembles the treatment of Thomas Quiney and William Hart. Shakespeare meant, I take it, that his daughter Susanna *and no one else* was to be the mistress of New Place.

What, then, were the provisions made for his widow? If we compare the will of Francis Collins, Shakespeare's lawyer, it would seem that he treated his wife more generously. Collins's widow was to be the mistress of the family home for the duration of her life, or until she married again. She was to share 'half the residue of my goods' with the eldest son, the other half going to the younger children. She was to be a coexecutor, with her eldest son. Shakespeare made his daughter and her husband his executors, not his wife, and his other arrangements were different as well. It is sometimes said that 'at common law a widow was entitled to a life-estate in one third of any and all those lands in which her husband had held an inheritable interest'. Lawyers warn us, though, that 'doubtless some widows were compelled by circumstance or consideration of relationship to accept other or lesser provision'.[5] In Collins's will the life-estate in one-third of the husband's heritable interest is spelled out, but not in Shakespeare's, where all lands and leases seem to go directly to Susanna and her husband.

Shakespeare's relationship with his wife, a major factor in the structure of the will, is not as invisible to us as is often suggested. Is it not significant that John and Mary Shakespeare, the poet's parents, produced children over a span of twenty-two years (with christenings from 1558 to 1580), whereas William Shakespeare and his wife stopped producing children after only three years of marriage? Though not infertile, they stopped when he was twenty-one and she twenty-nine or thereabouts – unusual, before the introduction of modern birth control. Biographers are now pretty well agreed that the poet's relationship with the dark lady of the Sonnets cannot be waved away as just a literary exercise; if they are right, this too is part of the story of his marriage. And is it not significant, again, that we find not a single reference in the will to any member of Anne Hathaway's family, apart from the terse mention of Anne herself?

When Shakespeare bought the Blackfriars Gate-House in 1613, three co-purchasers or trustees were named with him in the indenture, though he was to be the sole owner. What was the reason for this legal fiction? Legal experts explain that 'the use of trustees had the effect of barring Shakespeare's widow from any right to the property'.[6] This effect was no doubt intended, and it reinforces the impression given by the will.

Wills were by no means as stereotyped as we are sometimes led to believe, and Shakespeare's must be one of the most truly original of original wills. There are many signs in it of anger or

disappointment, obliquely expressed. Apart from Thomas Quiney
and William Hart, let us not forget Master Richard Tyler the elder,
who was to have received 26s. 8d. 'to buy him a ring' in the first
version of the will and whose name was simply struck out,
though he was still alive. Perhaps Shakespeare gave nothing to
the church because the church had very recently excommunicated
his daughter Judith and her husband and was about to humiliate
them again. They may have deserved it, yet it would not be too
surprising if Judith's father resented this public chastisement of
his family. Many details appear to fit into a larger pattern; the
treatment of Anne Hathaway may be a part of it. It is not a pretty
spectacle, the deathbed scene that I have sketched, with an
afflicted testator apparently so unforgiving. We can only hope,
though not too confidently, that the dead hand, as George Eliot
was to call it, does not point accusingly at Anne Hathaway, as
well as so many others.

Revising his will on 25 March 1616, the master playwright, it now
appears, staged his last play, a domestic drama: somewhat like
the Duke in act 5 of *Measure for Measure*, he tried to regain control
of a situation that had slipped from his grasp, and like the Duke
he could not be sure of the reactions of the principal performers.
He trusted his elder daughter, Susanna, and her husband, Dr John
Hall – but what of his wife and his younger daughter, Judith? Did
he have to wrestle, in his final illness, with a divided family? It is
a curious coincidence that Susanna resembled her father and that
Judith followed her mother's example in two significant ways.
Susanna's close likeness to her father was praised in her epitaph
(1649):

> Witty above her sex, but that's not all,
> Wise to salvation was good Mistress Hall:
> Something of Shakespeare was in that, but this
> Wholly of him, with whom she's now in bliss . . .

Judith, on the other hand, resembled her mother in marrying
late and in marrying a husband several years younger than
herself (Judith was born in 1585 and Thomas Quiney in 1589). It
may be that Anne Hathaway encouraged Judith to marry rather
than remain a spinster, and that Judith's father, with a keener eye
for human failings, distrusted Thomas Quiney even before his

relationship with Margaret Wheeler became known, and opposed the marriage. If Anne Hathaway took the view that any marriage is better than no marriage, is it not possible that this would remind her husband of Anne's own marriage to a youth of 18, eight years her junior and no doubt less experienced in the ways of the world? If the resulting marriage was not entirely satisfactory, might Anne's husband not perhaps ask himself whether the youth of 18 had been trapped, and would that not be a complicating factor in 1616 when he was uneasy about Judith's marriage, and when he dictated his will without a single reference, in the first instance, to the existence of his wife?

But, as Dr Johnson once exclaimed after pursuing speculation beyond the limits of the knowable, 'of these trifles enough!' We have still to grapple with a question that can and must be answered, and it is this: was the behaviour of 'gentle Shakespeare' on his deathbed, as I have described it, what we should have expected, or was it the very opposite, completely out of character?

Although biographers have been slow to recognize it, the tag 'gentle Shakespeare' only gives us one side of a complicated nature. What do we know of the other side? The very first allusion to him as a dramatist called him an upstart crow, one that 'with his tiger's heart wrapped in a player's hide supposes he is as well able to bombast out a blank verse' as the best writers of the day. Robert Greene adapted a line from *3 Henry VI*, 'O tiger's heart wrapp'd in a woman's hide' (I.4.138), because he saw gentle Shakespeare as a tiger, and he wanted to unmask the man he considered a relentless enemy. Commenting on Greene's attack, Henry Chettle explained that it was 'offensively taken' by Shakespeare and another (probably Marlowe), adding that 'with neither of them that take offence was I acquainted'; he offered his apologies to Shakespeare, for important people ('divers of worship') had come forward on his behalf. Years later Thomas Heywood used the same word as Chettle: Shakespeare was 'much offended' with Jaggard, the printer, who 'presumed to make so bold with his name'. Jaggard, as we know, had to remove the offending title page of the 1612 edition of *The Passionate Pilgrim*, which had so boldly and misleadingly printed Shakespeare's name – a second instance of decisive action when Shakespeare was angry. And the concluding lines of Jonson's great elegy made no secret of the less gentle side of 'my beloved'.

> Shine forth, thou star of poets, and with rage
> Or influence, chide or cheer the drooping stage.

A hard and angry Shakespeare is so utterly unlike the traditional image of a gentle dramatist that biographers have failed to notice how Robert Greene developed his complaint. Greene did so obliquely, in the fable of the grasshopper and the ant, where the 'waspish' and 'relentless' ant, like the tiger, stands for an absolute Johannes Factotum, who is in his own conceit 'the only Shake-scene in a country'. This may be the point of view of an enemy, it may be unpleasing and unwelcome, yet it is supported by other witnesses and therefore we cannot ignore it completely.[7]

The tiger, the waspishness, the resentment when others treat him badly, all come together in the deathbed scene as I have tried to reconstruct it. Am I correct in thinking that as a testator Shakespeare broke most of the rules? It is reassuring, at any rate, that in the only other record that equals his will in importance as a personal document he also went his own way, made up his own rules, and expressed both disappointment and anger: I mean in the account he gave of himself in the Sonnets. In the will and the Sonnets he emerges as unconventional and highly critical of those closest to him, the young man, the dark lady, as well as members of his own family. The traditional image of 'friendly Shakespeare', 'easy Shakespeare', 'gentle Shakespeare', presents him as he struck others when in congenial company; the will, like the Sonnets, gives us glimpses of the solitary inner man, and helps – just a little – to explain the sustained rage of a Hamlet or a Prospero.[8]

Afterword

Several friends and strangers have written to me with interesting comments on this paper (which, being intended as a twenty-minute paper, could not explore all the side issues). Here are a few of the points raised and some brief replies.

1 Was Thomas Quiney treated 'more humiliatingly' than Mrs Condell's son-in-law? After all, he was not named in Shakespeare's will. – I assume that all those concerned would know who was meant; his not being named can be interpreted as a considerate silence or as a gesture of contempt.

2 Was 'such husband' possibly a legal phrase? – Yes, but Shakespeare was familiar with legal terminology. The legal fences and trip-wires set up to protect Judith are perfectly visible in the will, and therefore all the more uncompromisingly hurtful.

3 If William Hart was a dying man, was there any need to leave him a bequest? – Yes, a greater need than if Hart had been in good health. Otherwise Shakespeare would seem to say to his brother-in-law, 'You're as good as dead, I can forget about you.'

4 Is it possible that Shakespeare wanted to protect his wife and his estate from pressure by the Hathaway family? – Yes, this is possible. It is also not impossible that Anne Hathaway was provided for before Shakespeare made his will, or was physically or mentally unfit to be an executor. Nevertheless, the absence of any direct reference to Anne, apart from the interlined bequest of the second-best bed, the fact that wives were normally treated quite differently, the signs in the will of resentment against others, and all the additional evidence about Shakespeare's relationship with his wife suggest, taken together, that we must not rule out the possibility that the testator and his wife were not at peace with one another.

In conclusion I must thank Dr Susan Brock and Professor Park Honan in particular for detailed comments and my brother, A. P. P. Honigmann, for advice on legal points.

Notes

Place of publication is London unless I state otherwise. The following sources are always cited using the abbreviated form of reference specified; for other sources, full details are given on first reference in each chapter, subsequent references being by surname of author or editor and title or short title.

Bradley, *Shakespearean Tragedy*. A. C. Bradley, *Shakespearean Tragedy* (1904).
Chambers, *William Shakespeare*. E. K. Chambers, *William Shakespeare: A Study of Facts and Problems* (2 vols, Oxford, 1930).
OED. *The Oxford English Dictionary*, ed. James A. H. Murray *et al.* (13 vols, Oxford, 1933).
Plutarch. *Shakespeare's Plutarch*, ed. T. J. B. Spencer (1964).
SR. *Transcript of the Registers of the Company of Stationers of London, 1554–1640*, ed. Edward Arber (5 vols, privately printed, 1875–94).

INTRODUCTION

1. S. T. Coleridge, *Biographia Literaria*, ch. 15.
2. A. Scoloker, 1604: see also my *Shakespeare's Impact on his Contemporaries* (1982) pp. 17–18.

1 IN SEARCH OF WILLIAM SHAKESPEARE: THE PUBLIC AND THE PRIVATE MAN

1. All the early allusions quoted in this chapter can be found, through the index, in Chambers, *William Shakespeare*. To avoid a clutter of footnotes I give references in only a few cases.
2. See Leslie Hotson, *'Shakespeare's Sonnets Dated' and Other Essays* (1949) p. 111ff.; and my *Shakespeare: the 'lost years'* (Manchester, 1985) p. 77ff.
3. See my '"There is a world elsewhere": William Shakespeare,

businessman' (in the Proceedings of the Third Congress of the International Shakespeare Association, ed. W. Habicht *et al.* (1988)).

4. A. C. Bradley, *Oxford Lectures on Poetry* (Oxford, 1909): 'Shakespeare the man'.
5. See my 'Sir John Oldcastle: Shakespeare's martyr', in *Fanned and Winnowed Opinions: Shakespearean essays presented to Harold Jenkins*, ed. J. Mahon and T. Pendleton (1987) p. 121.
6. Many (but not all) biographers believe that William Herbert (1580–1630), who became the third Earl of Pembroke in 1601, was the Young Man ('Mr W.H.') of the Sonnets. Clarendon, in his *History of the Rebellion*, said that Pembroke 'was immoderately given up to women. But therein he retained such a power and jurisdiction over his very appetite, that he was not so much transported with beauty and outward allurements, as with those advantages of the mind as manifested an extraordinary wit, and spirit.' Compare Shakespeare's picture of the Dark Lady's outward allurements and 'advantages of the mind'!
7. See my *Shakespeare's Impact on his Contemporaries* (1982) pp. 13–14.
8. Bradley, *Oxford Lectures on Poetry*, p. 321.
9. Chambers, *William Shakespeare*, II, 243. My italics.
10. Bradley, *Oxford Lectures on Poetry*, p. 322.
11. See my *John Weever: a biography of a literary associate of Shakespeare and Jonson* (Manchester, 1987) p. 26ff.
12. See my *Shakespeare's Impact*, pp. 9–11.
13. M. H. Spielmann, 'Shakespeare's portraiture', in *Studies in the First Folio*, ed. Sir Israel Gollancz (Oxford, 1924).
14. As in note 13. The discussion of Droeshout's engraving follows my 'Shakespeare and London's immigrant community *circa* 1600', in *Elizabethan and Modern Studies Presented to Willem Schrickx*, ed. J. P. Vander Motten (R.U.G. 1985). See also Samuel Schoenbaum, *Shakespeare's Lives* (Oxford, 1970) pp. 10–11.

2 POLITICS, RHETORIC AND WILL-POWER IN *JULIUS CAESAR*

1. T. S. Eliot, 'Shakespeare and the stoicism of Seneca', *Selected Essays* (ed. 1953) p. 136.
2. See Chambers, *William Shakespeare*, II, 210.
3. Harley Granville-Barker, *Prefaces to Shakespeare*, First Series (ed. 1948) p. 105.
4. Bradley, *Shakespearean Tragedy*, p. 60.
5. M. W. MacCallum, *Shakespeare's Roman Plays and their Background* (1910) p. 214.

3 THE POLITICS IN *HAMLET* AND 'THE WORLD OF THE PLAY'

1. *The Sources of 'Hamlet': with essay on the legend*, ed. Israel Gollancz (1926) pp. 225–7. All my quotations from Belleforest are taken from Gollancz's reprint of the seventeenth-century English translation, except where there is a special reason for quoting the French original (also reprinted by Gollancz), which was either Shakespeare's immediate source, or the source of his source.
2. Bradley noticed this 'curious parallelism' (*Shakespearean Tragedy*, p. 90).
3. Cf. V.1.138–57. Both princes are given the same epithet – 'young Fortinbras', 'young Hamlet' – and the play generally suggests that they are of roughly the same age.
4. J. E. Hankins, *The Character of 'Hamlet' and other Essays* (1941) p. 11.
5. Bradley, *Shakespearean Tragedy*, pp. 103, 107, etc.
6. For the contribution of the 'Fortinbras story', cf. also Hankins, *Character of 'Hamlet'*, pp. 244–5.
7. Ibid., p. 96. Unlike Wilson, Hankins recognised 'that the Danish king was chosen by some group', but, like Wilson (whose discussion of the same subject Hankins seems to have overlooked), he interpreted the politics of the play from a too inflexibly 'historical' viewpoint.
8. For instance, Shakespeare brings in at regular intervals words such as 'act', 'scene', 'stage', 'prompt', 'cue', 'tragedy'. Cf. S. L. Bethell's admirable account of the 'unreality' of Shakespeare's plays, *Shakespeare and the Popular Dramatic Tradition* (1944).
9. Cf. also H. D. F. Kitto, *Form and Meaning in Drama* (1956) p. 258: 'But surely it does not follow, as Wilson says it does, that Shakespeare must have composed the scene with the English constitution in mind. . . . It is surely the common experience that we go to the theatre willing to accept, without prepossessions, what the dramatist offers us . . . since nobody in the audience knew or cared what the Danish constitution was, in whatever century this is supposed to be, the dramatist could go ahead and assume what suited him best.'
10. The good Second Quarto includes the Council in the stage-direction for I.2: '*Florish. Enter Claudius, King of Denmarke, Gertrad the Queene, Counsaile . . . .*'
11. Quoted in Malone's Variorum *Shakespeare* (1821) VII, 200.
12. 'Claudius's description of Gertrude (I.2.9) as 'imperial jointress' is important . . . since the phrase signifies, not joint-monarch as some editors explain, but a widow who retains the jointure or life interest in the crown, and so points to the legal argument or quibble by means of which Hamlet was supplanted' – J. Dover Wilson, *What Happens in 'Hamlet'* (Cambridge, 1935) p. 38. Even if 'jointress' later acquired the meaning advocated by Wilson (cf. *OED*), this tells us little about Shakespeare's meaning, especially if, as seems likely, he invented the word. In Belleforest, incidentally, Old Hamlet and Claudius are joint governors ('Rorique . . . donna le gouvernement de Jutie . . . à deux

seigneurs . . . nommez Horvvendille et Fengon' – p. 180), which might have suggested joint monarchs for the play. But clearly Shakespeare wished only to stir vague thoughts about Gertrude's rights, not to define them meticulously.

13. 'It is permanently ambiguous. Indeed the very word "ghost", by putting it into the same class with the "ghosts" of Kyd and Chapman, nay by classifying it at all, puts us on the wrong track. It is "this thing", "this dreaded sight" . . .' – C. S. Lewis, 'Hamlet: the prince or the poem,' in *Proceedings of the British Academy*, XXVIII, 1942, p. 147.

14. 'The elder Hamlet had died two months before, at which time his son was presumably at Wittenberg . . . it is probable that in Hamlet's absence he [Claudius] had taken over control of affairs' (Hankins, *Character of Hamlet*, p. 98). Bradley, however, has shown that at the time of his father's death Hamlet was almost certainly not at Wittenberg (*Shakespearean Tragedy*, Note B). It therefore seems more likely that the shock of his mother's marriage stunned Hamlet's interest in the succession; but this matter lies genuinely 'outside the play', and so cannot be pursued.

15. Cf. A. C. Sprague, *Shakespeare and the Audience: a study in the technique of exposition* (1935) p. 243, and the excellent section on 'Testimony'. Bradley (*Shakespearean Tragedy*, p. 168) thought Claudius 'courteous and never undignified' as a king, an opinion that is, I believe, the accepted one.

16. Hankins (*Character of Hamlet*, p. 96) felt that when Fortinbras called 'the noblest to the audience' (V.2.379) this 'indicates that the kingdom's affairs were handled by a council of nobles'. In Belleforest, on the other hand, Hamlet is chosen king after his *harangue* 'en l'assemblée des citoyens' ('among the multitude of people') (pp. 264, 265).

17. Lewis, 'Hamlet: the prince or the poem', *Proceedings of the British Academy*, 1942, p. 147. After Lewis's lecture the 'mystery' and 'doubt' in *Hamlet* received even greater emphasis, in D. G. James's *The Dream of Learning* (1951), ch. 2 ('The new doubt'); Maynard Mack's 'The world of *Hamlet*', in *Tragic Themes in Western Literature*, ed. Cleanth Brooks (1955); Harry Levin's *The Question of 'Hamlet'* (1959); and elsewhere.

18. Probably a technical reason also dictated the allusions to Hamlet's popularity in Act IV. In several tragedies Shakespeare felt a need to rehabilitate his hero in the audience's sympathy at this point, partly, perhaps, because the tensions of Act III brought into notice some of the hero's less amiable qualities. Thus he invented Brutus's solicitude for the sleepy boy Lucius in *Julius Caesar* (IV.3.238ff.), and underlined Lear's humility in his reunion with Cordelia.

19. The technique is not unfamiliar. Kitto wrote 'We have to observe first how Shakespeare uses his Clowns much as the Greek dramatist used his Chorus; for they fill our minds with generalised thoughts about mortality and the vanity of human life, before we are brought, as by a gradual contraction of the focus, to the particular tragedy' (*Form and Meaning*, p. 283). Mack also explored 'umbrella speeches', 'mirror situations' and that 'inward action' which fills 'our minds with

impressions analogous to those which we may presume to be occupying the conscious or unconscious mind of the hero' ('The Jacobean Shakespeare', in *Stratford-upon-Avon Studies 1*, 1960).

20. Shakespeare also forces us to take note of misguided 'elections' in such memorable lines as 'Why, man, they did make love to this employment' (V.2.57), and the Queen's 'I will, my lord; I pray you, pardon me' (283), when warned not to drink.
21. Cf. Caroline F. E. Spurgeon, *Shakespeare's Imagery* (ed. 1958) p. 316; G. Wilson Knight, *The Wheel of Fire* (ed. 1960) pp. 17, 32; Maynard Mack (see note 17 above); R. A. Foakes, 'Hamlet and the court of Elsinore', *Shakespeare Survey*, IX (1956) 40.
22. Cf. P. Alexander, *Hamlet Father and Son* (1955) pp. 35, 169.
23. Cf. J. W. Draper, *The 'Hamlet' of Shakespeare's Audience* (1938) p. 13: 'For the first time, in *Hamlet*, Shakespeare fully and realistically portrays the political problems of a court: regicide, revolt, dynastic succession, and all the accompanying policy and intrigue'.
24. Cf. *Sources of 'Hamlet'*, pp. 199, 205, 217, etc. (Belleforest); in French, 'une grande et cauteleuse sagesse', 'Contre un desloial, il faut user de cautelle', etc.
25. Cf. Bradley, *Shakespearean Tragedy*, pp. 303–4, 333–4.

4　TRENDS IN THE DISCUSSION OF SHAKESPEARE'S CHARACTERS: *OTHELLO*

1. W. J. Harvey, *Character and the Novel* (1965) p. 192.
2. See Patrick Murray, *The Shakespearian Scene* (1969) p. 1; Christopher Ricks, *English Drama to 1710* (Sphere Library, 1971) p. 313.
3. For Stoll see J. I. M. Stewart, *Character and Motive in Shakespeare* (1949), p. 79ff.
4. M. C. Bradbrook, *Themes and Conventions of Elizabethan Tragedy* (1960) pp. 64–5.
5. See Stewart, *Character and Motive*, p. 143.
6. F. L. Lucas, *Literature and Society* (1951) p. 76.
7. See F. R. Leavis, *The Common Pursuit* (1952).
8. Dostoevsky, *The Brothers Karamazov*, book 8, ch. 3.
9. Bradley, *Shakespearean Tragedy*, pp. 186–7.
10. C. J. Carlisle, *Shakespeare from the Green Room* (Chapel Hill, NC, 1969) p. 205.
11. Ibid., p. 203.
12. T. S. Eliot, *Selected Essays* (1953) p. 130.
13. Montaigne, *Essays*, III.10.
14. Whitman, *Song of Myself*, XVI.
15. Bernard Beckerman, *Dynamics of Drama* (New York, 1970) p. 219.

5 THE UNIQUENESS OF *KING LEAR*: GENRE AND PRODUCTION PROBLEMS

1. Bradley, *Shakespearean Tragedy*, p. 53.
2. For example Susan Snyder, *The Comic Matrix of Shakespeare's Tragedies* (1977).
3. I assume that Cordelia rises when Lear kneels, and tries to help him to his feet.
4. Maynard Mack, *King Lear in our Time* (1966) p. 56.
5. Marvin Rosenberg, *The Masks of King Lear* (1972) pp. 264–5.
6. See G. Tillotson, *Essays in Criticism and Research* (Cambridge, 1942) pp. 41–8.
7. In this chapter I am indebted to T. W. Craik's discussion of the 'entry of Lear carrying Cordelia's inert body' in 'I know when one is dead . . . ' (British Academy Shakespeare Lecture, 1979, in the Academy's *Proceedings*, vol. lxv).

6 PAST, PRESENT AND FUTURE IN *MACBETH* AND *ANTONY AND CLEOPATRA*

1. See Geoffrey Bullough, *Narrative and Dramatic Sources of Shakespeare* (8 vols, 1957–75) VII, 451–4.
2. Shakespeare does not spell it out, though Antony says 'There's a great spirit gone! Thus did I desire it' (I.2.119). Plutarch wrote that everyone in Rome hated Antony for his 'naughty life', 'yet Caesar did somewhat bridle his madness and insolency . . . *And therefore* he left his dissolute manner of life, and married Fulvia, that was Clodius' widow.' Fulvia was domineering, 'sour and crooked of condition', and Antony married her under pressure (Plutarch, pp. 183–5; my italics).
3. Shakespeare seems to have omitted many essential stage-directions: see Chapter 10.
4. Cf. also II.6.112ff., III.7.3ff., 34ff.; III.10.29ff.; III.13.63ff., 88.
5. I return to Shakespeare's 'reaching out in all directions at once' in Chapter 9 (Shakespeare's 'mingled yarn'). Readers interested in Shakespeare's treatment of time should also consult Wolfgang Clemen's excellent 'Past and future in Shakespeare's drama', *Proceedings of the British Academy*, LII (1966); repr. in Clemen's *Shakespeare's Dramatic Art* (1972).

7 SHAKESPEARE SUPPRESSED: THE UNFORTUNATE HISTORY OF *TROILUS AND CRESSIDA*

1. For the 'private performance' theory see Peter Alexander, '*Troilus and*

Cressida, 1609', *The Library*, IX (1929) 267ff.; for the argument against it, Richard Levin, *New Readings vs. Old Plays* (1979) p. 167ff.

2. For the date see Chambers, *William Shakespeare*, I, 443; *Ben Jonson*, ed. C. H. Herford and Percy and Evelyn Simpson (11 vols, Oxford, 1925–52) I, 415. If *Poetaster* alludes to *The Whipping of the Satyre*, which was entered in SR on 14 August 1601, that would make *Poetaster* a little later than is usually thought. See my *John Weever: a biography* (1987) p. 40.

3. Chambers, *William Shakespeare*, I, 355.

4. See ibid., II, 326; and W. Barlow, *A Sermon Preached at Paules Crosse* (1601) sig. D5ᵇ.

5. G. B. Harrison, *Shakespeare's Tragedies* (1951) ch. 6.

6. See Chapman's translations, *Seaven Bookes of the Iliades* (1598), *Achilles Shield* (1598); Hugh Platt, *The Iewell House of Art and Nature* (1594); V. Saviolo, *V. Saviolo his Practise* (1595).

7. For Essex's tallness see G. Petau-Maulette, *Devoreux* (1597) sig. E4ᵇ.

8. Cf. R. Pricket, *Honors Fame* (1604) sig. B1ᵇ, B3ᵇ; G. B. Harrison, *A Last Elizabethan Journal 1599–1603* (1933) p. 156; E. M. Tenison, *Elizabethan England* (Leamington Spa, privately printed, 12 vols, 1933–61) X, 112, and XI, 244–6; P. M. Handover, *The Second Cecil: the rise to power 1563–1604* (1959) pp. 29, 230.

9. For Burghley as 'Nestor' see C. Ockland, *Elizabeth Queene* (1585) sig. D2ᵃ; *A Comparison of the English and Spanish Nation*, tr. R. Ashley, (1589) sig. D1ᵃ; Tenison, *Elizabethan England*, VIII, 329.

10. Lord Burghley appears not to have been Essex's political opponent, and Sir Robert Cecil only turned against Essex after Burghley's death (1598). But Cecil's role in opposing Essex became so clear in 1601 that it was natural to assume that a 'Cecil' faction had engineered his fall – an assumption shared by some later historians. See Tenison, *Elizabethan England*, X, 23, 307, and XI, 424, 470ff.

11. Shakespeare coined the word 'mappery' (*OED*); it may be significant that England's Nestor, Lord Burghley, particularly encouraged map-making, for political and military purposes.

12. Tenison, *Elizabethan England*, X, 314, and XI, 424.

13. Cf. *Troilus and Cressida*, III.3.205–6; and Tenison, *Elizabethan England*, XI, 477, 560.

14. Tenison, *Elizabethan England*, XI, 494.

15. Ibid., XI, 469–70, 532.

16. *Sir Fulke Greville's Life of Sir Philip Sidney*, ed. Nowell C. Smith (Oxford, 1907) p. 156.

17. See Tenison, *Elizabethan England*, XI, 526.

18. Quoted in W. B. Devereux, *Lives and Letters of the Devereux, Earls of Essex* (2 vols, 1853) II, 95.

19. Cf. also Jonson's allusion to Elizabeth and Essex in *Cynthia's Revels* (1601): *Ben Jonson*, I, 26ff.

20. Tenison, *Elizabethan England*, XII, 242.

21. Cf. ibid., XI, 243–6; Alan G. R. Smith, *Servant of the Cecils: the life of Sir Michael Hickes, 1543–1612* (1977) p. 122.

22. See *Troilus and Cressida*, II.3.138ff.

23. *State Papers Domestic*, 1598–1601, p. 573.
24. See W. W. Greg, *The Shakespeare First Folio* (Oxford, 1955) p. 347; Alice Walker (ed.), *Troilus and Cressida*, New Cambridge Shakespeare (Cambridge, 1957) p. 206. Also Greg, *The Shakespeare First Folio*, p. 165: 'It occasionally happens that a line or part of a line occurs twice over some way apart in a scene, and that its first appearance is a patent error . . . . ' Gary Taylor (cf. note 26) thinks that there is a 'simple theatrical motive for adding the Folio's half-line at the beginning of Ulysses' speech: without it . . . spectators may not know who Ulysses is talking about'. I find this hard to believe, since (i) Troilus is the one Trojan with a reason to 'look so heavy', and (ii) his extreme youth has been stressed throughout (I.2.79, 110, 112, 226, etc.).
25. See my *The Stability of Shakespeare's Text* (1965) ch. VI.
26. Gary Taylor, '*Troilus and Cressida*: bibliography, performance, and interpretation', *Shakespeare Studies*, XV (1982) 99–136.
27. See my 'Shakespeare's "bombast" ', in *Shakespeare's Styles: Essays in honour of Kenneth Muir*, ed. Philip Edwards *et al.* (Cambridge, 1980).
28. See S. Thomas in *Shakespeare Quarterly*, XXVII (1976) 186ff.
29. For the surviving copies of the Quarto see W. W. Greg, *A Bibliography of the English Printed Drama to the Restoration* (4 vols, 1939–57); and *A Short-Title Catalogue of Books Printed in England, Scotland, and Ireland . . . 1475–1640*, 2nd edn, vol. 2, ed Katharine F. Pantzer *et al.* (1976).
30. J. M. Nosworthy has written at length on the revision of *Troilus and Cressida* in *Shakespeare's Occasional Plays* (1965). We are closest, I think, in holding that Shakespeare began to write the play as a tragedy (Nosworthy, p. 75), but differ about the play's date and other matters.

8 *ALL'S WELL THAT ENDS WELL*: A 'FEMINIST' PLAY?

1. See Chambers, *William Shakespeare*, II, 249.
2. See Alfred Harbage, *Shakespeare's Audience* (ed. 1961) pp. 76–7.
3. See A. L. Rowse, *Sex and Society in Shakespeare's Age: Simon Forman* (1974).
4. I quote the source, 'Giletta of Narbon' (the thirty-eighth story in William Painter's *The Palace of Pleasure*), from G. K. Hunter's edition of *All's Well*, New Arden Shakespeare (1959) p. 145ff.
5. Quoted from Joseph G. Price, *The Unfortunate Comedy: a study of 'All's Well That Ends Well' and its critics* (Liverpool, 1968) p. 41.
6. Perhaps Helena reads two separate extracts from the letter, skipping some lines: 'this it says – /"When from my finger you can get this ring, / . . . And is by me with child" – and this is done!'
7. John Dryden, *An Essay of Dramatic Poesy*.
8. G. K. Hunter (ed.), *All's Well*, pp. xxiii, lix.

9 SHAKESPEARE'S MINGLED YARN AND *MEASURE FOR MEASURE*

1. T. S. Eliot, *Selected Essays* (ed. 1953) p. 116.
2. James Agate, quoted from *Sean O'Casey Modern Judgements*, ed. Ronald Ayling (1969) p. 176.
3. Sean O'Casey, *Blasts and Benedictions* (1967) p. 97.
4. Nevill Coghill, 'Six points of stage-craft in *The Winter's Tale*', *Shakespeare Survey*, XI (1958) 31–41.
5. *The Works of Thomas Deloney*, ed. F. O. Mann (Oxford, 1912) pp. 51–2.
6. *The Plays of John Marston*, ed. H. Harvey Wood (3 vols, 1939) III, 29.
7. Sir Philip Sidney, *An Apology for Poetry*, ed. G. Shepherd (1965) p. 116.
8. Johnson's *Life of Abraham Cowley*.
9. F. Würtenberger, *Mannerism* (1963) p. 239.
10. In 1981, when this lecture was delivered, the British Academy was located in Burlington House, near Piccadilly Circus.

10 ON NOT TRUSTING SHAKESPEARE'S STAGE-DIRECTIONS

1. Shakespeare in old spelling is cited from the Folio in this chapter, unless I state the contrary, and extracts in old spelling are identified by signature (Q and F).
2. For the use of Quarto 'copy' in the printing of some Folio texts, see Alice Walker, *Textual problems of the First Folio* (Cambridge, 1953).
3. Cf. *Timon*, 2hl^a: '*Some other. I know not*'; *Hamlet*, Q2, M1^{b}ff.: '*Other.*'
4. It is interesting that a 'Both' speech in *Hamlet*, Q2, was assigned to a single speaker in Q1 ('*Both.* Longer, longer' – Q2, C2^b; '*Mar.* O longer, longer' – Q1), and also a 'Both' speech in F1 ('*Hor. & Mar. within.* My Lord, my Lord' – F1; '*Hor.* My lord, my lord' – Q1). As these passages involve the Marcellus-actor, who may have been the Q1 pirate, Q1 could record what was said in the theatre.
5. Quoted from the Revels edition.
6. *A Trick to Catch the Old One* (1608) F1^b: 'Ha, ha, ha . . . Oh – o – o . . . True, true, true . . . .'
7. '*Stand forth*' in *A Midsummer Night's Dream* is more 'imperative' than in *Julius Caesar*, but this is in line with the text's other directions: '*Ly doune*', '*Sleepe*', '*Winde horne*', '*Shoute within . . . Winde hornes*' (El^a, F2^b, F4^a, F4^b)
8. R. Crane, *The Works of Mercy* (1621), the 'author's preface'.
9. For instance, in *The Stability of Shakespeare's Text* (1965) *passim*; 'The text of *Richard III*', *Theatre Research*, VII (1965) 48–55; 'On the indifferent and one-way variants in Shakespeare', *The Library*, XXII (1967) 189–204.

11 SHAKESPEARE AT WORK: PREPARING, WRITING, REWRITING

1. See K. J. Fielding, *Charles Dickens: a critical introduction* (ed. 1965) pp. 111–12.
2. See J. Limon, *Gentlemen of a Company: English players in Central and Eastern Europe, 1590–1660* (1985) pp. 22–3, 46; Philip Henslowe's *Diary*, *passim*.
3. See A. Harbage, *Theatre for Shakespeare* (1955) p. 82; also, the story that Shakespeare 'luckily cast his eye' on one of Jonson's plays, 'read it through' and recommended it (Chambers, *William Shakespeare*, II, 267).
4. See Chambers, *William Shakespeare*, II, 188.
5. Ibid., II, 210.
6. See also Gabriel Harvey's praise of *Venus and Adonis*, *Lucrece* and *Hamlet*, and Sir Edward Dyer's citation of the same passage from *Amores* (I.15.35): Chambers, *William Shakespeare*, II, 197.
7. See ibid., II, 249.
8. See my 'Shakespeare's "lost source-plays"', *Modern Language Review*, XLIX (1954) 293–307.
9. Chambers, *William Shakespeare*, I, 23.
10. See W. W. Greg (ed.), *Henslowe Papers* (A. H. Bullen, 1907) p. 84.
11. E. K. Chambers, *The Elizabethan Stage* (4 vols, Oxford, 1923) III, 445.
12. Harold Jenkins, *The Structural Problem in Shakespeare's 'Henry the Fourth'*, inaugural lecture, Westfield College, University of London, 1955 (Methuen, 1956) p. 18.
13. Fielding, *Charles Dickens*, p. 95.
14. See Chambers, *William Shakespeare*, II, 251.
15. W. W. Greg, *The Shakespeare First Folio* (Oxford, 1955) pp. 410, 352.
16. See Leslie Hotson, *I, William Shakespeare* (1937) pp. 237–59; and Chambers, *William Shakespeare*, II, 232.
17. See my *The Stability of Shakespeare's Text* (1965) p. 44.
18. Greg, *The Shakespeare First Folio*, p. 355.
19. Quoted in my *The Stability of Shakespeare's Text*, p. 22.
20. Ibid., p. 23.
21. *The Works of Thomas Nashe*, ed. R. B. McKerrow, revised by F. P. Wilson (5 vols, Oxford, 1958) III, 312, and I, 287.
22. See my *The Stability of Shakespeare's Text*, p. 25.
23. Quoted ibid., p. 28.
24. Scott McMillin, *The Elizabethan Theatre and 'The Book of Sir Thomas More'* (1987) pp. 135–59.
25. *Henslowe Papers*, pp. 56–69.
26. Fredson Bowers has suggested that 'fouler papers' might have preceded the foul papers, and that there could also have been 'intermediate fair copies' (see my *The Stability of Shakespeare's Text*, p. 17). My point here is that what others think of as a single, uniform foul-papers text could be a textual hybrid.
27. See my *The Stability of Shakespeare's Text*, p. 15.
28. Quoted ibid.

29. See ibid., p. 143.
30. *Shakespeare's Plutarch*, ed. T. J. B. Spencer (1964) p. 161. See also Brents Stirling, '*Julius Caesar* in Revision', *Shakespeare Quarterly*, XIII (1962) 187ff.
31. See my 'Shakespeare's "lost source-plays"', *Modern Language Review*, XLIX (1954) 299.
32. *The Early Letters of William and Dorothy Wordsworth*, ed. E. De Selincourt (Oxford, 1935) pp. 244–5.
33. Quoted in my *Stability of Shakespeare's Text*, pp. 60–1.
34. See for example Michael J. Warren, 'Quarto and Folio *King Lear* . . .', in *Shakespeare: Pattern of Excelling Nature*, ed. D. Bevington and J. L. Halio (Newark, NJ, 1978); Gary Taylor, 'The war in *King Lear*', in *Shakespeare Survey*, 33 (1980); *The Division of the Kingdoms: Shakespeare's two versions of 'King Lear'*, ed. Gary Taylor and Michael Warren (Oxford, 1983).
35. Nevill Coghill, 'Revision after performance', *Shakespeare's Professional Skills* (Cambridge, 1964) p. 198. See also my 'Shakespeare's revised plays: *King Lear* and *Othello*', *The Library*, 6th ser., IV (1982) p. 5. (*Note*: I have changed my mind about Coghill's argument, though not about the revision of *Othello* in more general terms: cf. my *The texts of 'Othello' and Shakespearian Revision* (1996), pp. 7–21.
36. Harold Jenkins (ed.), *Hamlet*, Arden Shakespeare (1982) p. 5.
37. *Hamlet, Prince of Denmark*, ed. Philip Edwards, New Cambridge Shakespeare (Cambridge, 1985) p. 30.
38. Greg, *The Shakespeare First Folio*, pp. 282, 334, 389.
39. See note 36.
40. Greg, *The Shakespeare First Folio*, p. 375.
41. Jenkins (ed.), *Hamlet*, p. 56.
42. Ibid., pp. 21–2.
43. J. Dover Wilson, *The Manuscript of Shakespeare's 'Hamlet' and the Problems of its Transmission* (2 vols, Cambridge, 1934) I, 29.
44. See Greg, *The Shakespeare First Folio*, p. 241.

12 SHAKESPEARE ON HIS DEATHBED: THE LAST WILL AND TESTAMENT

1. I return later to Shakespeare's relationship with his parish church. It should be added that though he may have acquired the right to be buried in the parish church when he purchased his sublease of Stratford tithes (1605), the significant fact remains that in his will he never alludes to the church or its officers or procedures, and he may well have felt that he had a legitimate grievance. Again, we should not overlook Richard Davies (Archdeacon of Coventry, not far from Stratford), who recorded that Shakespeare 'died a papist'. Davies probably wrote his notes on Shakespeare in the later seventeenth century, so is not a reliable witness; on the other hand, Shakespeare's parents must have married in a Catholic church,

in the reign of Queen Mary, and he may have been brought up as a Catholic.

2. E. K. Chambers, *William Shakespeare: A Study of Facts and Problems* 2 vols. (Oxford: Clarendon Press, 1930), 2:174ff.

3. See E. R. C. Brinkworth, *Shakespeare and the Bawdy Court of Stratford* (Chichester: Phillimore, 1972), 80.

4. But compare B. Roland Lewis: Shakespeare's will, 'more than any other one thing epitomizes the spirit of the man and mirrors his personality' (*The Shakespeare Documents*, 2 vols. [Stanford, California: Stanford University Press, 1940], 2:471). I differ, however, in approach and about 'the spirit of the man'.

5. Andrew Lewis in the *Times Literary Supplement*, 15 February 1991, 11.

6. See *The Reader's Encyclopedia of Shakespeare*, ed. O. J. Campbell and E. G Quinn (New York: Crowell, 1966), 72; also S. Schoenbaum, *William Shakespeare: Records and Images* (New York: Oxford University Press, 1981), 43.

7. For the fable of the grasshopper and the ant and related matters see chapter 1 of my *Shakespeare's Impact on his Contemporaries* (1982); also, pp. 10–11, above.

8. Most of the wills cited in this chapter are printed in *Playhouse Wills 1558–1642, An edition of wills by Shakespeare and his contemporaries in the London theatre*, ed. E. A. J. Honigmann and Susan Brock (Manchester, 1993). There are three exceptions, which I cite from the originals in the Public Record Office (Prerogative Court of Canterbury): Francis Collins 1617, Prob 10/347; John Combe 1612, Prob 10/325; and William Combe 1610, Prob 10/283. I have modernised the quotations.

Index

action, outer and inner, 39, 77, 79,
  81, 83, 88, 92, 101, 237
actor's vulgarisation, 183
Admiral, Lord, 114, 118
Agate, James, 242
Aleman, M., 199
Alexander, Peter, vii, 238–9
'All' speeches, 178–81, 187
Arber, Edward, 234
Arcimboldo, G., 158
argument of play, 191, 194–5
Ashley, R., 240
aside, 99, 176–8, 187
Aubrey, John, 14, 16–7
audience, 1, 45, 48–50, 52, 75, 78,
  83–4, 91, 113, 120, 135, 138–9,
  153, 159–60, 165–6, 168, 170,
  184, 208, 237
Augustine, St, 101
Austen, Jane, 188
author's notes, 193
Ayling, Ronald, 242

bad quartos, 181, 200, 212, 214–17,
  242
Balzac, H. de, 191
Barlow, W., 240
Beaumont and Fletcher, 145, 216–17
  Maid's Tragedy, The, 183
Beckerman, B., 72, 238
Beckett, S., 76–7
bed, second-best, 222, 227
bed-trick, 135–6, 155–7
Beeching, H. C., 13
Beethoven, L. van, 84
Belleforest, F. de, 44–5, 47–8, 236–8
Belott, S., 190
Bethell, S. L., 236
Bevington, D., 244
Bible, the, 62, 130, 210
Blackfriars theatre, 215
Blackstone, Sir W., 50
Blake, William, 154
blocking entry, 125–6

Blount, Edward, 199
blurring, 50, 106
Boccaccio, G., 136
body language, 163
bombast, 10, 124, 147
Boswell, James, 15
'Both' speeches, 182, 187, 242
Botticelli, Sandro, 159
Bowers, Fredson, 243
boy-actors, 42, 91
Bradbrook, M. C., 62
Bradley, A. C., 6–7, 12–13, 33, 46,
  59–61, 64–9, 72–3, 234–9
Brinkworth, E. R. C., 245
Brock, Susan, xii, 233, 245
Brockbank, P., 223
Brook, Peter, 76
Brooks, Cleanth, 237
Brown, J. Russell, viii
Bullen, A. H., 243
Bullough, Geoffrey, 239
Burbage, Richard, 119, 225
Burgh, N., 4
Burghley, Lord, 115, 136, 240

Camden, W., 195
Campbell, O. J., 245
cancelled passages, 201, 205–9
Capell, E., 169
Carlisle, C. J., 238
Catherine de Medici, 136
Cecil, Sir Robert, 114–19, 240
Centlivre, Mrs, 142
Chambers, E. K., 113–14, 190, 204,
  223–4, 227, 234–5, 240–3, 245
Chamberlain's Men, Lord, 113–14,
  125
Chanson de Roland, 196
Chapman, F., 188
Chapman, George, 115, 191–2, 237,
  240
character and role, xi, 66, 70
character, split, 68–70, 72
Charles I, 49

247